a Wolters Kluwer ᴸ

Corporate Manslaughter and Corporate Homicide Act 2007: A Guide

Wolters Kluwer (UK) Limited
145 London Road
Kingston upon Thames
Surrey KT2 6SR
Tel: 020 8247 1175
www.croner.co.uk

Published by
Wolters Kluwer (UK) Limited
145 London Road
Kingston upon Thames
Surrey KT2 6SR
Tel: 020 8247 1175
www.croner.co.uk

First published April 2008

© Wolters Kluwer (UK) Limited

British Library Cataloguing-in-Publication Data.

A catalogue record for this book is available from the British Library.

ISBN 978-1-85524-714-7

Typeset in-house at Wolters Kluwer (UK) Limited
Printed in the Netherlands by Alfabase, Alphen aan den Rijn

Contributors

Dr Roger K Bentley, BSc, PhD, CChem, FRSC, CFIOSH, worked in the chemical industry for 25 years, latterly as a loss prevention manager when he developed his experience of emergency planning at a COMAH top tier site. In 1994, he became an independent safety consultant and is now managing director of Astley Limited. His business activities include advising on chemical safety and risk assessment, emergency planning, occupational health and safety training, and security training and consultancy. Also, as an expert witness, he has provided expert chemical opinion in many cases involving incidents and exposures leading to injuries and diseases. He may be contacted by e-mail on *rkb@astley-services.demon.co.uk*.

Paul Clarke, BA(Hons), DPA, moved into the field of EU information after training as a librarian, and eventually became a Visiting Fellow at the European Business Centre at Anglia Ruskin University and the Managing Editor of the Lawtel EU database. In September 2001, he left Lawtel to set up EU Editorial Services Ltd. The author of several books on European topics, including the Structural Funds and publications on health and safety legislation, he now writes on a range of topics. Paul regularly runs training courses on EU legislation and has written and presented courses on funding for the European Commission. He may be contacted by e-mail on *paul@eueditorial.karoo.co.uk*.

Mike Everley, MA, MPhil, CFIOS, MIIRSM, LCG, is a health and safety consultant. He was a law examiner for NEBOSH and has also worked as a tutor on the MBA course run by Henley Management College. He regularly teaches on NEBOSH Diploma and Certificate courses and assists large, medium and small concerns with heath and safety issues. Further details can be found on his website at *www.mike.everley.freeuk.com*.

Peter Power is managing director of Visor Consultants Limited and a popular speaker and writer on crisis/business continuity management who often appears on TV and Radio programmes. He specialises in delivering highly successful exercises and workshops on the theme of corporate resilience. Peter has considerable experience gained at the front line of many serious incidents and is quoted in the UK Cabinet Office Guide on Integrated Emergency Management. He is also a special advisor to the UK Commission on national security and the primary author of the ubiquitous Gold, Silver and Bronze command structure. Peter can be contacted by e-mail on *info@visorconsultants.com*.

Norman Selwyn is one of the country's leading authorities on health and safety and employment law, and is well known as a popular lecturer, author and consultant, who has written extensively on employment law. He has served as a magistrate, chairman of the Social Security Appeal Tribunal and as an Immigration Adjudicator. He is the author of *Croner's The Law of Health & Safety at Work 2007/08*, now in its 16th edition. Norman can be contacted by e-mail on *juno@selwynfamily.co.uk*.

Robert Spicer, MA (Law), Diploma in Legal Studies, is an experienced public access barrister specialising in employment law and health and safety. He has published widely in these areas and has represented a number of clients in disputes related to their employment. He lives and works in Bristol. He may be contacted by e-mail on *RSp4593558@aol.com*.

Roy Thornley, MPhil, is a corporate risk consultant specialising in the field of corporate manslaughter by criminal negligence. In 2003, he was awarded a Masters Degree in Philosophy in recognition of a programme of work entitled *Corporate Manslaughter — A Reformulation of Criminal Law Policy*. His research into this complex area of the law has helped shape Government policy in reforming the law of involuntary manslaughter. He is registered with the Police National Crime and Operations Faculty at Bramshill and with Business Link Wessex. He is a member of the Advisory Council at the Centre for Corporate Accountability. Further details can be found on his website at *www.corporate-manslaughter.com*.

Karen Todd, BEng (Hons), PGDip, CEng MIMechE, is a self-employed Health and Safety Consultant and Consulting Engineer. As well as being qualified in Health and Safety, she is also a chartered mechanical engineer. Her work is extremely varied — she says that when her phone rings she never knows what to expect, but will take on anything within her capabilities, and if she can't help she has an excellent network of fellow colleagues who can. Her speciality is workplace personal injury accidents and their prevention. She acts as an expert witness in civil cases, and also does some insurance work as a liability surveyor. Further details can be found on her website at *www.athena-safety.co.uk*.

Foreword

By Norman Selwyn

The inability of the law to cope with manslaughter charges against all but smaller companies following deaths caused by inadequate health and safety procedures has long been a source of disappointment to pro-active campaigners. The reason is that, for manslaughter prosecution to succeed, there must be *mens rea* (ie a guilty mind) and a corporate body, being in essence a paper creation, can hardly be said to have a "mind". As far as smaller companies were concerned, it was easier to link the controlling mind of the director(s) as being the mind of the company, but the fact that only seven such prosecutions have succeeded over the years is an indication of the difficulties faced by enforcement authorities.

Since April 2008 all this has changed with the coming into force of the Corporate Manslaughter and Corporate Homicide Act 2007. Essentially, the Act enables corporate bodies to face manslaughter charges in appropriate circumstances if a death occurs because of the way in which the body manages or organises its activities constitutes a gross breach of the duty of care. The organisation will only be guilty of the offence if the way in which its senior managers manage or organise its activities is a substantial element in the breach.

The new offence is in addition to and an alternative to existing criminal liabilities, which indeed may be brought concurrently. On conviction, there is the possibility of an unlimited fine and, perhaps of greater significance, the imposition of a remedial and/or publicity order. Also, in the event that a corporate manslaughter charge fails, a jury may still convict a defendant organisation of breaches of appropriate health and safety rules.

The Act is by no means perfect. Critics will argue that a number of defects and omissions mean that its effectiveness will be limited. For example, it creates no new offence for individual directors who control corporate bodies, a failure to comply with a remedial order can be visited by a fine, which is strange, considering that the failure to comply with a prohibition order is punishable by imprisonment, and the opportunity to introduce alternative sanctions, eg a profit order, has been missed. Perhaps the most significant omission in the Act is the absence of specific health and safety duties placed on directors.

The essential question is, therefore, will the Act do any good? Will it reduce to any significant extent work-related deaths or serious accidents? The answer will clearly depend on a number of factors, which are outlined in this book and written about by authors with many years experience of health and safety law. It is estimated that there are likely to be about a dozen or so corporate manslaughter prosecutions each year, and it is felt that the clarification of the law will more than likely lead to these being successful. The failures of high-profile cases such as the Herald of Free Enterprise disaster in 1987 and the Southall rail accident in 1997, to name but two, are unlikely to be repeated.

But perhaps the Act will have its greatest impact on the health and safety culture of all major companies which engage in potentially dangerous activities. Health and safety must now be firmly placed at boardroom level. There is also a more level playing field, in that all corporate entities, whether large or small, including many government departments, are within the scope of the law and will have to ensure that adequate health and safety resources are provided, and that policies and procedures are reviewed on a regular basis.

A significant event which will indirectly affect the way in which the Act starts to bite has been the publication of guidance issued by the Institute of Directors and the Health and Safety Commission on leadership actions for directors and board members (*Leading Health and Safety at Work* available at *www.iod.com* or *www.hse.gov.uk/leadership*). This requires the board to accept formally and publicly its collective role in providing occupational health and safety leadership in its organisation, as well as the acceptance by each board member of his or her individual role in providing that leadership. In other words, there must not only be a health and safety policy but a genuine commitment to implement that policy. There must be active participation of all employees, with adequate feedback to the board director responsible for health and safety, so that the culture can permeate throughout the organisation. If this happens, there will be a greater chance of preventing major industrial accidents.

The New Act: A Personal Observation

An Introduction by Roy Thornley

I welcome the opportunity to write the introduction to the publication of this book on the new Corporate Manslaughter and Corporate Homicide Act 2007.

Few people will need reminding of the capsize of the Herald of Free Enterprise outside Zebrugge harbour in 1987 which killed 193 people, and the collapse of the manslaughter trial of 7 senior managers and the company that followed. The reasons why the prosecution failed to convict may not be so well known. But it is sufficient to say that, so far as the defendant company was concerned, present law proved inadequate by not allowing evidence of failure by omission of the senior managers to perform their duty to be collectively considered. The *Sheen Report* into the disaster recorded that:

> *"All concerned in management, from the members of the board of directors down to the junior superintendents, were guilty of fault in that all must be regarded as sharing responsibility for the failure of management. From top to bottom the body corporate was infected with the disease of sloppiness."*

This case may be considered the beginning of a 17-year debate on how to make companies more accountable to the communities in which they operate. In this time we have witnessed major train crashes claiming multiple loss of life and yet no large company has ever been convicted of manslaughter. Thankfully, with the advent of the new corporate manslaughter legislation this will now change. Its stringent provisions mean that a company's internal control of health and safety is a business risk that senior managers can no longer regard as a minor matter. Directors would be wise to act immediately, by raising the status of health and safety to one that assumes the same level of boardroom importance as other business risks.

The business case for the development of a rigorous health and safety system is wide and varied. However, there should be no greater incentive for individual or corporate employers to do everything possible to protect life, than to experience the harrowing account of how four teenagers died at sea in what has become known as the "Lyme Bay" tragedy.

On 22 March 1993, a group of eight children and their teacher set out in kayaks on an open sea crossing in Lyme Bay, Dorset. They were all novices attending an activity holiday operated by OLL Ltd. The two instructors who led the group were themselves untrained, inexperienced and without adequate safety equipment. After a short period of time the kayaks capsized and four children drowned.

In evidence, one of the survivors told the court, "The situation was deteriorating rapidly and people passed out within that last hour, they all deteriorated rapidly ... they were really strong and fighting all the time. The whole thing was one big nightmare and as a result I've lost four of my best friends."

On 4 December 1994, the managing director and the company were convicted of unlawful killing by gross negligence. It was the first conviction of a company for manslaughter in English legal history.

The investigation and trial exposed a systemic failure in the duty to take care, owed to the children. The trial judge, before passing a sentence of three years' imprisonment, told the defendant:

"...Whether by rules and procedures, adequate and properly qualified staff or by a close personal monitoring of the conduct of the centre, matters not, you must have known what was required of you and your company. I regret to say that it seems to me that there is force in the suggestion made in the course of this trial that to a degree you were more interested in sales than safety. Parents and teachers trusted you, and you betrayed that trust."

I was the senior investigating officer who made the decision to treat this incident as a crime as opposed to an accident at sea.

The human cost of this case remains incalculable. To experience the utter anguish of loving parents and family, sitting in stunned disbelief that their children, placed with trust in the care of others, should have their lives prematurely ended in such a devastating way, is to understand that this is a lifetime burden from which there is little escape. The fears and distress suffered by the survivors' clinging to life, while friends died around them are unimaginable, their return to normal life proved to be a long and painful journey. The young and inexperienced instructor trembled with remorse as she recounted in detail her traumatic memories of the ill-fated canoeing trip when giving evidence. And while time heals wounds, there will never be a moment when one can truly say that the events of that fateful day will be forgotten.

Naturally, public sentiment rests with the victims' families and survivors, but consider for a moment the shock and horror, the feelings of anticipation and anxiety, of the defendant and his family. Firstly learning of the deaths and then driven by events, having to cope with the sudden intense media coverage that such emotive incidents attract. Reading and viewing daily reports while reporters theorise and speculate in an effort to unravel the sequence of events. The realisation that the incident was to be treated as a criminal offence, followed in time by the arrest, charges of manslaughter and the final condemnation by a jury of peers in their finding of guilt. A prison sentence and enforced company closure, by the imposition of a fine that took every available penny out of the corporate account. To be shamed in the national and international media, as the man who wouldn't listen, reading headlines in the confines of a prison cell such as: "Director jailed for canoe trip manslaughter", "Fatal blunders that defy belief", "Boss is guilty", "Blunder after tragic blunder". This is merely the beginning of a sentence, the repercussions of which will be endured by the defendant forever.

The Lyme Bay incident was an unnecessary tragedy. So easily preventable had the company (through its managing director) devised, instituted, enforced and maintained a safe system of work, responded to complaints that highlighted corporate failings in safety and ensured that staff were properly supervised.

It would of course be considered ludicrous to suggest that a company wilfully intends to cause death. But a company's intentional acts, such as failing to protect people in their care, as we have seen, can lead to death. In any inquiry into a suspicious death, investigators will undoubtedly analyse evidence to identify individual liability. Where this cannot be proved, it is agreed that justice requires that companies be punished where death or serious injury results, where the conduct of a corporation has been seriously blameworthy in the circumstances. This is the notion of retribution — the vindication of the victim in recognition of the violation of their rights.

Relating the debilitating effects of such a tragedy on both victim and defendant should at this point have served its purpose of fastening senior managers to pay closer attention to safety in all of their corporate activities. If this has not been achieved, senior managers may wish to consider other reasons to support the business case for taking action.

New Corporate Manslaughter Legislation

The Corporate Manslaughter and Corporate Homicide Act 2007 became law on 6 April 2008. While this new book provides an essential guide to the requirements of the Act, senior managers should take immediate steps to review safety policies in response to a change in the basis of liability for the prosecution of companies for manslaughter.

Understanding the terms of the Act is absolutely critical. It includes the existing duties that employers and organisations already owe to their employees, in respect of workplace activities and the premises they occupy. It now accepts the collective decision-making processes of larger companies by disposing of the prerequisite under present law of proving gross negligent manslaughter at "controlling mind" level. It introduces liability based on the way corporate activities are managed or organised by its senior managers. Corporate prosecution is likely to follow if a person dies because the senior managers of the company fail to take effective steps to ensure that employees, when carrying on the business of the company, take proper safety measures.

Companies are fictitious entities; they cannot act for themselves and may only act through their directors and senior managers. In consequence, senior managers remain vulnerable to prosecution under present law in circumstances where death is allegedly caused by an individual's gross negligence. For example, one of the requirements of the new legislation is for senior managers to ensure mandatory compliance with health and safety legislation. In small to medium-sized companies where policy makers are more easily identifiable, individual directors may be especially at risk if they choose to disregard the health and safety requirements of their business.

Convictions, Fatal Injuries and Costs

Convictions for manslaughter by gross negligence at individual level are not as rare as one may think. According to the Centre for Corporate Accountability:

(a) there have been 22 incidents (involving at least one death) that have resulted in a conviction of a company, company director or business owner
(b) 51 deaths were involved in these convictions
(c) 7 companies were convicted
(d) 16 company directors were convicted
(e) 8 sole traders or partners were convicted.

There are three ongoing manslaughter prosecutions.

As a result of these convictions, 14 directors and business owners were immediately jailed to terms of imprisonment of various durations and, in one case, for 9 years. Others received suspended sentences or community service orders. A short analysis of these cases shows evidence of:

- failure to ensure sufficient training, resulting in lack of knowledge or experience to carry out the particular task
- failure to provide safety equipment
- failure to invest even minimum amounts of money in safety measures
- deliberate deactivation of safety cut outs
- removal of safety mechanisms designed to protect the operator of machinery
- failure to carry out vital repairs to equipment

- failure to isolate machinery for maintenance procedures
- failure to provide a safe system of work
- failure to maintain machinery
- failure to risk assess
- indifference to even basic health and safety precautions
- failure to maintain company vehicles
- failure to use correct safety equipment
- failure to use trained personnel
- failure to identify and respond to the "special needs" of staff
- allowing workers to work excessive hours
- failure to provide preventative equipment, supervision and training
- allowing company drivers to falsify records so they could work longer hours.

Whatever observations may be made with regard to these cases, one aspect that dominates is the preparedness of business owners to pursue a misguided bottom line. A willingness to throw all caution to the wind in the pursuit of profit; achieved by cutting corners, turning a blind eye and a general failure to invest in safety. In these cases it proved an ill-founded strategy that led to imprisonment.

New legislation unquestionably consigns apathetic and complacent attitudes towards safety into the corporate waste bin. Any prevailing thoughts of "it won't happen to me" used as an excuse not to set into place a safe system of work is strictly unthinkable. Work-related deaths have remained at a fairly constant level for a number of years, with at least one person fatally injured every other working day. The Health and Safety Executive (HSE) report, *Health and Safety Statistics 2006/07*, on work-related health and safety in Great Britain, includes the following facts.

- 241 workers were killed at work.
- 141,350 other injuries to employees were reported under RIDDOR (Reporting of Injuries, Diseases and Dangerous Occurrences Regulations 1995).
- 274,000 reported injuries occurred, according to the Labour Force Survey.
- 2.2 million people were suffering from an illness they believed was caused or made worse by their current or past work. Of these, 646,000 were new cases in the last 12 months.
- 2037 people died of mesothelioma (2005) and thousands more from other occupational cancers and lung diseases.
- 36 million working days were lost overall, 30 million due to work-related ill health and 6 million due to workplace injury.
- 1141 offences were prosecuted by the HSE and 2557 offences were prosecuted by local authorities (2005/2006).

While the numbers of people who die of workplace injuries remains unacceptably high, this in itself represents just a fraction of the overall loss of life accruing from the workplace. The HSE, in its publication *Driving at Work: Managing Work-related Road Safety*, highlights the carnage on our domestic roads, making it the largest category of work-related fatalities in the UK and estimates that:

> "... up to a third of all traffic accidents involve somebody who is at work at the time. This may account for over 20 fatalities and 250 serious injuries every week."

In *Driving for Work*, published by the Department for Transport, it is estimated that the full cost to the employer might be £8 to £36 for every pound paid on the insurance claim.

The extent to which a work-related accident could disrupt business ambitions, may be a topic not fully explored by directors. Company budgetary projections should take into account a full cost analysis of business continuity, should such an event occur. For example, directors should bear in mind that any contingency plan should include the provision of replacement personnel who are competent and qualified to undertake the task in hand. Directors would be considered negligent if they allowed unqualified personnel to take charge, making delegation to another member of staff who is untutored an unacceptable practice. This is merely one consideration among many others.

Companies operate in a global business market, therefore directors will readily appreciate the benefits to business by retention of the competitive edge over commercial rivals. An integral part of this strategy will be that of good marketing and publicity extolling the merits of the company.

It follows that bad publicity can severely damage the reputation and business potential of any company. Legislators have also recognised the damaging effects of stigma attached to a corporate conviction for manslaughter, by the inclusion of publicity orders as a part of the sentencing package. Such an order will require the company to publicise that it has been convicted, giving the details, the amount of fine and any terms of the remedial order made. Remedial orders are directives to the senior managers of the convicted company to remedy any management failure that led to death.

The requirement to comply with legal obligations and the scale of penalty that may be imposed for failure should provide further incentive for senior managers to protect people who may be killed from exposure to their business activities. For those who feel compliance is an insufficient reason to act, consideration should be given to the following possible consequences of non-compliance with health and safety legislation.

- Crisis management, etc, eg information gathering, public relations, media strategy plan, legal representation, assessment of accountability, dedicated director involvement following a serious incident.
- Compliance with the police investigation.
- Remedial work to remedy any deficiency in the company's safety policies which may be identified by the enforcement agencies during the investigation process.
- Defence costs.
- Fines and other penalties that may be imposed.
- Costs associated with civil claims.
- Loss of production.
- Insurance implications — is the company becoming too much of a risk?
- Loss of standing in the business community; arguably more acute in the small to medium-sized business.

Without doubt the Corporate Manslaughter and Corporate Homicide Act 2007 will achieve its purpose by making it easier to bring companies to account for manslaughter by gross negligence.

It emphasises government determination to bring the unnecessary loss of life that emanates from the workplace to an end. In consequence, it is expected that the Crown Prosecution Service will use the new basis of liability to reinforce this message by assessing evidence for prosecution under the Act as opposed to breach of regulation.

The effect of an increased level of corporate conviction and the added publicity given to it will send a strong message of intent to those companies who are reckless with matters of safety.

Companies who keep health and safety management at the front of their corporate agenda will have nothing to fear from the new legislation. There can never be a better time for senior managers to review their safety policies, with particular focus on how they manage and organise the company's activities. Protecting people inevitably means protecting you and your company.

This brings me back to the tragedy at Lyme Bay, the emotions of this case and the final words of Judge Ognall to the parents.

> *"Any lessons learned, or tributes paid to those who survived, can be of no comfort to the parents of Simon, Dean, Claire or Rachel. They have had to endure not only bereavement but the deeply harrowing rehearsal in this trial of the circumstances of their untimely deaths. None in this court could do other than grieve for them, and condolences are surely empty words. They died on the brink of their adult lives. In truth they were still only children. But despite that, each did all they could before they succumbed to be of brave heart, of good cheer, and of comfort and support to their companions. It must surely be said of each of them that they took back to the coiner the mintage of human kind."*

It is to the memory of Claire Louise Langley, Rachel Jane Walker, Simon James Dunne and Dean Mathew Sayer and to those who survived: Emma Louise Hartley, Marie Elaine Rendle, Samantha Stansbie and Joanne Willis that this introduction is dedicated, in the true hope that those who read this book will themselves not only share the sadness of this case but be motivated by it to become leaders in health and safety and promote best practice to protect the lives of people in their care.

Contents

Chapter 1

The Need for Change

Manslaughter — New Statutory Offence

- At one time it was thought that a company could not commit a criminal offence because it lacked the capacity to do the act and did not have a culpable mind.
- Companies and their directors were generally held to be at least partially to blame for a number of high-profile disasters in the last few decades. However, no individual was successfully prosecuted for causing any of the deaths.
- The problem with existing law was that, to convict a company of manslaughter, it had to be shown that a causal link existed between a grossly negligent act or omission by a person who is the "controlling mind" of the company and the immediate cause of death.
- The prosecution had to show that an act or omission by a controlling officer had created a dangerous situation and that proper precautions were not taken to guard against that danger.
- In 1996, the Law Commission proposed the introduction of a new offence of "corporate killing" which for the first time would make it unnecessary to identify a "controlling mind".
- The Commission also published a draft Bill on involuntary homicide which included a specific clause dealing with causation and stated that a management failure by a corporation may be regarded as a cause of a person's death.
- The Government accepted most of the Law Commission's proposals, but also decided that the new provisions should apply to all employing organisations.
- The Corporate Manslaughter and Corporate Homicide Act 2007 came into force on 6 April 2008 creating a new statutory offence of corporate manslaughter (or "corporate homicide" in Scotland). This replaces the common law offence of manslaughter by gross negligence.

1.1   At one time it was thought that a company could not commit a criminal offence because it lacked two crucial elements that are required to establish liability where most criminal offences are concerned:

- the capacity to do the act (*actus reus*)

- a culpable mind (*mens rea*).

1.2   However, in 1996 the Law Commission proposed the introduction of a new offence of "corporate killing" which for the first time would make it unnecessary to identify a "controlling mind" (also known as a "ruling mind" or a "directing mind").

1.3   The Corporate Manslaughter and Corporate Homicide Act 2007 came into force on 6 April 2008 creating a new statutory offence of corporate manslaughter (or "corporate homicide" in Scotland), replacing the common law offence of manslaughter by gross negligence.

In Practice

Limitations of the Legislation

The Controlling Mind

1.4 Under the Companies Act 1985, companies have a legal identity that is distinct from those who own or work for them. At one time it was thought that a company could not commit a criminal offence because it lacked two crucial elements that are required to establish liability where most criminal offences are concerned:

- the capacity to do the act (*actus reus*)
- a culpable mind (*mens rea*).

1.5 It has now been established, however, that a company can act through its controlling directors or managers.

Companies and their Directors

1.6 Companies and their directors were generally held to be at least partially to blame for a number of high-profile disasters in the last two decades, including the following.

- Football suffered both the Hillsborough Stadium disaster, where 95 people died, and the fire at Bradford City, which killed a further 49 people.
- The UK transport system was hit by a series of accidents, including:
  - the fire at King's Cross Underground station which resulted in 31 deaths
  - the Clapham train crash which killed 37 people and injured 500
  - the Paddington derailment where 31 passengers were killed and 250 injured
  - a train crash at Purley which saw a further 5 deaths added.
- The dredger Bowbelle collided with the Marchioness on the River Thames killing 51 party-goers and an explosion destroyed the Piper Alpha oil platform in the North Sea resulting in the death of 167 crew.

1.7 The common factor in these and other disasters, including the sinking of the Herald of Free Enterprise ferry, was that no individual was successfully prosecuted for causing any of the deaths.

Hatfield Rail Crash Prosecutions

1.8 Where prosecutions were brought, as in the case of the Hatfield rail crash when four people died, companies were convicted on health and safety grounds but no directors were held personally responsible for the deaths.

1.9 The judge in the Hatfield case, for example, ordered all manslaughter charges against the individuals concerned to be dropped halfway through the trial. He said that the conduct of the individuals was "at its highest, a bad error of judgement" and nowhere near the required standard of "gross negligence". He clearly recognised that his decision would be a major disappointment to the bereaved and those injured and went on to say "I have tried to explain why it is I am obliged by the existing law in my judgment to make these rulings. This case continues to underline the pressing need for the long-delayed reform of the law in this area of unlawful killing."

Causal Link Between a Grossly Negligent Act and Immediate Cause of Death

1.10   The problem with the existing law — which the Hatfield case judge highlighted — was that to convict a company of manslaughter it must be shown that a causal link exists between a grossly negligent act or omission, by a person who is the "controlling mind" of the company, and the immediate cause of death.

1.11   While that might be possible in the case of a building firm where the owner and managing director employs perhaps five or six workers, it clearly proved impossible to pinpoint who, if anyone, in Balfour Beatty was responsible for the mistakes that led to the Hatfield crash.

1.12   Similarly, P&O directors escaped prosecution despite Mr Justice Sheen saying in his report on the Herald of Free Enterprise incident that, "From top to bottom the body corporate was infected with the disease of sloppiness".

The Identification Principle

1.13   Under the law as it existed before the Act came into force, the prosecution had to show that an act or omission by a controlling officer had created a dangerous situation and that proper precautions were not taken to guard against that danger. This is known as the identification principle.

1.14   The problems which this placed in the way of a successful prosecution of a large company were highlighted in *R v HM Coroner for East Kent, ex p Spooner* [1989]. Lord Justice Bingham said in this case, "It is important to bear in mind an important distinction. A company may be vicariously liable for the negligent acts and omissions of its servants and agents, but for a company to be criminally liable for manslaughter … it is required that the *mens rea* and *actus reus* of manslaughter should be established not against those who acted for or in the name of the company but against those who were to be identified as the embodiment of the company itself."

1.15   The larger and more diffused a company's structure, the more difficult it is to attribute grossly negligent acts or omissions committed in the course of the company's operations to a controlling officer and, therefore, to the "embodiment of the company itself". Conversely, of course, the smaller the company the more likely it will be that such a causal link can be established. Since 1992 there have been more than 30 prosecution cases for work-related manslaughter but only 7 small organisations have been convicted.

1.16   Even the P&O European Ferries (Dover) Ltd case, in which the judge first ruled that a company might be properly indicted for manslaughter, ended in the acquittal of the defendant company.

First Companies Prosecuted for Manslaughter

1.17   It was December 1994 before OLL Ltd (formerly Active Leisure and Learning Ltd) became the first company in English legal history to be convicted of the common law crime of manslaughter. Its managing director, Peter Kite, also became the first director to be given a custodial sentence for a manslaughter conviction arising from the operation of a business when he was sentenced to two years' imprisonment. Four students canoeing at the Lyme Regis Activity Centre had drowned as a result of the unsafe practices allowed by Mr Kite at OLL.

1.18   Some of the other small companies convicted of corporate manslaughter include Jackson Transport (Ossett) Ltd, Teglgaard Hardwood Ltd, Nationwide Heating Systems Ltd and Keymark Services.

Injustice of the Legislation

1.19   It seems unjust that the owners of these firms should have been prosecuted because they were (or should have been) taking direct responsibility for health and safety matters, whereas directors of larger companies escaped simply because of the diffused management structures they had in place.

1.20   The Herald of Free Enterprise inquiry, for example, found that no single individual had responsibility for safety matters. If responsibility for the development of safety monitoring is not vested in a particular group or individual, of course, it becomes almost impossible to identify the "controlling mind" for whose shortcomings the company can be held liable. It has been suggested that shrewd and unscrupulous management might have taken advantage of that fact.

Crown Immunity

1.21   A further perceived injustice with the legislation is that Crown bodies, including government departments and other public sector organisations such as police forces, were excluded from potential prosecution by the concept of Crown immunity.

1.22   If they were involved in breaches of health and safety law which would have rendered a private company liable for possible prosecution, no action could be taken other than the Health and Safety Executive (HSE) issuing a Crown Censure. This exercise marked occasions where, but for Crown immunity, there would have been sufficient evidence to provide a realistic prospect of conviction in the courts.

1.23   It should be noted that many Crown bodies, such as government departments, lack a separate legal identity for the purposes of prosecution.

Law Commission Proposals

New Offence of "Corporate Killing"

1.24   In recent decades there has been a tendency for common law crimes to be replaced by statutory offences. The Law Commission has also been engaged in a long-term project to devise a statutory criminal code. As part of this exercise, it proposed in 1996 the introduction of a new offence of "corporate killing" which for the first time would make it unnecessary to identify a "controlling mind".

1.25   It is suggested in the Law Commission's report, *Legislating the Criminal Code: Involuntary Manslaughter*, that it should only be necessary to show that the organisation as a whole had failed to do what could be reasonably expected of it. The new offence would broadly correspond to the individual offence of killing by gross carelessness.

Draft Bill on Involuntary Homicide

1.26   The Commission also published a draft Bill on involuntary homicide which included a specific clause dealing with causation. This stated that a management failure by a corporation "may be regarded as a cause of a person's death notwithstanding that the immediate cause is the act or omission of an individual". The Commission argued that such express provision was necessary in order to make it clear that the ordinary principles of causation for homicide were applicable to the corporate offence. Accordingly, a jury could find that a corporation's management failure was the cause of death despite an intervention by an individual, eg the deliberate failure of an unsupervised frontline operator.

1.27   The Commission said that "there is a danger that, without [this provision] … the application of the ordinary rules of causation would in many cases result in a management failure being treated as a 'stage already set', and hence not linked in law to the death."

Government Proposals

1.28   The Law Commission's report provided the basis for the Government's subsequent consultation paper in 2000, *Reforming the Law on Involuntary Manslaughter: The Government's Proposals*. This accepted the wording of the core offence as suggested by the Law Commission, namely the following.
1. A corporation is guilty of corporate killing if:
    (a) a management failure by the corporation is the cause or one of the causes of a person's death
    (b) that failure constitutes conduct falling far below what can reasonably be expected of the corporation in the circumstances.
2. In this regard:
    (a) there is a management failure by a corporation if the way in which its activities are managed or organised fails to ensure the health and safety of persons employed in or affected by those activities
    (b) such a failure may be regarded as a cause of a person's death notwithstanding that the immediate cause is the act or omission of an individual.

Turnbull Guidance and Health and Safety Responsibilities

1.29   Nigel Turnbull, the Chairman of the Rank Group plc, produced *Internal Control: Guidance for Directors on the Combined Code*, published in 1999 by the Institute of Chartered Accountants in England and Wales. The Turnbull guidance, as it was known, was intended to help plcs to meet the London Stock Exchange listing rules.

1.30   The guidance was designed to assist finance and other directors to ensure their internal controls satisfied the needs of the company's business objectives, while safeguarding shareholder investments and company assets. The guidance marked a substantial change in the scope and formality of internal control evaluation and risk management reporting.

1.31   The guidance states, "Significant risks may, for example, include those related to market, credit, liquidity, technological, legal, health, safety and environmental, reputation, and business probity issues". The specific risks related to manslaughter therefore come under the remit of the Turnbull guidance.

1.32   Having established policies and procedures which ensure compliance with health and safety legislation, boards may delegate the task of implementing those policies and procedures to other individuals within the company, but, under the Turnbull principles, the directors should review regular reports on internal controls from those charged with day-to-day responsibility for health and safety management.

The Role of the Director

1.33   Further emphasising the importance of board involvement in health and safety, an October 2007 publication by the HSE and the Institute of Directors (IoD), was advertised as written by directors, for directors. *Leading Health and Safety at Work* carries on its front page the following two quotes that are central to the argument regarding corporate killing: "Board level involvement is an essential part of the 21st century trading ethic. Attitudes to health and safety are determined by the bosses, not the organisation's size" and "Health and safety is integral to success. Board members who do not show leadership in this area are failing in their duty as directors and their moral duty, and are damaging their organisation." The guidance is intended to help directors to plan, deliver, monitor and review health and safety in the workplace.

Political Support for Changes in the Law

1.34   At the Labour Party's first conference after its election victory in May 1997, the then Home Secretary Jack Straw announced that the Government intended to proceed with introducing the new offence of corporate killing.

Scope of the Bill

1.35   A working group of officials and lawyers was set up to consider how the proposed offences would work in practice. The result was the publication by the Home Office of its *Reforming the Law on Involuntary Manslaughter: The Government's Proposals* consultation paper.

1.36   While this accepted most of the Law Commission's proposals, the Government decided that the new provisions should apply to all employing organisations and not, as the Commission proposed, only to incorporated bodies. Bodies incorporated by private or local Act of Parliament (such as certain public utility companies) or special public Acts (including a number of organisations in the public sector, such as local authorities) and those established by Royal Charter (such as the BBC and some universities) as well as limited companies, should all be brought within the scope of the new Bill, the Government argued.

1.37   The new offence could be committed by "undertakings", as defined in the Health and Safety at Work, etc Act 1974, and could apply to "all employing organisations", including schools, hospital trusts, partnerships and unincorporated charities as well as one- or two-person businesses. This meant 3.5 million enterprises might become potentially liable for the offence of corporate killing.

1.38   The Law Commission had expressly removed the possibility of individuals being caught by the new offence. It said, "We intend that no individual should be liable to prosecution for the corporate offence, even as a secondary party. Our aim is, first, that the new offences of reckless killing and killing by gross carelessness should replace the law of involuntary manslaughter for individuals; and second, that the offence of killing by gross carelessness should be adapted so as to fit the special case of a corporation whose management or organisation of its activities is one of the causes of a death. The indirect extension of an individual's liability, by means of the new corporate offence, would be entirely contrary to our purpose."

1.39   In direct opposition to this proposal, however, the Government stated, "There is no good reason why an individual should not be convicted for aiding, abetting, counselling or procuring an offence of corporate killing."

Formal Proposal

1.40   The Labour Party promised a corporate killing law in three of its election manifestos, arguing that "companies and other organisations must be held properly to account for gross failings by their senior management which have fatal consequences". It was March 2005, however, before it eventually published a formal proposal.

1.41   The Government's formal proposal was based on the Law Commission's draft Bill, with some modifications, including provisions applying the new offence to Crown bodies. The Government later published an amendment to extend the scope of its Corporate Manslaughter and Corporate Homicide Bill to include deaths of people held in custody. The move followed a series of defeats in the House of Lords over the death in custody issue and was a late compromise to allow the new law to receive Royal Assent.

Reactions to the Act

1.42   The Corporate Manslaughter and Corporate Homicide Act 2007 received Royal Assent on 26 July 2007. It came into force on 6 April 2008 creating a new statutory offence of corporate manslaughter (or "corporate homicide" in Scotland), replacing the common law offence of manslaughter by gross negligence.

1.43   The Bill was widely welcomed, although trade unions and health and safety campaigners expressed concern about the absence of individual liability for directors and there was criticism of the extent to which public bodies are still exempt.

1.44   Campaigners in Scotland were also critical of the Government's decision to extend the Bill to their country despite the fact that separate legislation had been proposed. The Government argued that the Bill concerned health and safety and business associations, both of which are reserved matters under the Scotland Act 1998.

1.45   Professor Gary Slapper, director of the Open University law programme, said, "The new law is one of the most significant legislative changes to corporate responsibilities since the principles of the modern company were crystallised in the 14th century. The legislation makes it easier to convict culpable organisations. But the new law has not lowered the threshold of guilt: it criminalises only an organisation whose gross negligence results in death. Companies with good safety policies have nothing to fear from the new Act, even if someone dies in an awful accident."

1.46   The general secretary of the Trades Union Congress (TUC), Brendan Barber, argued that the parts of the Act relating to the individual liability of directors represented a failing. He stressed, however, that even though unions wanted individual directors to be made personally liable for safety breaches and would have liked penalties against employers committing safety crimes to be tougher, the new law should mean the start of a change in the safety culture at the top of the UK's companies.

Reputations at Risk

1.47   The Act contains a publicity order requiring firms convicted of corporate manslaughter to disclose their convictions in the public domain. A convicted firm will have to reveal the details not only of the offence and the amount of any fine but also the improvements it has been ordered to make to its health and safety culture.

1.48   Businesses are advised that if they do not meet current health and safety standards and have a poor safety culture then they should start restructuring and implementing the appropriate policies immediately. Health and safety needs to be taken seriously at all levels, especially at the executive level, so positive examples are set and a safety culture implemented from the top down. A health and safety director should be appointed to ensure concerns in this area as well as performance indicators, targets and failures are communicated directly to the board.

1.49   Under the legislation, the safety culture of an organisation is of greater importance than ever before. This will be especially true when defending a manslaughter prosecution under the Act, where documents such as internal memos, organisation charts, faxes and minutes of safety meetings will be vital in proving that poor management standards did not cause a breach of the duty of care.

List of Relevant Legislation

1.50
- Corporate Manslaughter and Corporate Homicide Act 2007
- Health and Safety at Work, etc Act 1974

Further Information

Publications

HSE Publications

The following is available from *www.hsebooks.com*.
- INDG417 *Leading Health and Safety at Work. Leadership Actions for Directors and Board Members*

Other Publications
- *Internal Control: Revised Guidance for Directors on the Combined Code*, Financial Reporting Council, 2005
- *Legislating the Criminal Code: Involuntary Manslaughter*, The Law Commission, Report No. 237

Organisations
- Institute of Chartered Accountants in England and Wales (ICAEW)
  Web: *www.icaew.co.uk*
  The Institute of Chartered Accountants in England and Wales is the largest professional accountancy body in Europe with over 128,000 members. The Institute was established by Royal Charter in 1880. The Institute is involved in a range of professional activities, including education, training, technical accounting issues and providing advice to its members.
- Institute of Chartered Accountants of Scotland (ICAS)
  Web: *www.icas.org.uk*
  The Institute of Chartered Accountants of Scotland is the world's first professional body of accountants.
- Institute of Directors (IoD)
  Web: *www.iod.com*
  The IoD provides a professional network for the business community.
- Health and Safety Executive (HSE)
  Web: *www.hse.gov.uk*
  The HSE and the Health and Safety Commission are responsible for the regulation of almost all the risks to health and safety arising from work activity in the UK.
- Law Commission
  Web: *www.lawcom.gov.uk*
  The Law Commission is an independent body that reviews the law of England and Wales and recommends reform when it is needed.

Chapter 2

Corporate Manslaughter and Corporate Homicide Act 2007

Corporate Manslaughter and Corporate Homicide Act 2007

- Prosecution for corporate manslaughter is the prosecution of a company as a result of a death or deaths for which the company is held responsible.
- Corporate manslaughter is a type of involuntary manslaughter (killing by gross negligence).
- Successful corporate manslaughter prosecutions are extremely rare because of the need to identify a "directing mind" of the company who is also guilty.
- The Corporate Manslaughter and Corporate Homicide Act 2007, which came into force on 6 April 2008, introduced a new offence for prosecuting companies and other organisations where there has been a gross failing in the management of health and safety with fatal consequences.
- Unlimited fines may be issued and the courts may force companies to publicise their convictions through a "publicity order", leading to severe damage to reputations under the new legislation.
- Under the new legislation, individual directors will not be liable for any deaths due to a general breach of the duty of care by the firm.
- Employers should take steps now to review their management structures and health and safety policies.

2.1   Prior to the introduction of the Corporate Manslaughter and Corporate Homicide Act 2007, which came into force on 6 April 2008, the state of the law surrounding the criminal liability of companies for corporate manslaughter was unclear and confusing, and successful prosecutions of companies for manslaughter were rare. These facts have been highlighted by the collapse or failure of manslaughter prosecutions against companies brought in the wake of high profile public disasters such as the sinking of the Herald of Free Enterprise.

2.2   There was public feeling that this state of affairs was unsatisfactory and that companies should be criminally liable if their behaviour results in fatalities.

2.3   The Government had been promising for many years to legislate to clarify the law of corporate manslaughter but the publication of draft legislation was continually delayed. Following a Law Commission Report in 1996, the Government did publish draft proposals in 2000 which represented a dramatic widening of the potential criminal liability of companies and their officers.

In Practice

The State of the Law Prior to the Act

Background — the Law of Manslaughter

2.4   In categorising criminal behaviour, English law required two elements to be present.
1. There had to be a criminal act, known to lawyers as the *actus reus*. In general, no crime can be committed unless there is a voluntary act or omission.

2. There had to be criminal intent, known to lawyers as the *mens rea*. Recklessness and gross negligence are sufficient to be included within the definition of criminal intent for manslaughter.

2.5 Manslaughter is divided into two types, voluntary and involuntary. It is the latter type which relates to corporate manslaughter.

2.6 Involuntary manslaughter occurs when there is an unlawful killing but there is no intent to kill or cause grievous bodily harm. Involuntary manslaughter is further sub-divided into unlawful act manslaughter and gross negligence manslaughter.

Unlawful Act Manslaughter

2.7 Unlawful act manslaughter occurs when the killing is the result of an unlawful or criminal act that all sober and reasonable people would realise would expose the victim to the risk of physical harm. It is irrelevant whether or not the accused knows the act is unlawful and criminal and whether or not he or she intends to do harm.

Gross Negligence Manslaughter

2.8 In gross negligence manslaughter, the following elements had to be present.
1. The accused had to owe a duty of care to the victim. The ordinary principles of the law of negligence applied in ascertaining whether such a duty exists.
2. The accused had to have breached that duty. A person could be liable for manslaughter by neglect of a positive duty arising from the nature of his or her occupation.
3. The breach had to have caused the death of the victim. This is a question of fact that the jury has to decide.
4. The breach had to be characterised as gross negligence or recklessness. In the words of Land J in *R v Stone and Dobson* (1997), "It is clear ... that the indifference to an obvious risk and appreciation of such risk coupled with a determination nevertheless to run it, are both examples of recklessness. What the prosecution have to prove is a breach of ... duty in circumstances that the jury feel convinced that the defendant's conduct can properly be described as reckless. That is to so say a reckless disregard of danger to the health and welfare of the infirm person. Mere inadvertence is not enough. The defendant must have been proved to have been indifferent to an obvious risk of injury to health, or actually to have foreseen the risk but to have determined nonetheless to have run it."

2.9 Failure to appreciate that the risk existed did not of itself amount to recklessness.

2.10 With effect from 6 April 2008, the common law offence of manslaughter by gross negligence in its application to corporations and other organisations was abolished.

Corporate Manslaughter

2.11 The most common entity in corporate manslaughter is a company or corporation but the law will also apply to other abstract entities such as councils. For example, Barrow Borough Council was charged with manslaughter in February 2004 following the death of seven people from legionnaires' disease.

2.12 A company is a separate legal entity in its own right but it is not a "real" person. Because it is not a real person, a company cannot commit voluntary manslaughter, nor can it commit unlawful act manslaughter. It can, however, commit manslaughter by gross negligence or recklessness.

2.13 The law of corporate manslaughter is separate from health and safety offences for which companies are liable and in respect of which companies are regularly prosecuted and fined. For example, Thames Trains was fined a record £2 million for breaches of health and safety law in respect of the Paddington rail crash.

The Identification Principle

2.14   Under existing law, a company could only be prosecuted successfully for manslaughter if the guilt of an identified human individual could be attributed to the company. In other words, the company must have had a criminal intent, or *mens rea*. In the words of Rose LJ in Attorney General's Reference (No 2 of 1999) (2000): "Unless an identified individual's conduct, characterised as gross criminal negligence, can be attributed to the company, the company is not, in the present state of the common law, liable for manslaughter."

2.15   This is known as the "identification principle" of corporate liability and was expounded in a ruling arising out of the failed prosecution of Great Western Trains for the Southall train crash. The effect of this is that the relevant person had to be so closely identified with the company as to amount to its alter ego and must be the company's "directing mind". In practice, for there to have been a successful manslaughter prosecution of a company it is necessary for there to be a successful prosecution of a company director or similar for manslaughter.

2.16   In small companies, where there are one or two directors, identifying an individual who is a directing mind of the company is relatively straightforward. Indeed, the seven successful corporate manslaughter prosecutions previous to the introduction of the new Act, were all of small companies.

2.17   However, in a large company, where structures can be very complex and responsibilities are divided, identifying specific individuals who can be characterised as the embodiment of the company and who have been grossly negligent or reckless is often impossible. This is why prosecutions for corporate manslaughter were rarely brought and often failed, even in the highest profile cases.

2.18   The first successful prosecution of a company for manslaughter occurred as recently as 1994, when the company OLL Ltd was found guilty in relation to the deaths of four teenagers who drowned during a canoeing trip off Lyme Regis. The managing director was also found guilty of manslaughter and imprisoned.

2.19   The most high-profile failed corporate manslaughter prosecution was of P&O Ferries in relation to the sinking of the Herald of Free Enterprise. Although the judge commented that P&O was "infected from top to bottom with the disease of sloppiness" and was guilty of "staggering complacency", no controlling mind could be identified and so no criminal guilt could be attributed to the company.

Manslaughter Penalties

2.20   Although the courts could impose unlimited fines, in practice the fines imposed upon companies convicted of manslaughter were low, possibly reflecting the size of the companies.

Corporate Manslaughter Legislation

2.21   The Corporate Manslaughter and Corporate Homicide Act 2007 introduced a new offence across the UK for prosecuting companies and other organisations where there has been a gross failing, throughout the organisation in the management of health and safety with fatal consequences (known as corporate manslaughter in England and Wales and corporate homicide in Scotland).

2.22   The law applies to all organisations that employ people and this includes partnerships, clubs, trade unions, schools and other educational institutions, local authorities, hospital trusts and individuals who employ others in small businesses. Its applicability is very wide.

2.23 Under the new Act, companies, organisations and, for the first time, government bodies, face an unlimited fine if they are found to have caused death due to their gross corporate health and safety failures.

2.24 The introduction of the Corporate Manslaughter and Corporate Homicide Act 2007 has the following effects:
1. It is now easier to prosecute companies and other large organisations when gross failures in the management of health and safety lead to death, by delivering a new, more effective basis for corporate liability.
2. It allows unlimited fines to be issued and enables the courts to force companies to publicise their convictions through a "publicity order", leading to severe damage to reputations.
3. It has reformed the law so that a key obstacle to successful prosecutions has now been removed because both small and large companies can be held liable for manslaughter where gross failures in the management of health and safety cause death, not just health and safety violations.
4. It complements the existing law under which individuals can be prosecuted for gross negligence manslaughter and health and safety offences, where there is direct evidence of their culpability.
5. It is designed to complement existing health and safety legislation so new regulations are not imposed on business.
6. It lifts Crown immunity to prosecution meaning that Crown bodies — such as government departments — will be liable to prosecution for the first time.
7. It will apply to companies and other corporate bodies, in the public and private sector, government departments, police forces, and certain unincorporated bodies — such as partnerships — where these are employers.

2.25 Safety culture is a key factor for juries to consider in deciding whether or not there has been a gross breach in health and safety management. The individuals within the company are not liable to prosecution under the new Act.

Who Will Prosecute?

2.26 The police and the health and safety enforcing authority, eg the Health and Safety Executive, investigates most workplace fatalities and such investigations may lead to corporate manslaughter prosecutions. Previously, only the police and the Crown Prosecution Service could carry out this role.

Penalties for Corporate Killing

2.27 Under the new Corporate Manslaughter and Corporate Homicide Act 2007, unlimited fines may be issued, and the courts may force companies to publicise their convictions through a "publicity order", leading to severe damage to reputations.

Evasion of Liability

2.28 Most prosecutions for the offence are likely to be against companies, which gives rise to the real risk that corporate structures could be exploited to try to evade liability, eg by establishing financially weak subsidiary companies to carry out risky activities or by dissolution or insolvency of a guilty company. The Government is anxious that enforcement action should be a real deterrent.

2.29 The law applies to foreign companies doing business in the UK so that it is not possible for a company incorporated overseas but carrying out activities here to escape prosecution. The Government recognises that there may be practical problems in taking enforcement action against such companies.

2.30   Criminal proceedings may be brought against parent companies or other companies within a group if their management failings contributed to the death. This will prevent group structures from being used for evasion, eg for establishing subsidiary companies to carry out risky business or by establishing financially weak subsidiary companies with insufficient assets to pay any fine.

2.31   The Act makes provisions against criminal liability evasion by dissolving a company or making it insolvent before the prosecution takes place. Companies could be subject to legal proceedings to freeze their property and assets and that such proceedings could be taken before a prosecution commences, to prevent assets being transferred or dissipated.

The Individual

2.32   The law makes companies, not directors, liable for any deaths due to a general breach of the duty of care by the firm. Individual directors are not personally liable, as the new manslaughter offence will apply only to corporations, including public bodies.

Territorial Extent

2.33   With one or two exceptions, English criminal law applies only to England and Wales so that the courts do not have jurisdiction over criminal acts committed outside England and Wales. One of the exceptions to this rule is that the courts have jurisdiction over homicide offences, which include manslaughter, committed abroad.

2.34   However, the new corporate manslaughter law applies only to offences of corporate killing committed in the UK and if a corporate killing by a UK company takes place overseas it will be a matter for the courts of the particular country concerned.

Crown Immunity

2.35   Under the Act, Crown immunity has been lifted. This means that Government bodies are under the remit of the law and face an unlimited fine if they are found to have caused death due to their gross corporate health and safety failures.

Private Prosecutions for Corporate Manslaughter

2.36   The consent of the Director of Public Prosecutions will be required for all prosecutions brought under the new legislation.

Reckless or Grossly Careless Transmission of a Disease

2.37   There is increasing pressure on companies and employers to protect the workforce in the wake of the string of public diseases in recent years, where complacency and neglect have been seen to be contributory factors to fatalities. If a company's management failure leads to the transmission of a fatal disease, the company may be guilty of corporate manslaughter.

Preparing for the Legislation

2.38   The legislation came into force on 6 April 2008.

2.39   Undertakings, and not just companies, should consider the following steps.

1. Review existing systems, policies and organisational arrangements so that responsibilities for health and safety are clear, are understood by everybody in the company and are implemented. This should be an ongoing process.
2. Ensure that health and safety policies are properly recorded and accessible. Policies should be properly disseminated so that everyone understands what the policies are, who is responsible for what and where to find the necessary information.
3. Consider arranging an external health and safety audit by specialist advisors.

List of Relevant Legislation

2.40
- Corporate Manslaughter and Corporate Homicide Act 2007
- Local Employment Act 1960

Further Information

Publications
- *Legislating the Criminal Code: Involuntary Manslaughter*, The Law Commission, Report No. 237
- *Reforming the Law on Involuntary Manslaughter: The Government's Proposals*, The Home Office

Organisations
- Centre for Corporate Accountability
  Web: *www.corporateaccountability.org*
  The Centre for Corporate Accountability is a charitable organisation that monitors worker and public safety, and undertakes research and provides advice on law enforcement and corporate criminal accountability.
- Home Office
  Web: *www.homeoffice.gov.uk*
  The Home Office is the government department responsible for internal affairs in England and Wales.
- Crown Prosecution Service (CPS)
  Web: *www.cps.gov.uk*
  The CPS is responsible for prosecuting people in England and Wales charged with a criminal offence.
- Health and Safety Executive (HSE)
  Web: *www.hse.gov.uk*
  The HSE and the Health and Safety Commission are responsible for the regulation of almost all the risks to health and safety arising from work activity in the UK.

Directors' Responsibilities

- Directors have legal responsibilities for health and safety under the Health and Safety at Work, etc Act 1974, the Regulatory Reform (Fire Safety) Order 2005 and the Companies Act 1985 (as amended).
- Directors can be prosecuted under these Acts, under relevant subsidiary legislation and under common law for manslaughter.
- Directors should ensure that health and safety is included in the overall corporate social responsibility programme.
- Directors should provide health and safety leadership and accept their individual roles in providing this leadership.
- Directors should actively support the participation of employees in improving health and safety and be kept informed of health and safety risk management issues.
- An organisation's competent person can use a number of arguments to ensure that directors are committed to health and safety.

2.41   Directors have a critical role to play in ensuring that health and safety is properly managed and that risks are controlled. The Health and Safety Commission has been taking action to motivate boardrooms to improve health and safety for some time. It is now recognised that boardrooms and directors need to take greater responsibility for health and safety within their organisations.

2.42   The most fundamental factor affecting health and safety performance is what is commonly referred to as "safety culture". There is little doubt that the strongest influence on safety culture within most businesses is "the message from the top". The directors of a company send out signals, either consciously or subconsciously, of what they expect of their employees. Strong leadership from the top is vital in delivering effective control of risks to health and safety.

2.43   Directors need to be made aware of the need to ensure that health and safety is taken into account when business decisions are taken.

In Practice

Legal Responsibilities

Health and Safety at Work, etc Act 1974

2.44   Under s.37, if an offence is committed with the consent or connivance of, or if an offence is attributable to any neglect on the part of, any:
- director
- manager
- company secretary
- other similar officer of the body corporate
- any person acting in one of these capacities
- they, as well as the body corporate, shall be guilty of the offence and can be proceeded against and punished accordingly.

2.45   This also applies where the affairs of a body corporate are managed by its members. The acts and defaults of a member in connection with his or her functions of management can be treated as if he or she were a director of the body corporate.

Companies Act 1985

2.46 According to the Companies Act 1985 (as amended by the Companies Act 2006), the Secretary of State may prescribe cases whereby directors' reports will contain information about the arrangements in force for that year for:
- securing the health, safety and welfare at work of the employees of that company (and any subsidiary company)
- protecting other persons against risks to health resulting from the activities at work of the employees.

Company Directors Disqualification Act 1986

2.47 The court may disqualify a person from being a director of a company if he or she is convicted on an indictable offence, whether on indictment or summarily, if the offence was in connection with the management of the company.

2.48 A magistrates' court may impose a disqualification for up to 5 years, while higher courts may disqualify for up to 15 years.

Common Law

2.49 Under common law, a director may be prosecuted for manslaughter.

Corporate Social Responsibility

2.50 There is increasing pressure on businesses to:
- promote greater transparency in corporate reporting and in the marketplace
- answer public concern about directors' and organisations' behaviour
- stimulate good practice.

2.51 The Government's strategy document, *Revitalising Health and Safety*, recognises that health and safety management needs to be set in the wider context of corporate social responsibility. Therefore it is seen as one of the indicators of a company's performance. This has been seen as an opportunity to work with investors and stakeholders to promote health and safety and to establish it as an important factor in corporate social responsibility. This has potential for influencing health and safety performance.

2.52 Corporate social responsibility and investors'/stakeholders' influences now impact on health and safety. Therefore those with corporate responsibility (ie directors) should be aware of how the safety performance of the organisation and the commitment given to health and safety by directors will impact on their business functions.

2.53 As part of this process, the Health and Safety Executive launched the Corporate Health and Safety Performance Indicator (CHaSPI), which aims to help in the assessment of how well an organisation manages its risks and responsibilities towards its workers, the public and other stakeholders.

2.54 There is a clear opportunity for companies and directors to demonstrate their commitment to corporate social responsibility through proactive occupational safety and health policies. There is also an opportunity to win over consumers at the same time.

Prosecution of Directors

2.55   Directors, managers and company secretaries are personally under a duty to ensure that the company's statutory duties are performed. Prosecution will normally occur under s.37 of the Health and Safety at Work, etc Act 1974 but other legislation may be employed. Directors may also be prosecuted under common law, particularly for manslaughter.

2.56   It should be noted that anyone who acts in a managerial capacity may be held liable under s.37 of the Health and Safety at Work, etc Act 1974 whatever title he or she may have. For example, if the affairs of the body corporate are being managed by its members (eg a workers' co-operative) the acts of a member which are in connection with his or her managerial functions are within the meaning of s.37.

2.57   Persons who purport to act as directors, managers, secretaries or similar officers are also equally liable. Therefore if a person acts as a director even though he or she has been disqualified from doing so under the Companies Act 1985, he or she is purporting to act as such.

Appointment of Third Parties

2.58   A director does not escape responsibility for health and safety matters by appointing a third party to carry out the necessary duties. The director must make sure that an independent third party is competent and properly supervised. However, the director still has to accept greater responsibility for the safety of employees and others, eg those who are engaged on a part-time basis to assist.

Offences

2.59   An offence will be committed under the following circumstances.

- A director consents to the commission of an offence, ie he or she is well aware of what is going on and agrees to it.
- A director connives to an offence, ie he or she is well aware of what is going on and his or her agreement is tacit, not actively encouraging of what happens but letting it continue and saying nothing about it.
- A director is under a duty to do something and fails to do it, or does it in a negligent manner. In this case an act of neglect is committed.

2.60   Directors may also be disqualified for breaches of safety legislation (eg a failure to comply with a prohibition notice). The disqualification can be in addition to any other penalty imposed.

HSE Guidance on Directors' Responsibilities

2.61   The HSE's publication *Successful Health and Safety Management* (HSG65) highlights the need for senior management to take the lead. It states that "visible and active support, strong leadership and commitment of senior managers and directors are fundamental to the success of health and safety management".

2.62   Boardrooms and directors are expected to take a number of actions in respect of health and safety.

- The board is expected to accept its collective role in providing health and safety leadership within the organisation. This should be done formally and in public.
- The individual members of the board need to accept individual roles in providing health and safety leadership.
- Board decisions need to reflect health and safety intentions, as articulated in the health and safety policy statement.

- The active participation of employees in improving health and safety must be recognised.
- The board should ensure that it is kept informed of, and alert to, health and safety risk management issues.

2.63   In support of the guidance *Directors' Responsibilities for Health and Safety*, the HSE has produced *Director Leadership — Case Studies* highlighting the vital role that directors play in health and safety. These can be accessed on the HSE website.

Importance of Strong Leadership

2.64   Strong leadership is vital in delivering effective health and safety risk control. Everyone should know and believe that directors are committed to continuous improvements in health and safety performance. Expectations must be explained along with the procedures to deliver them.

2.65   Board members need to ensure that actions and decisions at work always reinforce the messages in the health and safety policy statement. Any mismatch between individual attitudes, behaviour and the organisation's health and safety policy will undermine good health and safety practice and workers' beliefs. A director's personal responsibilities and liabilities under health and safety law must be recognised.

New Plant, Premises, Processes or Products

2.66   Many business decisions will have health and safety implications. It is particularly important that the health and safety ramifications of investment in new plant, premises, processes or products are taken into account as decisions are made.

Legal Responsibility Rests with the Employer

2.67   It is important for boards to remember that, although health and safety functions can (and should) be delegated, legal responsibility for health and safety rests with the employer.

Active Participation of Workers

2.68   Effective health and safety risk management requires the active participation of workers. Directors should encourage workers at all levels to become actively involved in all aspects of the health and safety management system. Worker involvement supports a positive health and safety culture where health and safety is everyone's business. The best form of participation is a partnership for prevention, where workers and their representatives are involved in identifying and tackling potential or actual problems. This is much better than consulting workers and their representatives only after decisions have already been taken.

Appointing a Health and Safety Director

2.69   Appointing a health and safety director creates a board member who can ensure that health and safety risk management issues are properly addressed, both by the board and by the organisation as a whole.

2.70   The chairman and/or chief executive have a critical role to play in ensuring that risks are properly managed and that the health and safety director has the necessary competence, resources and support of other board members to carry out his or her functions.

2.71   It is important that the role of the health and safety director should not detract either from the responsibilities of other directors for specific areas of health and safety risk management or from the health and safety responsibilities of the board as a whole.

Health and Safety Policy

2.72   The health and safety responsibilities of all board members should be clearly articulated in the organisation's statement of health and safety policy and arrangements.

2.73   The Health and Safety Commission suggests that any board and directors will need to:

- review the health and safety performance regularly
- ensure that health and safety policy statements reflect current board priorities
- ensure that management systems provide effective monitoring and reporting procedures
- be kept informed about significant health and safety failures and of the outcome of the investigations into their causes
- ensure that implications in respect of health and safety are addressed in all decisions
- ensure that risk management systems for health and safety are in place and effective (periodic audits can provide information on their operation and effectiveness).

Getting Directors' Commitment

2.74   One of the challenges to be faced is convincing staff at a senior level that health and safety is a boardroom issue and that those with corporate roles do have a responsibility for health and safety both collectively and as individuals.

2.75   Senior staff need to ensure that the actions and decisions they take reinforce the safety message. An expressed attitude needs to be supported by observed action. A mismatch will undermine employees' trust and belief and thus make the task of implementing an effective safety management system that much harder. Visible management and good communication are essential.

2.76   Commitment by directors will increase motivation and concern throughout the organisation for health and safety. It is best indicated by the proportion of resources and support allocated, including time, staff and finances. Typically this will be done by:

- arranging for a director or the chairman to sign the health and safety policy
- arranging for a senior director to chair the committee on safety
- ensuring that sufficient financial resources are allocated to health and safety
- ensuring that staff are fully involved in health and safety
- appointing and training sufficient competent persons.

2.77   For success to be achieved, it is crucial that the competent person within the organisation will:

- wield control and authority, with the support of the board of directors
- have a direct line of communication to directors on matters of policy.

Corporate Recognition of Health and Safety

2.78   Those with health and safety responsibilities will be required to support their case for safety and the application of risk reduction measures. Highlighting legal responsibilities and subsequent case law can be a convincing tool to utilise when striving to make health and safety a corporate issue. Clearly a balance must be drawn between health and safety and business needs. Health and safety should be seen as a business asset by directors. The following arguments can be used for convincing directors to take responsibility for health and safety. They can also be used to show how health and safety can be of benefit to the business.

2.79   Positive arguments include the following.
- Reduction in exposure of the company and key personnel to criminal liability.
- Minimising the likelihood of prosecution and consequent penalties.
- Reduction in the risk of directors' disqualification from office.
- Reduction in exposure of the company and senior managers to civil liability for death or injury.
- Control over insured losses to the satisfaction of insurers to ensure that policy cover remains valid.
- Reduction in financial risks and improved control over uninsured losses (such as lost production time, repair costs to plant and equipment, replacement costs for spoiled materials, rework costs for damaged products, etc).
- Control over risks of loss in market share.
- Improvement of the organisation's reputation in the eyes of customers, competitors, suppliers, other stakeholders and the wider community.
- Reduction in risks to company share values, etc.

Training

2.80   Training for directors should concentrate on the following topics.
- The legal responsibilities of directors.
- The potential outcomes for the individual if prosecution occurs (to include case law).
- The need to integrate health and safety in all business decisions.
- The benefits of health and safety to the overall business function.
- The actions expected of directors in respect of health and safety.
- How directors can show commitment to health and safety.

List of Relevant Legislation

2.81
- Regulatory Reform (Fire Safety) Order 2005
- Management of Health and Safety at Work Regulations 1999
- Health and Safety (Consultation with Employees) Regulations 1996
- Safety Representatives and Safety Committees Regulations 1977
- Company Directors Disqualification Act 1986
- Companies Act 1985
- Health and Safety at Work, etc Act 1974

Further Information

Publications

HSE Publications

The following are available from *www.hsebooks.co.uk*.
- HSG65 (rev 1997) *Successful Health and Safety Management*
- INDG343 *Directors' Responsibilities for Health and Safety*

Other Publications
- *Internal Control: Guidance for Directors on the Combined Code*, Institute of Chartered Accountants for England and Wales

The Corporate Health and Safety Performance Indicator can be accessed at *www.chaspi.info-exchange.com/default.asp*.

Director Leadership — Case Studies can be accessed at *www.hse.gov.uk/corporateresponsibility/casestudies*.

Step-by-step Guide: How to Fulfil Directors' Responsibilities

- Show directors' commitment to health and safety by ensuring that the safety policy is signed by the chief executive/chairman.
- Highlight directors' responsibilities to health and safety in the safety policy.
- Arrange for a director to chair the health and safety committee, if established.
- Show commitment to health and safety through resources, management style and communication.
- Review health and safety performance regularly, ensure that policy statements reflect current board priorities and ensure that implications in respect of health and safety are addressed in all decisions.
- Ensure that training and information is provided on directors' responsibilities.

Conviction Criteria

- Organisations can be found guilty of corporate manslaughter (or corporate homicide) if the way in which their activities are managed or organised by its senior management is a substantial element in the breach of the duty of care owed.
- Provisions under the Act should mean that it will be easier to bring successful prosecutions of companies whose gross management failings lead to the death of an employee, or a member of the public, to whom a duty of care is owed.
- In many instances senior managers will play a more significant role in managing activities than their title might suggest, and perform duties above and beyond the content of their job description.
- To avoid prosecution, companies will need to show that they have an effective health and safety management system, transparent procedures and defined lines of reporting and responsibility.
- A duty can be said to be owed if forseeability, proximity, and reasonable grounds to impose such a duty are all present.
- Whether a particular organisation owes a duty of care to a particular individual is a question of law.
- A breach of a duty of care by an organisation is a "gross" breach if the conduct alleged to amount to a breach of that duty falls far below what can reasonably be expected of the organisation in the circumstances.

2.82   If a person's death is caused by a substantial breach in the health and safety duty of care owed by an organisation's senior management, they will be liable to prosecution under the Corporate Manslaughter and Corporate Homicide Act 2007.

Employers' Duties

2.83   The Corporate Manslaughter and Corporate Homicide Act 2007 places senior managers and organisations at risk of prosecution if their gross management failings lead to the death of an employee or a member of the public to whom a duty of care is owed.

2.84   The legislation states that there has to be a relevant duty of care owed by the organisation in the law of negligence to the deceased, and a gross breach of that duty of care leading to that person's death.

2.85   The Health and Safety at Work, etc Act 1974 (HSWA) requires employers to ensure "so far as is reasonably practicable" the health, safety and welfare of their employees and other persons who may be affected by their work. This includes sub-contractors and the general public.

Employees' Duties

2.86   The HSWA requires that employees must take reasonable care for the safety of themselves and of other persons who may be affected by their acts or omissions. They should co-operate with their employers and others in carrying out their statutory obligations.

In Practice

Management and Organisation of Activities

2.87   Organisations to which the Corporate Manslaughter and Corporate Homicide Act 2007 applies will be guilty of the offence of corporate manslaughter (or corporate homicide, as applicable) if the way in which they manage or organise their activities leads to a person's death, and amounts to a gross breach of a relevant duty of care owed by the organisation to the deceased.

2.88   However, they will only be guilty if the way in which their activities are managed or organised by senior management is a substantial element in the breach of the duty of care owed.

2.89   While the usual principles of causation in criminal law apply (the management failure need not be the sole cause of death), management failure must be a cause *R v Pagett* [1983]. Essentially, a management failure must have caused the death and have been more than a minimal contribution.

2.90   Intervening acts may break the chain of causation in certain circumstances. For instance, in the case of *Lambert v Lewis* [1982], the claimant's conduct in continuing to use a trailer coupling after it had broken severed the chain of causation which linked the defendant's breach (in supplying the defective coupling) and the loss claimed (for liability to persons injured when the coupling gave way).

Clarification of Senior Manager

Removal of Key Obstacle to Successful Prosecutions

2.91   The Act has removed a key obstacle to successful prosecutions by removing the need to identify an individual senior manager who embodies the company. Up until now this meant that, particularly in larger organisations, it was virtually impossible to prosecute a company for deaths arising out of the gross management failings of a company where no one senior manager could be identified as being responsible.

2.92   The more well-known cases include the Southall, Paddington and Ladbroke Grove rail crashes and the Herald of Free Enterprise disaster. The Centre for Corporate Accountability (CCA) gives details of failed prosecution cases.

2.93   The only successful prosecutions have involved directors of small companies comprised of one or two directors, where the management structure was unsophisticated and therefore the "controlling mind" was easily identifiable.

2.94   In the case of larger companies, senior managers and directors may be able to take comfort in the fact that they will not face individual prosecution under the Act for corporate manslaughter, even if it could be shown that their acts or omissions contributed to the relevant management failures that led to the death. From this point of view, some feel that the Act in its current form is a missed opportunity.

New Provisions

2.95 The new provisions should mean that it will be easier to bring successful prosecutions of companies whose gross management failings lead to the death of an employee or a member of the public to whom a duty of care is owed. Crown bodies such as government departments and the police will also be liable for prosecution for the first time. Such bodies had previously been immune.

Who is a Senior Manager?

2.96 The Act defines a senior manager as a person who plays a significant role in an organisation in:

- making decisions about how the whole or a substantial part of its activities are to be managed or organised
- managing or organising the whole or a substantial part of those activities.

2.97 This definition is wide ranging and covers day-to-day operational managers as well as strategic decision makers. Some senior managers are easily identifiable, eg chief executive, finance director, production manager, etc. However, it may be more difficult to decide whether the likes of foreman, site manager (construction), transport manager (haulage), charge hand, lead operator, supervisor, etc are in fact senior managers, as in many instances they will play a more significant role in managing activities than their title might suggest, and perform duties above and beyond the content of their job description.

2.98 There has been speculation that the senior manager test might lead to unscrupulous delegation of health and safety functions to junior management as a means of escaping liability. However, it is hard to believe that the courts would allow the legislation to be thwarted in this manner and it is not inconceivable that such conduct might in itself be held to be so irresponsible and reckless as to amount to gross negligence.

2.99 In large organisations, or organisations where there are many tiers of management or complex management structures (eg on a construction site where there are large numbers of sub-contractors), higher level managers may not be aware of what is happening at lower levels. In addition, information from the top may not be fed down the management chain.

2.100 The flow of information between different levels in the organisation and between different departments is essential for good communication — in other words, the left hand must know what the right hand is doing.

Effective Health and Safety Management Systems

2.101 To avoid prosecution, companies will need to show that they have adhered to an effective health and safety management system, transparent procedures and defined lines of reporting and responsibility.

2.102 An effective health and safety management system may be demonstrated by ensuring the following.

- Risk assessments, systems of work and all other policies and procedures are comprehensive, workable and documented.
- Clear and effective lines of communication are maintained at all levels.
- All company roles and responsibilities are defined and understood.
- Staff and management at all levels are trained not only in the specifics of their job, but also in all relevant health and safety policies and procedures.

- Regular and effective systems of reviewing all policies and procedures, and monitoring and enforcing the requisite compliance, are implemented and maintained.

Duty of Care

2.103   Liability for corporate manslaughter is not strict; the mere fact that a fatality occurs will not lead to a conviction under the Act. There has to be a relevant duty of care owed by the organisation in the law of negligence to the deceased, and a gross breach of that relevant duty of care leading to that person's death.

Duty of Care Case Law

2.104   Negligence has been defined as, "the omission to do something which a reasonable man, guided upon those considerations which ordinarily regulate the conduct of human affairs would do; or doing something which a prudent and reasonable man would not do" in *Blyth v Birmingham Waterworks* [1856].

2.105   The law as to who owed a duty of care, to whom and in what circumstances derives from the famous case of the snail found in a bottle of ginger beer in *Donoghue v Stevenson* [1932]. Lord Atkin stated in his judgement in this case that, "The rule that you are to love your neighbour becomes in law, you must not injure your neighbour; and the lawyer's question, who is my neighbour receives a restrictive reply. You must take reasonable care to avoid acts or omissions which you can reasonably foresee would be likely to injure your neighbour. Who, then, in law is my neighbour? The answer seems to be — persons who are so closely and directly affected by my act that I ought reasonably to have them in my contemplation as being so affected when I am directing my mind to the acts or omissions which are called in question."

2.106   Lord Atkin then went on to approve specific cases in which the duty was to avoid physical injury to persons or property, and is known as the "neighbour principle".

2.107   In modern times, the Donoghue principle has been restated by the House of Lords in *Caparo Industries Plc v Dickman* [1990].

Features of a Duty of Care

2.108   A duty can be said to be owed if the following are present.
- Foreseeability.
- Proximity.
- Reasonable grounds to impose such a duty.

Foreseeability

2.109   For the requirement of foreseeability to be satisfied, it must be foreseeable that harm would result from the act in question, and what type of harm might be caused.

Proximity

2.110   Proximity means sufficient closeness. This is a difficult concept. It may be satisfied if there is temporal and geographic proximity. Proximity means "closeness", but in a legal sense to denote circumstances when the law will recognise that a duty should exist, it is therefore to some extent a question of policy as to how "proximity" would be defined, to establish a duty or not.

Reasonable Grounds to Impose Duty

2.111   It must be just and reasonable for the law to recognise that a duty should be owed by the defendant not to cause this particular type of harm. However, the courts are also concerned not to open the floodgates.

Owing a Duty of Care

2.112   The question of whether the defendant owes a duty not to cause the harm suffered can depend on the type or nature of the harm actually suffered. An example would be in the construction of a building where the builder has a duty to take care to avoid injury due to the property's (latent) defects. Such defects may cause injury to people who subsequently use or come within the vicinity of the premises. These people are those who the builder would reasonably consider as likely to suffer such injury if reasonable care is not taken.

2.113   There is no question of liability where the management of an activity includes reasonable safeguards and a death nonetheless occurs. Therefore a fatality which could not have been prevented by the senior management doing all that would be reasonably expected of the relevant organisation, in terms of safeguards and precautions, will not elicit a prosecution under the Act.

2.114   The Act specifies where a duty of care is owed and examples include the duty owed by:

- an employer to his employees and non-employees, eg visitors, sub-contractors, etc to provide a safe system of work
- an occupier of buildings and land to people in or on, or potentially affected by, the property
- the supplier of a product to the end user
- contractors to those who might be affected by their work activities, eg members of the public and other contractors
- transport companies to their passengers.

2.115   Whether a particular organisation owes a duty of care to a particular individual is a question of law. The judge must make any findings of fact necessary to decide that question.

Gross Breach

2.116   A breach of a duty of care by an organisation is a "gross" breach if the conduct alleged to amount to a breach of that duty falls far below what can reasonably be expected of the organisation in the circumstances. To assess this, the proposed law will require a consideration of the organisation's compliance with health and safety legislation.

2.117   Rather than consider the knowledge and motives of senior managers, the risk of death from any failure to comply with legislation will need to be evaluated. Attention will then be given to the attitudes, systems, policies and accepted practices within the organisation which may have encouraged or tolerated non-compliance with the legislation.

2.118   There are a number of factors for the jury to take into account. These include the following.

- Whether the evidence shows that the organisation failed to comply with any health and safety legislation that relates to the alleged breach and if so:
  - how serious that failure was
  - how much of a risk of death it posed.

- The extent to which the evidence shows that there were attitudes, policies, systems or accepted practices within the organisation that were likely to have encouraged any failure to comply with health and safety legislation relating to the breach, or to have produced tolerance of it.
- Any health and safety guidance (eg an Approved Code of Practice, guidance or manual produced by an enforcing authority) that relates to the alleged breach.
- Any other matters they consider relevant.

2.119 When considering breaches of health and safety duties, juries may consider guidance on how those obligations should be discharged. Guidance does not provide an authoritative statement of required standards and therefore the jury is not required to consider the extent to which this is not complied with. However, where breaches of relevant health and safety duties are established, guidance may assist a jury in considering how serious these are.

2.120 It may be expected from the Bill which preceded the Act that relevant considerations will include:

- whether senior managers knew, or ought to have known, that the organisation was failing to comply with that legislation or guidance
- whether they knew, or ought to have known, of the risk of death or serious harm posed by the failure to comply
- whether they sought to cause the organisation to profit from that failure.

List of Relevant Legislation

2.121
- Corporate Manslaughter and Corporate Homicide Act 2007
- Health and Safety at Work, etc Act 1974

Further Information

Organisations

- Centre for Corporate Accountability
  Web: *www.corporateaccountability.org*
  The Centre for Corporate Accountability is a charitable organisation that monitors worker and public safety, and undertakes research and provides advice on law enforcement and corporate criminal accountability.
- Health and Safety Executive (HSE)
  Web: *www.hse.gov.uk*
  The HSE and the Health and Safety Commission are responsible for the regulation of almost all the risks to health and safety arising from work activity in the UK.

Enforcement

- The main enforcement bodies for health and safety are the Health and Safety Executive (HSE) and the relevant local authority. Other enforcers may include the fire authority.
- The enforcement powers of these bodies are detailed in the Health and Safety at Work, etc Act 1974.
- Enforcement is primarily by means of workplace inspections, conducted by health and safety inspectors from the HSE or environmental health inspectors from the local authority.
- Inspectors can enter premises at any reasonable time and do not need to make an appointment.
- When inspecting a premises, an inspector may take photographs, request to see records, ask questions, take samples or remove items of equipment.
- The powers of inspectors include issuing of enforcement notices, as well as the ultimate power to prosecute a company.
- All staff should be familiarised with the role of enforcing authorities and the powers of inspectors, so that they are aware of the need to co-operate with them.
- Enforcement is based upon the principles contained within the Cabinet Office Enforcement Concordat.

2.122   The appropriate use of enforcement powers is an important influence on any health and safety management system. The purpose of enforcement is to:

- ensure that duty holders take action to deal with serious risks immediately
- promote and achieve sustained compliance with the law
- ensure that when any breach occurs, those responsible may be held accountable.

2.123   Responsibility for the enforcement of health and safety legislation is split between the Health and Safety Executive (HSE) and local authority inspectors (environmental health officers). The split is dependent on the main activity of the premises being inspected and is detailed in the Health and Safety (Enforcing Authority) Regulations 1998.

2.124   In general, the HSE is the enforcing authority for operations which include industrial premises, construction activities, mines and quarries, agriculture, railway operations, educational establishments and hospitals. Separate inspectorates within the HSE's Field Operations Division deal with particular activities, such as offshore, mines, agriculture and railways. Shops, offices, catering, entertainment and certain services are the responsibility of local authorities.

2.125   Inspectors from the HSE and the local authority have the same powers of enforcement as detailed in the Health and Safety at Work, etc Act 1974 (HSWA). Employers should be aware that they also face enforcement by other inspectors, such as the Fire and Rescue Authority. They have similar, but not necessarily identical, powers.

Employers' Duties

2.126   Under the HSWA, employers must:
- allow inspectors to exercise their powers

- not obstruct inspectors (obstruction may lead to prosecution)
- obey the reasonable directions of inspectors
- comply with any enforcement notices served on them by inspectors.

Employees' Duties

2.127   Under the HSWA, employees must:
- co-operate with inspectors
- allow themselves to be interviewed by an inspector and answer questions
- give a written statement to an inspector, if requested, unless they are under caution.

In Practice

Health and Safety Inspections

2.128   An enforcement inspector may visit premises in a number of circumstances, for example:
- following a reported incident
- as a consequence of a complaint
- as part of a routine inspection.

Following a Reported Incident

2.129   A visit usually follows a serious incident. However, a visit may follow less serious incidents if the inspector sees merit in a formal investigation.

As a Consequence of a Complaint

2.130   The complaint might be from an employee, including a safety representative, or from members of the public. The complaint might be anonymous and, in most cases, inspectors will not disclose the fact that they are visiting the premises to investigate a complaint.

As Part of a Routine Inspection

2.131   Both the HSE and local authorities have a programme of inspection that determines the regularity of visits. This depends on the level of risk presented by the activity undertaken at the premises. The frequency of visits will depend on the management's:
- previous compliance
- accident record
- attitudes.

2.132   Most organisations will not be visited very often. For a typical medium-sized organisation, a routine inspection may only occur every five years, or sometimes after a longer interval.

Powers of Entry

2.133   Inspectors may enter premises at "any reasonable time". This means that the inspector may enter the premises at any time while the premises are open, including during any night-shift work. It would be unreasonable, however, for the inspector to require entry during the night if the premises are not usually open at this time.

2.134   The inspector does not need to make an appointment and often does not. Unlike the police, the inspector does not need to obtain a court order for entry to the premises. The inspector should carry a warrant that shows their identity, as well as their authority. It is good practice for the employer to ask to see the inspector's warrant if there is any doubt as to their identity.

2.135   Any attempt by the employer to prevent inspectors from entering the premises can result in prosecution for obstruction.

2.136   Inspectors may take a police constable with them if they anticipate any serious obstruction. Inspectors may also take another inspector with them, or another authorised person, such as a specialist inspector or medical doctor from the Employment Medical Advisory Service (EMAS).

What an Inspector Might Do

2.137   On entry, inspectors can perform a number of tasks, including the following.
1. They can take measurements, photographs and records/details, as they see fit. This might include photographs of the scene of an accident and dimensions of plant or machinery.
2. Samples of substances can be taken. This might include atmosphere monitoring such as personal monitoring for an employee, eg for a harmful dust.
3. Inspectors are able to take samples of articles, including any components involved in an accident or incident.
4. They can require a piece of equipment to be dismantled if they feel that it might have caused, or will cause, a danger to health and safety.
5. The inspector can take items into possession. This might include equipment or components involved in an accident or incident. The item(s) taken into possession may be scientifically tested or examined.
6. Samples of substances may also be taken and tested.
7. Inspectors have the power to require that a scene is left undisturbed, eg the scene of an accident. This power may be invoked by telephone before they arrive on-site.
8. Records, such as plant inspection reports, results of surveys, etc, may be requested by inspectors. Other requested documents could be health and safety policies or risk assessments.
9. Inspectors may request the use of facilities and assistance, eg the use of an office for interviewing purposes.

Interviews by Inspectors

2.138   Inspectors have the power to require persons who they feel may help their enquiries to answer questions. It is an offence to refuse to answer such questions. They might also require that signed statements be given. Inspectors use the same rules of evidence collection that the police use, ie those under the Police and Criminal Evidence Act 1984. For example, interviews may be tape-recorded. If, during their enquiries, inspectors have reasonable cause to believe that an individual might have committed an offence and therefore is liable to prosecution, the inspectors must also caution that person. In these circumstances, the person under caution can refuse to provide a statement or answer questions. However, such refusals may be seen as implying some guilt.

Other Powers of Inspectors

2.139   Section 20(2)(m) of the HSWA gives inspectors "any other power which is necessary" for them to be able to carry out their responsibilities.

2.140   Inspectors are given additional power in s.25 of the HSWA, to deal with situations of "imminent danger". In such circumstances, inspectors may "seize and render harmless" any article or substance. This action might simply consist of an inspector switching off a machine, or alternatively, making detailed arrangements for the disposal of a harmful substance.

2.141   Inspectors are given a lot of power under the HSWA and employers and others need to be aware of inspectors' powers and how to approach a visit.

2.142   Following an inspection, if the inspectors are not satisfied with the organisation's health and safety arrangements, they may issue an enforcement notice. The ultimate power of an inspector is the power to prosecute.

Methods of Enforcement

2.143   The range of enforcement methods includes the following.

- Prosecution — in the event of a serious accident or persistent failure to comply with legislation.
- Improvement notice — served where the inspector is of the opinion that there is a contravention of the law and it is likely that the contravention will continue or be repeated.
- Prohibition notice — issued in circumstances where there is a risk of serious personal injury. Notices may be deferred for a specified time or they may take immediate effect if the risk is imminent.
- Written confirmation — to ensure that requirements are clearly specified and recorded. Written confirmation may be used in evidence to support a notice or prosecution if the written advice is ignored.
- Oral advice — only when the contraventions are simple and minor. Generally there will only be oral confirmation that conditions are satisfactory or that specific items have received adequate attention.

Enforcement Notices

2.144   There are two types of enforcement notices that can be served by inspectors. These are a prohibition notice or an improvement notice. Both of these notices can be served on the spot but it is usual for the improvement notice to be served by post. Failure to comply with a notice will always result in prosecution.

Prohibition Notices

2.145   A prohibition notice can be served when an inspector is of the opinion that there is a risk of serious personal injury. The notice will prohibit the continuance of a particular activity. The notice will:

- specify the matter that the inspector believes is, or will give rise to, a risk of serious personal injury
- outline whether the HSWA, or any regulations have been breached
- order that the particular activity should not be carried out.

2.146   Prohibition notices are issued in relation to serious matters such as unguarded or inadequately guarded machinery or activities such as poor control when working at height or entering a confined space. These notices are also issued for any other matter where an inspector believes that if a notice is not issued, someone is likely to be seriously injured.

2.147   Prohibition notices generally take effect immediately, ie the activity in question must cease immediately. In some cases, however, the notice might be deferred. For example, an inspector might defer the notice until a production run is completed, if it is deemed unsafe to stop in the middle of a run.

2.148   The inspector is likely to attach a schedule to the notice giving directions on how the notice can be complied with, eg "improve guarding at a machine". Failure to comply with the notice is a serious criminal offence and can lead to a fine and/or imprisonment for up to two years.

Improvement Notices

2.149   Improvement notices are issued on a range of activities where an inspector believes a breach of the HSWA has occurred. The notice does not stop a particular activity from continuing but requires an improvement in the health and safety arrangements for the activity. An improvement notice might also require the provision of risk assessments or improvements being made to an organisation's safety policy.

2.150   The improvement notice will:
- describe the activity that requires improvement
- detail the statutory provisions that are being breached
- specify the date by which the improvement should be completed.

2.151   The receiver of an improvement notice must remedy the situation by the time specified in the notice, which cannot be earlier than 21 days after it is served. This period of time allows an appeal to be lodged, if required.

2.152   As with prohibition notices, inspectors may attach a schedule to the notice advising the employer on how the notice might be complied with. Failure to comply with the notice on time is a criminal offence, which can lead to a fine and/or imprisonment for up to two years. Inspectors can extend the time limit on the notice, at the request of the employer. In these cases, inspectors will issue an official notice of extension.

Appeals Against Notices

2.153   There is a facility for appeals against notices if the employer feels that the notice is invalid in some way. Appeals must be lodged within 21 days of the notice being served and are heard in the employment tribunal.

2.154   The principal grounds for appeal against enforcement notices are:
- the inspector misinterpreted the law
- the inspector exceeded his or her enforcement powers
- breach of law is accepted, but is of such a minor nature that the notice should be cancelled, eg the measure is not reasonably practicable.

2.155   The tribunal may:
- cancel the notice
- affirm the notice in the original form
- affirm the notice with modifications by way of omissions, amendments or additions.

2.156   In the case of an improvement notice, the notice is suspended once an appeal is lodged.

2.157   In the case of a prohibition notice, the notice stands throughout the appeal, ie the prohibited activity would continue to be stopped. For this reason, such appeals are usually held promptly. The tribunal has the power to withdraw the notice. However, it is relatively rare for such appeals to be successful.

Prosecutions

2.158   Inspectors of the HSE, or the relevant local authority, can bring prosecutions. In Scotland, any prosecution will be based on the decision of the Procurator Fiscal, usually on the recommendation of the enforcing authority.

2.159   Prosecution or the recommendation to prosecute will normally be taken where certain circumstances (one or more of the following) apply, including:

- death as a result of the breach of legislation
- the gravity of an alleged offence together with the seriousness of any actual or potential harm
- there has been reckless disregard of health and safety requirements
- there have been repeated breaches which gave rise to significant risk or persistent and significant poor compliance
- work has been carried out without, or in serious non-compliance with, an appropriate licence or safety case
- a duty holder's standard of managing health and safety is far below what is required
- failure to comply with an improvement or prohibition notice
- false information has been supplied in an attempt to deceive an inspector
- inspectors have been intentionally obstructed in the lawful course of their duties.

2.160   Most offences under the HSWA and associated regulations are "triable either way". This means that there is a legal facility for the cases to be transferred to a higher court where the potential penalties are higher. In England and Wales, cases are first heard in the magistrates' court and can, depending on the seriousness of the charge, be transferred to the Crown Court, where a judge and jury will hear the case(s). In Scotland, the same principles apply. However, for historical reasons, Scotland has its own distinctive legal system and court structure.

Penalties

2.161   The table below, *Penalties for Breaches of Health and Safety Law*, illustrates the fines and prison sentences available to the courts at present:

Penalties for Breaches of Health and Safety Law

Offence	Magistrates' Court	Crown Court
Health and Safety at Work, etc Act 1974 ss.2–6	£20,000	Unlimited
Health and Safety at Work, etc Act 1974 ss.7–9	£20,000	Unlimited
Breach of regulations	£5000	Unlimited
Contravening the requirements of a prohibition or improvement notice	6 months (maximum sentence)	2 years (maximum sentence)

2.162   Imprisonment is not a penalty that is available across the board. It is available for a few offences only, including the contravention of enforcement notices.

Crown Immunity

2.163 Prior to the introduction of the Corporate Manslaughter and Corporate Homicide Act 2007, there was still some Crown immunity in the UK. This meant that the Crown body in question, such as the Ministry of Defence, could not be prosecuted. It did not mean that the body was immune from complying with the legislation; the HSE had the power to issue Crown enforcement notices. In extreme situations, the HSE could also issue a Crown Censure. This is a formal record of the fact that, if it were not for Crown immunity, there would have been a prosecution.

2.164 Under the Act, Crown Immunity has been lifted. This means that Government bodies are under the remit of the law and face an unlimited fine if they are found to have caused death due to their gross corporate health and safety failures.

The Role of the Police

2.165 The police will usually attend the scene of any sudden death in the workplace in order to assess whether or not a charge of manslaughter may be brought. This is in addition to any enforcement action by the HSE or relevant local authority.

Fire Authorities and Enforcing Authorities

2.166 Fire authorities have a duty to enforce the Management of Health and Safety at Work Regulations 1999 and the Regulatory Reform (Fire Safety) Order 2005 in the majority of premises (although the HSE does have some enforcing duties under such legislation).

2.167 Under fire safety legislation, an appeal can be made against any enforcement or prohibition notice within 21 days from the day on which the notice was served. Such an appeal must be made to the local magistrates' court (in England and Wales) or the sheriff within whose jurisdiction any relevant workplace is situated (in Scotland). The bringing of the appeal has the effect of suspending the operation of an improvement notice until the appeal is finally disposed of or the appeal is withdrawn. Prohibition notices remain in force until after the appeal hearing. The court may either cancel or affirm the notice and, if it affirms it, may do so either in its original form or with such modifications as the court may think fit.

Enforcement Concordat

2.168 Enforcement is based upon the principles contained within the Cabinet Office Enforcement Concordat. The principles are as follows:

- Proportionality — this relates enforcement action to the risks and takes into account how far the duty holder has fallen short of what the law requires. The measures taken to control risks will be judged according to what is "reasonably practicable". The authorities will search for evidence that good practice was followed.
- Targeting — this means ensuring that those employees whose activities give rise to the most serious risk, are adequately regulated.
- Consistency — this means following a similar approach in similar circumstances to achieve similar ends.
- Transparency — this means helping duty holders to understand what is expected of them and what they should expect from the enforcing authority upon inspection.
- Accountability — regulators are accountable to the public and policies should be in place against which their performance can be judged.

Training

2.169 All staff should be given appropriate training in the role of the enforcing authorities and the powers of inspectors so that they are aware of the need to co-operate with them.

List of Relevant Legislation

2.170
* Corporate Manslaughter and Corporate Homicide Act 2007
* Health and Safety (Enforcing Authority) Regulations 1998
* Health and Safety at Work, etc Act 1974

Further Information

Publications

HSE Publications

The following is available from *www.hsebooks.co.uk*.
* HSC14 *What to Expect When a Health and Safety Inspector Calls: A Brief Guide for Businesses, Employees and Their Representatives*

Employers' Factsheet: Enforcement Powers of the HSE and Provisions of the Police and Criminal Evidence Act 1984 (PACE)

Statutory Background

Health and Safety at Work, etc Act 1974

Enforcement of the Health and Safety at Work, etc Act 1974 (HSWA), and related legislation, is shared between the Health and Safety Executive (HSE) and local authorities. The general rule is that the "enforcing authority" in the case of industrial premises is the HSE and in the case of commercial premises within its area, the local authority.

Each enforcing authority is empowered to appoint suitably qualified persons as inspectors, for the purpose of exercising enforcement powers granted by the HSWA.

Inspectors are appointed under s.19 of the HSWA and can be requested to produce details of their identity and authority (when exercising any of their powers under the HSWA). Inspectors appointed by local authorities will usually be suitably qualified Environmental Health Officers.

Powers of inspectors (s.20)

This is a key provision in the HSWA, setting out the very extensive powers of inspectors.

Of particular note, inspectors have a right:
- of entry to premises (at any reasonable time) without any need to give notice
- to carry out investigations and examinations
- to require any person to answer questions relevant to any examination/ investigation and to sign a declaration as to the truth of the answers
- to require the production of and inspection of books and documents (eg accident book, plant maintenance schedules and risk assessments)
- to require any person to give general facilities and assistance.

Anyone obstructing an inspector carrying out s.20 powers will be guilty of a criminal offence (s.33 of the HSWA).

Interviewing powers in more detail

Section 20(2)(j) enables an inspector to question any person who the inspector believes has information relevant to any examination/investigation.

In particular:
- such a person cannot refuse to answer questions put to him/her under s.20 powers
- a person questioned can nominate another person to be present at the interview (eg his or her manager or supervisor)
- no answer given under a "Section 20 interview" is admissible in evidence against that person in any legal proceedings

- it is a specific offence for a person to prevent any other person from appearing before an inspector or from answering any question to which an inspector may require an answer (s.33).

The inspector is not obliged to conduct any interview under s.20 powers and in some circumstances it would be inappropriate (eg where someone is about to be charged with an offence). Interviews not conducted under s.20 powers will be subject to the Police and Criminal Evidence Act 1984 (PACE).

Police and Criminal Evidence Act 1984

Section 66

Section 66 provides for codes of practice to be followed by the police in regard to:
- detention and questioning
- identification of persons
- searching of premises
- statutory powers of stop and search.

Section 67(9)

"Provides that persons other than police officers who are charged with the duty of investigating offences or charging offenders, shall in the discharge of that duty have regard to any relevant provision of such a code."

This brings in, therefore, inspectors carrying out investigations under the HSWA.

Code of Practice on questioning

The code stresses the absolute right of persons to obtain legal advice or to communicate with anyone outside of the police station. This right applies not only to those voluntarily assisting the police with an investigation, but also to those under detention.

A person who wants legal advice may not be interviewed, or continue to be interviewed, until he or she has received it (paragraph. 6.6 of Code C).

A caution is required on, or immediately before, an arrest:
- when there are grounds to suspect a person of an offence
- following a break in questioning — if there is doubt as to whether the suspect appreciates that he or she is still under caution
- upon being charged with an offence

Legal obligations on company directors and potential personal liabilities

The potential liability of companies and directors is increasing. It is much easier to prosecute the company, rather than the director or manager in a senior position. In order to succeed in a prosecution of an individual there has to be:
- positive consent
- specific knowledge
- neglect.

Where a company is relatively small, and a director can be easily identified as having day-to-day control of the company, that director is much more vulnerable to prosecution. Directors may be criminally liable by virtue of s.37 of the HSWA.

Manslaughter

Where someone has killed another person(s) unintentionally by gross recklessness, in breach of health and safety legislation, he or she can be found guilty of a statutory offence as well as the common law offence of manslaughter.

What businesses should do when an accident occurs in the workplace

- Be aware that certain categories of workplace injury and disease, together with specified dangerous occurrences and gas incidents, must be reported to the relevant enforcing authority (the Reporting of Injuries, Diseases and Dangerous Occurrences Regulations 1995 (RIDDOR)).
- Notify your Insurers (public liability and employers' liability).
- Carry out your own immediate investigation (including taking photographs and making sketch plans), but do not disturb or interfere with anything which may subsequently be needed to be seen by the enforcing authority, (ie the HSE or local authority) and the police. It must be stressed, in this context, that any reports or comments will be fully discoverable in any civil proceedings and will probably be open to the enforcing authority/police unless the investigation and report is carried out solely for the benefit of obtaining external solicitor advice.
- Make an appropriate entry in the accident book.
- Appoint one person in the organisation to be the co-ordinator of the investigation and the contact point with the enforcing authority.
- In serious cases, liaise with your public liability and employers' liability insurers, with a view to instructing external solicitors.
- Consider if the circumstances warrant possible disciplinary action against any employee(s).
- Review procedures, risk assessments, working practices and systems of work in light of the accident.
- Be aware of the investigatory powers of the HSE, local authority and the police.
- If possible, seek advice prior to any interviews taking place.
- If the police are involved in the investigation, external solicitors should generally be instructed.
- If the HSE or local authority is conducting interviews, ascertain under what powers (s.20 of the HSWA or under "general" investigative powers). If the former, ensure that the interviewee is aware of his/her rights to have a third party present with him/her. In the case of general investigative powers, be aware of the relevant provisions of PACE (which, for example, permits unlimited access to legal representation).
- Ensure that the interviewee is aware of the need to read any written statement very carefully and only to sign it if completely satisfied that it is a completely accurate record.
- Ask for copies of any statements given (or if the interview is tape recorded, ask for a copy tape).

Note:
This factsheet is merely an overview. If an accident occurs in your workplace and the HSE and/or the police are about to carry out an investigation, you must seek appropriate professional advice.

Investigation and Prosecution

- Where a work-related death occurs and there is evidence that a serious criminal offence has been committed, various public bodies liaise with each other to make decisions related to the investigating, charging and prosecuting of offences.
- The Work-related Deaths Protocol sets out the principles for effective liaison between the bodies.
- The Health and Safety Executive (HSE), local authorities, the police and the Crown Prosecution Service (CPS) have different responsibilities in relation to a work-related death.
- Where there is an indication that an offence of manslaughter or another serious criminal offence has been committed, the police will conduct an investigation.
- Investigations should be managed professionally, with the continuous maintenance of communications between the signatory organisations.
- In large-scale investigations, a strategic liaison group will be formed to ensure effective inter-organisational communication and to share relevant information and experiences.
- Where the CPS, HSE and enforcing authority seek to prosecute, a decision as to which body will take main responsibility for the prosecution will be made at a conference which will discuss the management of proceedings.
- Arrangements will be made for ensuring that bereaved relatives of the deceased and witnesses are kept informed.
- Instructions to the prosecuting advocate will be given.
- Where the CPS has decided not to prosecute, the HSE or other enforcing authority will await the result of the coroner's inquest before charging any other health and safety offences, otherwise the case would be prejudiced.

2.171   Where a work-related death occurs and there is evidence that a serious criminal offence other than a health and safety offence has been committed, the following bodies must liaise with each other to make decisions related to the investigating, charging and prosecuting of offences.

- The police.
- The Crown Prosecution Service (CPS).
- The Health and Safety Executive (HSE).
- The local authority or other enforcing authority.

In Practice

Work-related Deaths Protocol

2.172   The Work-related Deaths Protocol has been agreed between the Crown Prosecution Service, Health and Safety Executive, the Association of Chief Police Officers, the British Transport Police and the Local Government Association. It sets out the principles for effective liaison between the bodies.

2.173   The HSE, local authorities, the police and the CPS have different responsibilities in relation to a work-related death.

43

HSE and Local Authorities

2.174   Section 18 of the Health and Safety at Work, etc Act 1974 (HSWA) provides that the HSE and local authorities are responsible for making adequate arrangements for the enforcement of health and safety legislation, with a view to securing the health, safety and welfare of workers and protecting others, mainly the public. Each has specific areas of responsibility.

Rail Accident Investigation Branch

2.175   The Rail Accident Investigation Branch (RAIB) is the independent railway accident investigation organisation for the UK. It investigates railway accidents and incidents on the UK's railways to improve safety, rather than establish blame. The Protocol does not deal with liaison and co-operation with the RAIB.

Other Organisations Following the Protocol

2.176   Other organisations, for example the Civil Aviation Authority and the Maritime and Coastguard Agency, are not signatories to the Protocol but have agreed to follow its principles.

Police Investigation

2.177   Where there is an indication that an offence of manslaughter or another serious criminal offence has been committed, the police will conduct an investigation. A police officer attending an incident involving a work-related death should arrange the following.

- Identifying, securing, preserving and taking control of the scene.
- Supervising and recording all activity.
- Informing a senior supervisory officer.
- Enquiring whether the employer or other responsible person in control of the premises or activity has informed the HSE, the local authority or other investigating authority.
- Contacting and discussing the incident with the HSE and other enforcing authority, agreeing arrangements for controlling the scene, considering access to others and local handling procedures to ensure the safety of the public.

Management of the Investigation

2.178   The HSE will conduct an investigation relating to possible offences under the HSWA. The HSE will pass to the police any information relating to a serious criminal offence.

2.179   Investigations should be managed professionally, with the continuous maintenance of communications between the signatory organisations.

2.180   Throughout the investigation, the police, HSE and the enforcing authority should keep the progress of the investigation under review.

2.181   In large-scale investigations, a strategic liaison group should be formed to ensure effective inter-organisational communication and to share relevant information and experiences. This will include the following.

- The CPS and the HSE will co-ordinate in deciding whether or not to prosecute, taking into account the criteria contained in the Code for Crown Prosecutors. The decision will be made without undue delay.

- Bereaved families and witnesses will be kept informed of developments. When the police are considering charging a company with corporate manslaughter, the CPS must be consulted.
- When the CPS decides not to prosecute, the HSE must be notified as soon as possible. The public announcement of a decision not to prosecute should be co-ordinated with the HSE.
- When the CPS decides to prosecute, the HSE will be informed of the progress of the case and notified of the result.
- When the CPS brings a charge following a work-related death, the HSE will disclose to the CPS a copy of any report or other document submitted to the coroner. This report must not be disclosed to any other party without the consent of the HSE.

Prosecution

2.182   Where the CPS, HSE and enforcing authority seek to prosecute, there should be a conference to discuss the management of proceedings and in particular the following.

- Which body will take main responsibility for the prosecution.
- The wording of the charges and any alternative charges.
- Matters relating to the disclosure and retention of evidence.
- A timetable for case management.
- Arrangements for ensuring that bereaved relatives of the deceased and witnesses are kept informed.
- The announcement of the decision to prosecute.
- An agreement as to a mechanism for consultation if the proceedings are discontinued or no evidence is offered.
- Instructions to the prosecuting advocate.

The Coroner

2.183   The Protocol makes the following points about the relationship of enforcing authorities with the coroner.

- When a serious criminal offence arising out of a work-related death has been charged, the police or the CPS will notify the coroner.
- The coroner may then adjourn the inquest until the end of the criminal prosecution.
- The Director of Public Prosecutions (DPP) may ask the coroner to adjourn the inquest where proceedings relating to the death have started in the magistrates' court.
- Where the CPS has decided not to prosecute, the HSE or other enforcing authority will await the result of the coroner's inquest before charging any other health and safety offences otherwise the case would be prejudiced.

List of Relevant Legislation

2.184

- Corporate Manslaughter and Corporate Homicide Act 2007
- Health and Safety at Work, etc Act 1974

Further Information

Organisations

- Association of Chief Police Officers (ACPO)
  Web: *www.acpo.police.uk*
  The ACPO is an independent, professionally-led strategic body. It works in the public interest and, in equal and active partnership with government and the Association of Police Authorities, leads and co-ordinates the direction and development of the police service in England, Wales and Northern Ireland.
- British Transport Police
  Web: *www.btp.police.uk*
  The British Transport Police is the national police force for the railways providing a policing service to rail operators, their staff and passengers throughout England, Wales and Scotland.
- Civil Aviation Authority (CAA)
  Web: *www.caa.co.uk*
  The CAA is the UK's independent aviation regulator, with all civil aviation regulatory functions (economic regulation, airspace policy, safety regulation and consumer protection) integrated within a single specialist body.
- Crown Prosecution Service (CPS)
  Web: *www.cps.gov.uk*
  The CPS is responsible for prosecuting people in England and Wales charged with a criminal offence.
- Director of Public Prosecutions
  Web: *www.cps.gov.uk/about/dpp.html*
  The Director of Public Prosecutions (DPP) is responsible for ensuring the independent review and prosecution of criminal proceedings started by the police in England and Wales.
- Health and Safety Executive (HSE)
  Web: *www.hse.gov.uk*
  The HSE and the Health and Safety Commission are responsible for the regulation of almost all the risks to health and safety arising from work activity in the UK.
- Local Government Association (LGA)
  Web: *www.lga.gov.uk*
  The LGA was formed in 1997 and represents the 500 or so local authorities of England and Wales. The authorities represent over 50 million people and spend around £78 billion per annum.
- Maritime and Coastguard Agency (MCA)
  Web: *www.mcga.gov.uk*
  The MCA is responsible throughout the UK for implementing the Government's maritime safety policy.
- Rail Accident Investigation Branch
  Web: *www.raib.gov.uk*
  The Rail Accident Investigation Branch (RAIB) is the independent railway accident investigation organisation for the UK. It investigates railway accidents and incidents on the UK's railways, aiming to improve safety rather than establish blame.

Penalties and Sentencing

- A trial involving corporate manslaughter charges will be governed by the normal rules of evidence and procedure for trials on indictment, ie matters of law are decided by the judge and questions of fact are dealt with by the jury.
- The jury must consider whether the evidence shows that the organisation failed to comply with any health and safety legislation which relates to the alleged breach and if so, how serious that failure was and how much of a risk of death it posed.
- Any guilt must be proven beyond reasonable doubt.
- A number of recent Court of Appeal cases have considered the matter of levels of fines in health and safety cases where deaths have been caused. It is thought that these may be relevant to sentencing under the Corporate Manslaughter and Corporate Homicide Act 2007.
- The Centre for Corporate Accountability has proposed that organisations convicted of killing should face the threat of fines in excess of 10% of the annual global turnover of the company.
- The Sentencing Advisory Panel recommends that offending companies should be required to supply detailed accounts for a three-year period so that the court can accurately assess its financial position.
- The Panel has also suggested that the significance of previous warnings of danger as an aggravating feature may affect levels of fines.
- Fines imposed on bodies such as local authorities or hospital trusts may divert resources and result in a worsening of safety standards.
- Where an organisation is convicted of corporate manslaughter or corporate homicide, the court may make a remedial order instructing the organisation to take specified steps to remedy the breach or cause of it.
- The court may make a publicity order which requires the organisation to publicise the fact of its conviction.
- The Act does not make specific provision for appeals, and general principles will therefore apply.

2.185   Any organisation that is guilty of corporate manslaughter or corporate homicide is liable on conviction on indictment to an unlimited fine. A number of recent Court of Appeal cases have considered the matter of levels of fines in health and safety cases where deaths have been caused, and have stated general principles applicable to companies. It is likely that these cases will form the basis of fines, penalties and sentencing on those organisations found guilty under the Corporate Manslaughter and Corporate Homicide Act 2007.

In Practice

Court Proceedings

2.186   Section 1 of the Corporate Manslaughter and Corporate Homicide Act 2007 (the Act) states that an organisation that is guilty of corporate manslaughter or corporate homicide is liable on conviction on indictment to a fine. This means that prosecutions must be brought in the Crown Court. It also states that the offence of corporate homicide (the Scottish version) is indictable only in the High Court of Justiciary.

2.187   A trial involving corporate manslaughter charges will be governed by the normal rules of evidence and procedure for trials on indictment. In general terms, this means that matters of law are decided by the judge and questions of fact are dealt with by the jury.

2.188   Any guilt must be proven beyond reasonable doubt.

Matters for Consideration by the Jury

2.189   Section 8 of the Act sets out specific matters for consideration by the jury, as follows.

- Where it is established that an organisation owed a relevant duty of care to a person, and it falls to the jury to decide whether there was a gross breach of duty, the jury must consider whether the evidence shows that the organisation failed to comply with any health and safety legislation which relates to the alleged breach and if so, how serious that failure was and how much of a risk of death it posed.
- The jury may also consider the extent to which the evidence shows that there were attitudes, policies, systems or accepted practices within the organisation which were likely to have encouraged any such failure or to have produced tolerance of it.
- The jury may also have regard to any health and safety guidance which relates to the alleged breach.
- This does not prevent the jury having regard to any other matters which they consider relevant.

Note:
"Health and safety guidance", for these purposes, means any code of practice, guidance, manual or similar publication which is concerned with health and safety matters and which is made or issued by an authority responsible for the enforcement of any health and safety legislation.

Health and Safety Prosecutions

2.190   While the practical implications of these provisions remain to be seen, companies may still be prosecuted for breaches of specific health and safety law as well as, or as an alternative to, corporate manslaughter.

2.191   The new offence is aimed at complementing rather than replacing existing offences under the Health and Safety at Work, etc Act 1974.

Fines and Penalties

2.192   Any organisation that is guilty of corporate manslaughter or corporate homicide is liable on conviction on indictment to an unlimited fine. This is because the new statute applies only to organisations and not to individuals, so imprisonment is not an option.

Relevant Case Law

2.193   A number of recent Court of Appeal cases have considered the matter of levels of fines in health and safety cases where deaths have been caused. Some of these cases deal specifically with health and safety regulations, but a number have stated general principles applicable to companies. It is thought that these may be relevant to sentencing under the new Act.

R v Howe and Son (Engineers) Ltd [1998], Court of Appeal

2.194   H was a small precision engineering company. In 1996, an employee was electrocuted while cleaning H's factory. The company pleaded guilty to a number of charges. It was fined a total of £48,000. It appealed to the Court of Appeal. That court stated that it was not possible to lay down any tariff or to say that fines should specifically relate to the net profit or turnover of a defendant company.

2.195   The court made the following points of general significance with reference to the factors which were relevant in assessing levels of fines.

- A deliberate breach of health and safety law with a view to cost cutting or increasing profit was a serious aggravating feature.
- There was evidence that safety standards in small organisations might be lower than in larger ones. The degree of care required in matters of safety was not affected by the size, financial strength or weakness of a company.
- Fines should reflect public disquiet at an unnecessary loss of life.
- Aggravating features included failures to heed warnings and deliberately profiting from a failure to take necessary health and safety measures.
- Mitigating elements included a prompt admission of responsibility, a guilty plea, steps to remedy deficiencies and a good safety record.

2.196   The fine would be reduced to £15,000. This was a small company with limited resources. The full burden of the fine fell on the company because the fine was not deductible for tax purposes.

R v Balfour Beatty Rail Infrastructure Services Ltd [2006], Court of Appeal

2.197   The charge in this case involved breach of duty as a cause of the Hatfield rail disaster in October 2000 when 4 passengers were killed and 102 injured.

2.198   A train from London to Leeds was rounding a bend at 115 miles per hour when two sections of track disintegrated and the train was derailed. The track had failed because of brittle fractures. The track was owned by Railtrack plc which had primary responsibility for the safety of the track. Balfour Beatty was responsible for inspections of the track. It had failed to adequately inspect the track and had failed to appreciate from the result of inspections that action was called for. The most relevant action which it had failed to take was to impose a speed restriction on the stretch of track where the accident happened.

2.199   Balfour Beatty was fined £10 million. It appealed to the Court of Appeal. The fine was reduced to £7.5 million on appeal. The following points made by the court are likely to be of relevance.

- The knowledge that breach of duty could result in a fine of sufficient size to impact on shareholders would provide a powerful incentive for management to comply with that duty.
- The fine must not always be large enough to affect dividends or share price, but must reflect both the degree of fault and the consequences, so as to raise appropriate concern on the part of shareholders at what had happened.
- Such an approach would satisfy the requirement that the sentence should act as a deterrent. It would also satisfy the requirement, which would rightly be reflected by public opinion, that a company should be punished for culpable failure to pay due respect for safety, and the consequences of that failure.
- In the present case, there had been a serious systemic failure on the part of a company, the contractual duties of which were directed at securing the safety of rail travellers. The consequence had been 4 deaths and more than 100 injured passengers.
- Balfour Beatty was a very substantial company. Its overall remuneration under its 7-year contract was £368 million. It was therefore hard to say that a fine of £10 million, although severe, was wrong in principle.

R v Yorkshire Sheeting and Insulation Ltd [2003], Court of Appeal

2.200 Y was a company which specialised in roofing work. It had been contracted to work on a project. A self-employed roofing sheeter engaged by Y fell through a rooflight and was killed. Y was fined £100,000. It appealed to the Court of Appeal. That court reduced the fine to £55,000 and made the following points of general application.

- Y was a responsible company which, on this one occasion, had contributed to a failure to take the reasonable and practical steps required to ensure the safety of those who had been working on the roof.
- Although there had been serious default, in that the problem giving rise to the risk had been identified before the day on which the death had occurred, and that the problem had not been addressed by the provision of netting, the covering of all relevant rooflights and the demarcation of safe areas, such default had, to a significant extent, been due to a lack of communication between all those involved, including the main contractor.

Level of Fines

2.201 The Sentencing Advisory Panel has made the following recommendations in relation to fines.

2.202 The starting points should be:
- the imposition of a publicity order
- a fine of 5% of the company's average annual turnover.

2.203 This appears to conflict with the statement in *R v Howe*, to the effect that fines should not relate to the net profit or turnover of a company. The Panel's view is that annual turnover is the most appropriate measure of a company's ability to pay fines.

2.204 The Centre for Corporate Accountability (CCA) has commented that this level is too low. It has proposed that organisations convicted of killing people should face the threat of larger fines than those which are found to be in breach of European competition law. This is currently an administrative fine of 10% of the annual global turnover of the company.

2.205 The CCA has also commented that the current sentencing provisions in the Act fail to address the need for a full range of effective corporate penalties available to the courts. The new publicity orders should be seen simply as a first step towards more effective sentencing reforms.

Financial Information

2.206 There can be difficulties in obtaining accurate information about a company's finances. It has been proposed that the court should be able to require a professional assessment of a company's finances from an expert. The cost of this should be met by the company. This could be described as a "pre-sentence report".

2.207 The Sentencing Advisory Panel recommends that offending companies should be required to supply detailed accounts for a three-year period so that the court can accurately assess its financial position.

2.208 It is important to note that the Act is a new piece of legislation with many novel features. It remains to be seen how many prosecutions will be brought under the Act and the way in which courts approach sentencing.

Warnings

2.209   The Sentencing Advisory Panel has also discussed the significance of previous warnings of danger as an aggravating feature which may affect levels of fines. For example, previous incidents of a similar nature, to which an organisation should have responded, may amount to warnings and may result in increased fines.

2.210   In the case of Kite (1996), a company which operated an activity centre, two instructors at the centre resigned as a protest over poor safety standards. One of them warned the company's managing director, in writing, that there could be danger to life if safety standards were not improved. The company did not heed these warnings. One year later, four school pupils died from drowning during a trip organised by the company. The company was fined £60,000 for common law manslaughter. The managing director was sentenced to three years imprisonment. This was reduced to two years on appeal.

2.211   In 1997, a construction company was warned by the Health and Safety Executive (HSE) that a gang foreman was not working with the correct equipment. Two years later the same worker was killed when he fell through a rooflight. The company had not heeded the warning from the HSE. It was fined £25,000 for common law manslaughter.

Deliberate Breaches of Appropriate Standards of Care

2.212   Where a company has deliberately breached the appropriate standard of care for profit motives, this is a seriously aggravating factor. For example, where a haulage company's drivers falsified tachographs and records and worked excessive hours, and a driver fell asleep on the motorway and killed himself and two other workers, the company was fined £50,000. The company's managing director was imprisoned for seven years.

Public Bodies

2.213   The courts have sometimes taken the view that breaches of health and safety law are more serious where there is a significant public element, for example public safety.

2.214   While Crown organisations are exempt from the Health and Safety at Work, etc Act 1974, the new statute applies to many Crown organisations but their liability is limited in a number of respects. It is important to be aware that fines imposed on bodies such as local authorities or hospital trusts may divert resources and result in a worsening of safety standards.

Remedial Orders

2.215   Section 9 of the Act deals with remedial orders. Significant points are as follows.

- Where an organisation is convicted of corporate manslaughter or corporate homicide, the court may make a remedial order instructing the organisation to take specified steps to remedy:
  - the relevant breach
  - any matter which appears to the court to have been a cause of the death and which has resulted from the relevant breach
  - any deficiency, in relation to health and safety matters, in the policies, systems or practices of the organisation of which the relevant breach appears to the court to be an indication.

- Such an order may only be made on an application by the prosecution which specifies the terms of the proposed order.
- The terms of a remedial order must be such as the court considers appropriate, having regard to representations and evidence in relation to the matter.
- Before the prosecution applies for a remedial order, it must consult with the appropriate health and safety enforcement authorities.
- Remedial orders must specify a timeframe for the specified steps to be taken.
- The order may require the convicted organisation to provide the appropriate enforcement authority with evidence that the steps have been taken.
- Organisations may apply to the court for time periods specified in relation to remedial orders to be extended.
- Failure to comply with a remedial order is in itself an offence punishable with an unlimited fine.

2.216 The Sentencing Advisory Panel has made the following comments on remedial orders.

- The overall aim of remedial orders is the rehabilitation of offending companies by setting out steps to be taken to ensure that the failures which resulted in death are dealt with.
- Remedial orders will provide an additional safeguarding power in the limited number of cases where companies have failed to respond.
- The costs of complying with a remedial order should not result in a decrease in any fine which has been imposed for the same offence. Remedial orders are rehabilitative. Reductions in fines would reward companies which have failed to comply with health and safety standards.

2.217 Again, it should be noted that this power is new and that it will no doubt be the subject of judicial interpretation.

Publicity Orders

2.218 Publicity orders are dealt with under s.10 of the Act.

2.219 Where an organisation is convicted of corporate manslaughter or corporate homicide, the court may make a publicity order which requires the organisation to publicise the following.

- The fact of the conviction.
- Details of the offence for which it has been convicted.
- The amount of any fine which it has been ordered to pay.
- Details of any remedial order.

2.220 Before a court makes a publicity order, it must consult the appropriate health and safety authority and have regard to representations made by the prosecution or the defence.

2.221 A publicity order must specify a period of time within which its requirements must be complied with. It may require the organisation to supply evidence of compliance with its requirements to the relevant health and safety authority.

2.222 Failure to comply with a publicity order is an offence punishable with an unlimited fine.

2.223 The aim of publicity orders is to provide the public with information as to what has been done to deal with an organisation's shortcomings. It is hoped that the availability of such orders will encourage organisations to avoid management failures and will deter them from disregarding their health and safety responsibilities.

2.224 The Sentencing Advisory Panel makes the following comments in relation to publicity orders.

- Concern remains over the sufficiency of the impact of fines on large companies. The power to make publicity orders already exists in Australia, Canada and the US.

- It is thought that publicity orders will normally be made in addition to fines, but they can be imposed alone.

- Publicity orders are aimed at deterrence because of the impact they can have on the public reputation of a company through damage to consumer confidence, equity value and market share.

- The HSE already has a "name and shame" database which provides a public record of all health and safety convictions and the names of convicted companies.

- It is thought that the wording of publicity orders will normally be a matter for consultation with the family of the victim.

- Publicity orders may be useful where the court has reduced a fine because of a company's financial circumstances, or where a company has a poor record of compliance with the law, or where it is thought that the customers, creditors and shareholders of the company should know about the conviction.

- A publicity order should be made in all cases where there are convictions for corporate manslaughter.

- Options for the form of the order may include publication on television, radio and the press, publication on the company's website, notice to shareholders and written notice to customers and suppliers of the company.

- Publicity orders will involve costs for the convicted company. The indirect financial costs may be large and are difficult to estimate.

2.225 Critics of the new publicity order regime have stated the view that the orders will result in greater damage to the reputation of the company, causing lower share prices, higher insurance premiums, difficulty in recruiting and greater difficulty when tendering for future work.

Compensation Orders

2.226 Courts have powers to make orders requiring defendants to pay compensation for any personal injury, loss or damage resulting from the offence. These powers, conferred by the Powers of Criminal Courts (Sentencing) Act 2000, will also apply to the new corporate manslaughter statute. Courts are required to give reasons if they do not make such orders.

2.227 The following points may be particularly relevant to corporate manslaughter cases.

- Compensation orders may be made in favour of the relatives and dependants of the deceased for bereavement and funeral expenses.

- An order for the payment of funeral expenses may be made for the benefit of anyone who has incurred them.

- Compensation for bereavement may only be made in favour of persons who may claim under the Fatal Accidents Act 1976, that is, the spouse of the deceased or, where the deceased was a minor, the parents of the deceased.

- The maximum sum which can be claimed for compensation for bereavement is £10,000.

- The amount of compensation which may be ordered is a matter for the discretion of the court.

- In cases where both a fine and a compensation order are imposed, and the defendant does not have the means to pay both, then the compensation order takes priority over the fine.

- Any compensation paid is deducted from damages received in civil proceedings.

2.228 The Sentencing Advisory Panel takes the view that in cases of corporate manslaughter, compensation issues are likely to be complex, and better dealt with through civil proceedings.

Appeals

2.229 The Act does not make specific provision for appeals, and general principles will therefore apply. Appeals from the Crown Court can be made to the Court of Appeal (Criminal Division) within 28 days of the decision to be appealed. The notice of appeal must state the grounds of appeal. The application is initially considered by a single judge who decides whether or not to grant or refuse leave to appeal. Where leave to appeal is refused, the appellant may ask the full Court of Appeal to reconsider.

2.230 The appeal is not a rehearing of the trial. The Court of Appeal considers written and oral arguments but will only rarely hear fresh evidence. It will only intervene in an appeal against conviction where the conviction is shown to have been unsafe. Where an appeal is against sentence only, the Court of Appeal has no power to increase the sentence but will only reduce it where it is shown to have been wrong in principle or manifestly excessive.

2.231 The prosecution can refer serious cases to the Court of Appeal where it is considered that the Crown Court sentence was unduly lenient. In such cases, the Court of Appeal has the power to increase the sentence.

2.232 A further appeal may be made to the House of Lords in the very limited circumstances that a point of law of general public importance is involved.

Director of Public Prosecutions

2.233 The consent of the Director of Public Prosecutions (DPP) is required before proceedings are brought under the Act.

2.234 The practicalities of the "DPP consent" requirement are well-illustrated by the notorious case of *R v Director of Public Prosecutions and others ex parte Jones* [2000], High Court. This case concerned the offence of common law manslaughter.

2.235 The facts of the case, in summary, were that in 1998, J was sent by an employment agency to work at Shoreham docks. He was employed by Euromin, whose managing director was M. J's work involved the unloading of bags of cobblestones from the hold of a ship. The system for this involved workers standing near an open grab bucket attached to a crane. The lever in the driver's cab for closing the bucket was very sensitive. When it was operated, the bucket closed in one second. J was decapitated when the grab bucket closed on him.

2.236 The HSE and the police investigated the matter. The HSE issued improvement and prohibition notices and decided to prosecute Euromin for statutory offences. The DPP decided not to prosecute the company or M for negligent manslaughter. This decision was challenged in the High Court by an application for judicial review. That court ruled as follows.

- The DPP's decision not to prosecute should be quashed.
- The DPP had been wrong in applying a test of subjective culpability rather than objective liability for the dangerous system of work.
- The test for negligent manslaughter was objective. Negligence would be criminal if, on an objective basis, the defendant demonstrated a failure to advert to a serious

risk going beyond mere inadvertence in respect of an obvious and important matter which the defendant's duty demanded he should address.

2.237 The common law offence of manslaughter by gross negligence is abolished in its application to corporations by s.20 of the Act. The Jones case illustrates how the decision of the DPP, in relation to workplace deaths, may be successfully challenged by judicial review. It is anticipated that this case will continue to be relevant.

List of Relevant Legislation

2.238
- Corporate Manslaughter and Corporate Homicide Act 2007
- Powers of Criminal Courts (Sentencing) Act 2000
- Fatal Accidents Act 1976
- Health and Safety at Work, etc Act 1974

Further Information

Organisations
- Centre for Corporate Accountability
  Web: *www.corporateaccountability.org*
  The Centre for Corporate Accountability is a charitable organisation that monitors worker and public safety, and undertakes research and provides advice on law enforcement and corporate criminal accountability.
- Health and Safety Executive (HSE)
  Web: *www.hse.gov.uk*
  The HSE and the Health and Safety Commission are responsible for the regulation of almost all the risks to health and safety arising from work activity in the UK.
- Sentencing Advisory Panel
  Web: *www.sentencing-guidelines.gov.uk/about/sap/index.html*
  The Sentencing Advisory Panel is an independent body which provides advice to the Sentencing Guidelines Council.

Compensation Claims

- An injured person is increasingly likely to make a claim for financial compensation following an accident.
- Claims can also be made for medical conditions, such as asbestosis, or for mental conditions, such as work-related stress.
- Claims are usually based on common law, eg the common law duty of care. They can also be based on breaches of statutory duty.
- The injured party will generally use the law of tort to make a claim. This includes the tort of negligence and the tort of breach of statutory duty.
- There are a number of possible defences to these claims, such as contributory negligence (where the claimant was partly to blame for the accident). This may mean damages are reduced.
- There may be claims where the employer is liable for the negligence of its employees, called vicarious liability.
- There may also be claims where the employer might not have been negligent at all, called strict liability.
- Claims for personal injury or death must be made within three years from the date of the accident.
- Claims for diseases and occupational ill health must be made within three years of the disease being diagnosed. Asbestosis may be diagnosed 30 years after exposure.
- Claimants must send 2 copies of a standard letter of claim to the defendant and the defendant must acknowledge this letter within 21 days.
- The defendant has three months to investigate the claim and must then disclose specific information, such as accident book entries.
- If this exchange of information does not result in an agreement, the case will proceed to court.
- Employers will stand a better chance of winning cases if they have taken a proactive approach to health and safety and have kept suitable records.
- Employers are required to have insurance that provides at least minimum cover for these claims.

2.239   In the event of an incident, the injured person, whether an employee or not, is increasingly likely to make a claim for compensation. Solicitors and trade unions often actively encourage and promote personal injury claims and with no-win/no-fee arrangements many prospective claimants perceive that there is nothing to lose by making a claim. The subsequent increase in claims has meant that the employer's liability insurance premium has increased for many organisations. It is important that safety practitioners and managers understand the legal principles behind personal injury claims and know how best to defend and win these claims.

Employers' Duties

2.240   Employers must comply with:
- the requirements of the Civil Procedure Rules (as amended by the Woolf reforms)
- the Employers' Liability (Compulsory Insurance) Act 1969 under which it is compulsory to have employers' liability insurance.

2.241   These are in addition to the requirement to comply with the Health and Safety at Work, etc Act 1974 (HSWA) and all health and safety regulations, under which claims may also be made.

In Practice

Legal Principles Governing Claims

Duty of Care

2.242   The fundamental starting point for most personal injury claims was established in the groundbreaking case of *Donoghue v Stevenson* (1932). This is the famous "snail in the bottle" case which established that a duty of care is owed to our "neighbours". The case described neighbours as being those who we could reasonably foresee being affected by our acts and omissions. Typical neighbour relationships include:

- employer to its employees
- employer to others' employees
- employer to contractor
- occupier to authorised visitors
- occupier to unauthorised visitors, eg trespassers
- employer to members of the public.

2.243   The common law duty of care owed by an employer to its employees was further defined in the case of *Wilsons and Clyde Coal Co v English* (1938). In particular the case considered the personal nature of the duty. In this case, the employer was compelled by law to employ a colliery agent who was in charge of safety in the mine. Nonetheless, when an accident occurred, the employer was held liable. The case decided that the employer's duty of care to his employees was personal to the employer and could not be delegated, eg to a manager or safety advisor. In other words the common law duty of care established in *Donoghue v Stevenson* is primary and cannot be transferred to someone else, diluted or delegated to employees. The case went on to say that employers must provide:

- a safe place of work and equipment
- safe systems of work
- reasonably competent employees.

2.244   The two cases mentioned above are regularly cited in claims for personal injury. Since these cases occurred, there have been many others that have further developed and interpreted the common law duty of care. For example, in *Paris v Stepney Borough Council* (1951) a one-eyed man lost his other eye while working on the underside of a vehicle. None of the workforce had been provided with protective goggles. The injured man claimed damages and it was deemed that employers owe the duty of care to each employee individually. If the employer knows of a condition in an employee that makes that employee more susceptible to injury, or makes the consequences of injury more severe than usual, extra precautions must be taken. Consequently, employers must take into account any significant "special needs" in an employee and take extra precautions. Employees with "special needs" might include (depending on the circumstances):

- young and inexperienced workers
- pregnant employees

- employees with learning difficulties
- employees with a medical condition or a disability.

2.245   In a more recent case, *Walker v Northumberland County Council* (1995), an action under common law for work-related stress was successful. Consequently, employers today must take into account mental well-being as well as physical well-being.

What Kind of Claims May be Made?

2.246   In practice, the law of tort will be used to bring claims. "Tort" means a wrongdoing in civil law. Two particular torts are usually used when someone brings a claim for personal injury. These are the tort of negligence and the tort of breach of statutory duty. These two torts are often used together and this is commonly referred to as a "double-barrelled" claim.

The Tort of Negligence

2.247   A claim for compensation based upon the tort of negligence requires three conditions to be proved by the claimant, as follows.
1. A duty of care must be owed by the defendant to the claimant.
2. The duty of care must have been breached.
3. The injury or loss suffered by the claimant, must have been due to the breach of duty of care.

2.248   There are some points to note about these three conditions in practice.
1. The first condition is not usually an issue, especially for employees suing their employers (a duty of care clearly exists between employer and employee).
2. The second condition involves the court deciding whether the defendant took reasonable care of the claimant. All too often defendants are not in a position to prove the positive action they have taken because the evidence in the form of records is not available. Managers have a particularly important role here to keep the necessary records.
3. In the third condition, the main potential contention is whether the injury or loss was related to the acts or omissions of the defendant. For example, someone suing an employer for a back injury must be able to show that the injury was work-related rather than due to an activity or incident which occurred in the claimant's own time, eg when playing sport. Alternatively, there may be no injury at all. Medical evidence is particularly important in these cases.

Tort of Breach of Statutory Duty

2.249   An alternative route when making a claim for personal injury is for the claimant to show that the defendant was in breach of a relevant statute and therefore liable to pay compensation. The general principle of being able to cite statute law in a civil claim was first established in *Groves v Lord Wimborne* (1898). In this case, a boy employed at the defendant's factory was caught in an unguarded cogwheel. His arm was amputated. It was held that the applicable statute required the secure fencing of dangerous parts of machinery and therefore the statute was relevant to the boy's civil claim.

Civil Liability Exclusions

2.250   Not all statutes can be used in a civil claim. Notably, the main sections of the Health and Safety at Work, etc Act 1974 (HSWA) cannot be used because of the civil exclusion clause at s.47 of the HSWA. This essentially means that breaches of these statutory provisions cannot be used to make a compensation claim.

2.251 There were exclusions in the Management of Health and Safety at Work Regulations 1999 (MHSWR), but these were removed in October 2003. The MHSWR retain an exclusion for "persons not in employment", eg members of the public who therefore still cannot cite the regulations in making a civil claim. Otherwise regulations on health and safety can be used without restriction.

Conditions to be Met for Breach of Statutory Duty

2.252 It is important to note that a breach of a statute is not sufficient on its own to prove the tort of breach of statutory duty in a civil claim. The following conditions must be fulfilled.

1. The statute cited must apply to the claimant, eg an employee must use a statute which applies to employees, a member of the public must use a statute which applies to the public, etc.
2. The statute cited must have been designed to prevent the type of injury incurred by the claimant. For example, the Control of Substances Hazardous to Health Regulations 2002 are unlikely to be suitable in a case where the injury relates to manual handling.
3. The statute must have been breached. If there has been a prosecution by the appropriate enforcing authority, this may aid the claimant's case.
4. The injury must have been caused by the breach of statute. This is often referred to as the causation rule. For example, a claimant's hearing loss must be due to a breach of the Control of Noise at Work Regulations 2005 by his or her employer, and not was it due to the claimant attending pop concerts in his or her own time.

Defences Against a Claim

2.253 There are a number of possible defences that may be applicable to a particular case. The claimant might not be able to show negligence or breach of statutory duty. For example, the employer did take reasonable care of his employee, or the injury sustained was not due to a breach by the employer.

Contributory Negligence

2.254 One of the more important defences is that of "contributory negligence". This is based on the Law Reform (Contributory Negligence) Act 1945 which states that if claimants are partly to blame for an accident through their own negligence, then the amount of compensation should be reduced. For example, if claimants failed to wear protective clothing issued to them, or if they did not follow procedures or protocols, then they may be open to a charge of contributory negligence and the damages award may be reduced or even withheld. Where it can be shown that the injury sustained was due to the sole fault of the claimant, the defendant will not be liable at all.

"Volenti" Rule

2.255 The use of *volenti non fit injuria* is often misunderstood as a potential defence in compensation claims. The term means that the employee has consented to the risks at his or her workplace. The "*volenti*" rule once predominated but it is no longer a realistic defence in most cases today. However, it can be used where employees have a specific legal duty placed on them. The case of *ICI Ltd v Shatwell* (1964) is an example of this. The Quarries (Explosives) Regulations 1959 required that no electrical testing for shot firing be carried out unless all persons in the vicinity had withdrawn to a safe area. This duty was placed on *employees*. Two employees were injured when they acted in breach of these regulations and of the employer's instructions. In the civil claim that followed it was held that the employers could successfully use the defence of "*volenti*". Whatever the defence open to the employer, none will succeed unless there is evidence available.

Vicarious Liability: When the Employee is Negligent

2.256 There are some situations where an employer is liable for the negligence of its employees with respect to some other person being injured. This is referred to as vicarious liability. The key conditions for this liability to third parties are that:

- the employee must have been negligent
- the employee must have been acting in the course of employment, in other words acting on behalf of the employer.

2.257 In the case of *Rose v Plenty* (1976) the employer prohibited milkmen from letting children ride on milk floats. In blatant breach of this instruction and unknown to the employer, a milkman engaged a young boy to help him deliver and collect milk bottles during the round. The boy was injured due to the negligent driving of the milkman. It was held that the employer was liable for the employee's negligence as the employee was acting "in the course of employment", ie acting on behalf of the employer. In the recent case of *Mattis v Pollock* (2003), a nightclub doorman who stabbed a person in the vicinity of the club, in revenge for an earlier attack on him in the club, committed the act "in the course of employment". Consequently, the club owner (the employer) was vicariously liable for the doorman's actions.

Strict Liability: When the Employer is Not Negligent

2.258 There are other situations where the employer is liable even though it has not been negligent. This is often referred to as "strict liability". The Employers' Liability (Defective Equipment) Act 1969 says that where an employee is injured using equipment which has a latent defect, the employer will be liable even though they may have taken all the necessary steps to ensure that the equipment was obtained from a reputable supplier. It will be up to the employer, not the injured employee, to pursue the manufacturer through the courts.

Limitations on Timescales for Claims

2.259 Any action for personal injury or death must be commenced within three years from the date of the accident. This comes from the Limitation Act 1980 and from the Prescription and Limitations (Scotland) Act 1973. In some cases, it may be difficult to ascertain a precise date when an injury was sustained, eg noise-induced deafness. In these cases, the date when the claimant became aware of the injury may be used. This often relates to the date of diagnosis by a medical practitioner. In the case of a death, the Fatal Accident Act 1976 allows close relatives to make a claim on behalf of the deceased.

Damages

2.260 Damages can be considerable and there are two broad types.
1. Pecuniary: these involve monetary losses such as loss of earnings, medical and travel expenses.
2. Non-pecuniary: these involve compensation for pain and suffering and loss of amenity such as changes to lifestyle.

Procedures When a Claim is Made

2.261 New rules were put in place in 1999 following Lord Woolf's enquiry into the reasons why the legal system for dealing with claims was slow and unfair. The new rules made it clear that litigation should be a last resort and introduced a number of "pre-action protocols" to provide for the early exchange of information. Parties who fail to comply with the protocols can be penalised by the courts. A summary of the intended sequence of events is as follows.

- Letter of claim received.
- Defendant must reply (at least acknowledge) within 21 days.
- Claim investigated.
- Admit liability and settle out of court.
- Deny liability either completely or partially.
- Relevant documentation disclosed.
- A "statement of truth" must be signed by someone from the defendant's organisation.

Letter of Claim

2.262   Following the decision to make a claim, the claimant must send two copies of a standard "letter of claim" to the defendant. The letter contains information relating to the general circumstances of the claim including the nature of any accident, a description of injuries sustained and the documents which the claimant would like to be disclosed. The defendant must acknowledge the letter of claim within 21 days. If the defendant does not reply within this timescale, the claimant will be entitled to begin legal proceedings. The court will take into account the fact that the defendant did not follow the protocol's rules. This puts an important onus on companies who may be named as defendants to react quickly to letters of claim. They must therefore have the necessary procedures in place in order to facilitate this prompt action.

Information That Defendants Must Disclose

2.263   Following the initial acknowledgement by the defendant of the letter of claim, the defendant has three months to investigate the claim before replying. The protocols set out in some detail specific information that defendants must disclose. For workplace injury claims, this includes:

- accident book entries
- first-aid reports
- foreman/supervisor's report.
- Reporting of Injuries, Diseases and Dangerous Occurrences Regulations 1995 (RIDDOR) report to the enforcing authority.

2.264   Where specific regulations apply, the protocols require additional documents to be produced. For example, in respect of the MHSWR, the following should be disclosed:

- pre-accident risk assessment required by regulation 3
- post-accident risk assessment required by regulation 3
- accident investigation report
- health surveillance records required by regulation 6.

2.265   In cases where the Control of Substances Hazardous to Health Regulations 2002 are relevant, a similar disclosure of documentation is required by the protocols. This includes:

- the risk assessment carried out to comply with the requirements of regulation 6
- documentation relating to the maintenance of personal protective equipment.

2.266   For claims involving the Workplace (Health, Safety and Welfare) Regulations 1992, the documents required to be disclosed include:

- repair and maintenance records required by regulation 5
- housekeeping records to comply with regulation 9.

2.267　If companies are unable to produce the relevant documentation, it may harm their case. If they have complied with the law, they must keep the appropriate records to be able to prove it.

The Three "Tracks"

2.268　In situations where the pre-action protocols do not result in agreement or settlement, the case will be allocated to one of three "tracks" as follows.
1. Small claims track jurisdiction with a financial limit of £5000.
2. A fast track for relatively straightforward cases up to £15,000 with strictly limited timetables set up by the court.
3. A multi-track for cases over £15,000 providing hands-on management by judicial teams.

2.269　It is hoped that this system will ensure speedy settlements of cases and that positive direction and management of cases by the courts will help bring cases to a conclusion.

The Expert Witness

2.270　The pre-Woolf situation regarding the use of expert witnesses was that each side appointed its own expert witnesses. These witnesses were then required to argue their client's case from their own expert perspective. This generally led to disagreement and argument. Typically, in a health and safety claim, health and safety experts would be appointed by each side and possibly medical experts as well. Although these experts were obviously bound to answer questions truthfully in a court of law, they also had loyalties to their clients. The Woolf Report, however, encourages the joint selection of experts. There is still the flexibility for either side to obtain its own expert report, with leave of the court. However, it will be up to the court to decide whether the cost of more than one expert report is justified and recoverable. The Woolf measures mean that the expert witness will be acting for the courts rather than for a particular client and as such will be more accountable to the courts. This is an underlying but fundamental change to the role of the expert witness. In practice the Woolf Report may halt the growth in the expert witness industry.

Winning the Cases

2.271　Employers and other defendants need to consider carefully their approach to civil claims if they are to win more claims and reduce the accompanying costs of accidents, including insurance premiums. The collection of evidence on the whole range of positive actions that may have taken place on health and safety is necessary, making an increase in record keeping and consequent bureaucracy inevitable. The following points may comprise a sensible strategy in order to win more claims and to deter others.
- Be proactive on health and safety.
- Generate a positive health and safety culture and ensure that health and safety is a high priority alongside other key business objectives.
- Keep records and make sure they are up to date and retrievable.
- Remember those people with "special needs" such as young persons or those with relevant medical conditions.
- Be scrupulous on recruitment and ensure that having a positive attitude to health and safety is a criterion for the job.

- Include health and safety as a personal performance appraisal issue.
- Use discipline where necessary for breaches of health and safety procedures and protocols.
- Train staff, especially managers (including senior managers).

Role of Insurance

2.272   Employers are required to have insurance that provides at least minimum cover for compensations claims.

- Most employers are required to have insurance by virtue of the Employers' Liability (Compulsory Insurance) Act 1969.
- Exemptions include a number of public sector bodies such as government departments.
- A current certificate of insurance must be displayed.
- An insurance "excess" may be agreed with your insurance company and this may help to keep the premium manageable.
- This insurance is designed to provide at least a minimum level of cover in the event of accidents or incidents and consequent claims by employees.
- Cover must be at least £5 million.
- Copies of certificates of insurance must be kept for at least 40 years either as paper copies or electronically.
- The Health and Safety Executive enforces the law on employers' liability insurance.
- Employers without insurance can be fined up to £2500 for each day they do not have suitable insurance.
- Public liability insurance is designed to give cover in the event of claims by non-employees.

Training

2.273
- Managers and other relevant staff must be given training in the Woolf protocols for dealing with claims.
- This training should include the need for claims to be dealt with quickly, ie within no more than 21 days.

List of Relevant Legislation

2.274
- Management of Health and Safety at Work Regulations 1999
- Limitation Act 1980
- Fatal Accident Act 1976
- Health and Safety at Work, etc Act 1974
- Law Reform (Contributory Negligence) Act 1945
- Employers' Liability (Compulsory Insurance) Act 1969
- Employers' Liability (Defective Equipment) Act 1969

- Civil Procedures Rules (as amended by the Woolf reforms)

Further Information

Publications

HSE Publications

The following are available from *www.hsebooks.co.uk*.
- HSE39 *Employers' Liability (Compulsory Insurance) Act 1969: a Guide for Employees and Their Representatives*
- HSE40 (rev 1) *Employers' Liability (Compulsory Insurance) Act 1969: a Guide for Employers*

Other Publications
- *The Law of Health and Safety at Work*, Selwyn, N. Croner Publications

Chapter 3

Health and Safety Management Systems

Demonstrating an Effective Health and Safety Management System

- To avoid prosecution under the Corporate Manslaughter and Corporate Homicide Act 2007 (the Act), a demonstrable and effective health and safety management system should be in place.
- When considering whether or not a gross breach has taken place, the Act requires juries to consider, among other matters, the attitudes, policies, systems or accepted practices likely to have encouraged the failure.
- The organisation needs to establish an effective health and safety management system to implement their health and safety policy. It needs to be proportionate to the hazards and risks they need to combat.
- The health and safety management system should be based on effective risk assessment and be subject to robust systems of internal control and review, with all findings being effectively used.
- The health and safety roles and responsibilities of senior managers need to be clearly outlined, and their performance should be measured and evaluated to ensure they have the necessary competencies to carry out their roles and responsibilities effectively.
- The attitude of those at director level plays an important part in developing the organisation's culture and its tolerance of breaches of safety legislation.
- Managers need to ensure that all employees, at all levels, are motivated and empowered to work safely.
- A systematic review of performance, based on the information obtained from monitoring and auditing, is required if an organisation is to learn from all relevant experience.
- Only when directors and senior executives give a positive commitment to any changes that need to be implemented will those occupying other managerial levels follow suit.

3.1   In order to ensure that an organisation's health and safety management system operates efficiently and in a way that provides a defence under the requirements of the Corporate Manslaughter and Corporate Homicide Act 2007 (the Act), it is essential that evidence can be obtained, when required, that demonstrates that effective management systems are in place and that those occupying senior management positions are both competent and fully committed to ensuring the effectiveness of the health and safety management system.

Employers' Duties

Corporate Manslaughter and Corporate Homicide Act 2007

3.2   The Corporate Manslaughter and Corporate Homicide Act 2007 places senior managers and organisations at risk of prosecution if any gross management failings lead to the death of an employee, a member of the public or another to whom a duty of care is owed.

3.3   The legislation states that there has to be a relevant duty of care owed by the organisation in the law of negligence to the deceased and a gross breach of that relevant duty of care leading to that person's death.

3.4   In order to ensure that the organisation's health and safety management system operates efficiently and in a way that provides a defence under the requirements of the Act, it is essential that evidence can be obtained, when required, that demonstrates that effective management systems are in place and that those occupying senior management positions are both competent and fully committed to ensuring the effectiveness of the health and safety management system.

Management of Health and Safety at Work Regulations 1999

3.5   The Management of Health and Safety at Work Regulations 1999 provide the legal framework for a health and safety management system. Employers are required to make and give effect to such arrangements as are appropriate — having regard to the nature of their activities and the size of the undertaking — for the effective planning, organisation, control, monitoring and review of the preventive and protective measures.

3.6   Where the organisation employs five or more employees, these arrangements must be recorded.

Health and Safety at Work, etc Act 1974

3.7   The Health and Safety at Work, etc Act 1974 requires employers to ensure "so far as is reasonably practicable" the health, safety and welfare of their employees and other persons who may be affected by their work. This includes sub-contractors and the general public.

Employees' Duties

3.8   Employees must inform their employer, or other employees with a responsibility for health and safety, of any work situation where there is a serious and immediate risk to health and safety. Similarly, they must inform employers of any shortcomings in the employer's protection arrangements.

In Practice

3.9   The emphasis in the Corporate Manslaughter and Corporate Homicide Act 2007 is on effective management of health and safety and therefore it is vital that senior management can demonstrate that they have an effective system in place.

Gross Breach of Care

3.10   To be guilty of an offence under the Act, an organisation's activities must be managed or organised in such a way as to amount to a gross breach of a relevant duty of care owed by the organisation to the deceased.

3.11   A "gross" breach involves conduct that falls far below what can reasonably be expected of the organisation in the circumstances. Furthermore, the way in which the organisation's activities are managed or organised by its senior management must form a substantial element in the breach.

3.12   "Senior management" is defined as persons who play significant roles in the making of decisions about how the whole, or a substantial part, of an organisation's activities are to be managed or organised, or the actual managing or organising of the whole, or a substantial part, of those activities.

3.13   When considering whether or not a gross breach has taken place, the Act requires juries to consider, among other matters, the following.
- Failure to comply with any relevant health and safety legislation and, where this occurs, the seriousness of the failure and the risk of death it posed.
- Attitudes, policies, systems or accepted practices likely to have encouraged the failure to comply with the relevant health and safety legislation, or led to a tolerance of this failure.
- Any relevant health and safety guidance.
- Any other matters they consider relevant.

Relevant Duty of Care

3.14   A "relevant duty of care" is taken to mean any of the following duties owed by an organisation under the law of negligence.
- The duty owed to an employee or to other persons working for the organisation or performing services for it.
- The duty owed as an occupier of premises.
- The duty owed in connection with the supply of goods or services, the carrying on of construction or maintenance operations, the carrying out of other activities on a commercial basis or the keeping of any plant, vehicle or other thing.

3.15   Therefore, in order to defend the organisation against such a charge, it is necessary for senior managers to ensure that they have evidence to demonstrate a transparent and effective health and safety management system is in place and that its policies and procedures are translated into positive action on a day-by-day basis.

3.16   In line with the requirements of the Turnbull Report, *Internal Control: Guidance for Directors on the Combined Code*, it is essential that the health and safety management system is based on effective risk assessment and is subject to robust systems of internal control and review. It is also essential for senior managers to ensure that the health and safety management system covers the full range of duty of care situations outlined and, as a minimum, ensures compliance with all relevant health and safety legislation and guidance.

The Role, Responsibilities and Competency of Senior Managers

Combined Negligence

3.17   It is important to remember that a "gross" breach under the Act need not purely relate to the failures of one individual, rather the negligence of several individuals may add up to gross negligence, particularly where the individuals occupy senior management positions. Therefore, it is essential that the health and safety roles and responsibilities of senior managers are clearly outlined, that their performance is measured and evaluated and that they have the necessary competencies to carry out their roles and responsibilities effectively.

Directors' Responsibilities

3.18   Those operating at director level in organisations (titles may differ depending on whether the organisation is in the private or public sector and on its legal status) have a critical part to play in ensuring that health and safety is effectively managed. For example, they are responsible for ensuring robust internal monitoring, that reviews take place and that effective risk assessments are undertaken. Additionally, the attitude of those at director level plays an important part in developing the organisation's culture and its tolerance of breaches of safety legislation and organisational rules and procedures.

Impact of Health and Safety Director Role

3.19   Some organisations may choose to appoint a specific director to manage the health and safety responsibilities. This has the advantage of providing a focal point for health and safety within the organisation and allows that person to provide authority and credence to health and safety initiatives. However, it may also lead to others at director level feeling that they have no health and safety responsibilities.

3.20   In reality, health and safety factors need to be taken into account when all business decisions are made, they should not be considered in isolation. For example, when deciding on the purchase of equipment, the health and safety issues related to the various items of equipment under consideration need to be taken into account along with factors relating to purchase costs, maintenance requirements, training needs and installation costs, etc.

3.21   Health and safety impacts on the decisions made by directors with a diverse range of responsibilities and not merely on the director allocated health and safety responsibilities.

No Directing Mind, No Excuse

3.22   In order for any health and safety management system to be effective, it is essential that those at senior management level take the lead and provide visible and active support, strong leadership and commitment. Where this is lacking, line managers will perceive that health and safety is a "cosmetic" rather than a genuine concern for the organisation and a sloppy culture, which tolerates rule breaking, will quickly be generated.

3.23   This was highlighted by the Herald of Free Enterprise disaster where it was found that all those concerned in management, from the members of the board of directors down to the junior superintendents, were guilty of fault. From the top to the bottom, the body corporate was infected with the "disease of sloppiness".

3.24   In the past, the need to identify a particular individual at the directing mind level, whose negligence directly caused death, meant that this combined negligence was not enough to successfully prosecute an organisation for manslaughter. However, under the Act, the total of the various examples of individual negligence may, taken together, count as gross negligence. This is particularly true where senior managers are involved. The Act makes it easier to successfully prosecute in cases such as the Herald of Free Enterprise. Therefore, it is essential that those at senior management level set positive examples and ensure that others in the management chain do likewise.

Health and Safety Commission's Guidance

3.25   The Health and Safety Commission's (HSC) guidance, INDG343 *Directors' Responsibilities for Health and Safety*, advises that:

- directors formally and publicly accept a role in providing health and safety leadership
- directors accept their individual roles in relation to health and safety
- all board decisions reflect the board's health and safety intentions (as stated in policy)
- directors accept a role in engaging active participation of their staff in improving health and safety
- directors ensure that they are kept informed of, and are alerted to, relevant health and safety issues.

3.26   The HSC also recommends the appointment of a health and safety director.

The Health and Safety Management System

3.27   As juries will need to consider the extent of health and safety legislative breaches when deciding if gross negligence led to the death, it is clear that no new or additional standards have been introduced by the Act.

3.28   Senior managers need to ensure and be able to demonstrate to enforcement authorities and the courts that the health and safety management system in operation meets the requirements of current health and safety standards and legislation.

3.29   Organisations with a positive attitude towards health and safety will, of course, be doing this already. However, they will still need to ensure that they have evidence available to demonstrate that this is the case. In organisations lacking such a positive attitude, a lot more work will be required.

The Management of Health and Safety at Work Regulations 1999

3.30   There is a plethora of specific health and safety legislation relating to, eg the control of hazards such as chemicals, noise, vibration, work at height, electricity and equipment, etc which must be adhered to. However, the main requirements of the Management of Health and Safety at Work Regulations 1999 (MHSWR) apply to health and safety management systems. These include the following.

- Assessments of the risks to employees and others (Regulation 3).
- Principles of prevention (Regulation 4).
- Health and safety arrangements (Regulation 5).
- Health and safety assistance (Regulation 7).
- Procedures for serious and imminent danger (Regulations 8 and 9).
- Information for employees (Regulation 10).
- Co-operation and co-ordination between employers (Regulations 11 and 12).
- Capabilities and training of employees (Regulation 13).

3.31   Employers are required to make and give effect to such arrangements as appropriate — having regard to the nature of their activities and the size of the undertaking — for the effective planning, organisation, control, monitoring and review of the preventive and protective measures. Where the organisation employs five or more employees, these arrangements must be recorded. The MHSWR provides the legal framework for a health and safety management system.

3.32 According to the accompanying Approved Code of Practice (ACOP), the effective management of health and safety will depend on a suitable and sufficient risk assessment being carried out and the findings being effectively used.

Planning

3.33 The health and safety management system should ensure the implementation of their health and safety policy, the contents of which should be proportionate to the hazards and risks they need to combat.

3.34 This will involve:

- adopting a systematic approach to risk assessment with deadlines for completion
- using risk assessment methods to set priorities and objectives for hazard elimination and risk reduction
- selecting appropriate methods of risk control
- setting deadlines for the design and implementation of the preventive and protective measures
- developing performance standards for the completion of risk assessments and the implementation of the preventive and protective measures.

Organisation

Consultation and Communication

3.35 The organisation needs to involve employees and, where appropriate, their representatives in the carrying out of risk assessments and in the selection and implementation of the preventive and protective measures. It also needs to establish effective means of communication and consultation that make clear the commitment to health and safety. This communication will ensure that employees receive sufficient information to implement effectively the control measures that have been introduced.

Provision of Information and Training

3.36 The provision and evaluation of information, instruction and training should ensure the competence of employees, particularly those involved in risk assessment and the selection and implementation of the preventive and protective measures. Where necessary, this competence will need to be supported by the provision of health and safety assistance or advice.

Control

3.37 In order to establish effective control, an organisation should:

- clarify health and safety responsibilities and ensure those with such responsibilities clearly understand what they need to do and have the time and resources required to discharge them
- co-ordinate the activities of various individuals
- set standards to judge the performance of those with health and safety responsibilities
- ensure adequate supervision is provided.

Monitoring

3.38 Organisations should monitor:

- how well their health and safety policy is being implemented

- how well identified risks are being controlled
- how successfully a positive safety culture is being developed.

3.39   This will include both proactive and reactive monitoring, eg:

- planning and carrying out routine inspections to check the effectiveness of the preventive and protective measures
- investigating the immediate, underlying and root causes of incidents and accidents to ensure that remedial action is taken
- recording and analysing the findings of proactive and active monitoring in order to identify themes or trends.

Review

3.40   Organisations should carry out reviews in the following circumstances.

- In order to establish priorities for any remedial action identified as a result of proactive or reactive monitoring.
- In order to periodically check the effectiveness of the entire health and safety management system.

A Model for a Health and Safety Management System

3.41   The HSE's guidance, HSG65: *Successful Health and Safety Management*, outlines the following key elements that should be incorporated into an effective health and safety management system.

Policy

3.42   Setting a clear direction for the organisation to follow in terms of health and safety.

Organising

3.43   Ensuring that all employees, at all levels, are motivated and empowered to work safely. This relies on effective involvement and participation and is sustained by effective communication and the promotion of competence.

3.44   A positive health and safety culture needs to be fostered through the visible and active leadership of senior managers.

Planning and Implementing

3.45   Risk assessment methods should be used to decide priorities and to set objectives for eliminating hazards and reducing risks. Performance standards need to be established and used for measuring achievement.

Measuring Performance

3.46   Performance needs to be measured against agreed standards through the use of proactive and reactive monitoring techniques.

3.47   Monitoring should consider hardware, in terms of premises, plant and substances, and software, in terms of people, procedures and systems. In addition, monitoring should consider individual behaviour and performance, including that of senior managers in respect of health and safety.

3.48   The objectives of monitoring are to determine the immediate causes of sub-standard performance, and to identify the underlying causes and their implications for the design and operation of the health and safety management system.

Auditing and Reviewing Performance

3.49 A systematic review of performance, based on the information obtained from monitoring and auditing, is required if an organisation is to learn from all relevant experience. This not only ensures that the organisation adopts a philosophy of continuous improvement, but also forms the basis of self-regulation implied in the Health and Safety at Work, etc Act 1974 (HSWA).

3.50 The results of the review can be incorporated into any annual reports that are required to be produced. This is also in line with the requirements of the Turnbull Report.

Securing Commitment at Board and Senior Executive Level

3.51 In order for an organisation to effectively manage health and safety in a way that will offer a defence against a possible prosecution under the Act, it is essential that senior management give a positive commitment to any changes that need to be implemented. Only then will those occupying other managerial levels follow suit.

3.52 In order to secure such a commitment from those at board or senior executive level, the following approach could be adopted.
1. The preparation and delivery of a presentation, at board or senior executive level, outlining the implications of the Act and providing detailed recommendations concerning the action that needs to be taken to defend the organisation.
2. Preparation of a brief for a board or senior executives meeting that, in order to focus their attention and interest, outlines the likely outcomes of a failure to defend a prosecution under the Act, such as the following.
   (a) Fines may be in the order of 2.5% to 10% of annual turnover if the recommendations of the Sentencing Advisory Panel are followed. Where the organisation pleads not guilty, the starting point may be 5% for a first offence. Turnover is calculated from the average of three years. The panel suggests that the fine imposed needs to be set at a level significantly higher than for an offence involving a death under the HSWA, because the new offence involves more serious instances of management failure. The sentencing guidelines will lead to far more significant fines as the largest current fine under health and safety legislation is the £15 million awarded against Transco (in 2005, for safety breaches that led to the deaths of four members of a family), which represented less than 1% of the organisation's annual turnover.
   (b) Brand image could be seriously damaged if the courts impose a publicity order on every organisation convicted as has been suggested. This might require publicity on television, in local and national newspapers, in the trade press and in notices to shareholders or letters to customers.
3. Preparation of a report for consumption at board or senior executive level that reviews the effectiveness of the existing health and safety management system. This should consider the following.
   (a) Whether the policy is up to date and translated effectively into action.
   (b) Whether health and safety roles and responsibilities are clearly identified at all levels and those allocated with these roles and responsibilities understand them and have the competencies to discharge them effectively.
   (c) All relevant health and safety legislation, guidance and standards and how well they are being complied with.

(d) The status of risk assessments, ie if they have been completed and if the reviews are up to date.

(e) The disciplinary records relating to rule-breaking, etc.

(f) Whether key performance indicators are established and are being met.

(g) Whether training needs analysis has been undertaken, training provided and training records kept.

(h) The effectiveness of the proactive and reactive monitoring regimes with regard to inspections, safety sampling, accident and incident investigations, etc.

(i) Whether all identified remedial work has been actioned and follow-up monitoring instigated.

(j) The effectiveness of the auditing and review process.

(k) Whether current insurance arrangements are sufficient to cover possible defence costs.

4. Preparation of costed and prioritised recommendations for action that needs to be taken, for consideration at a board or senior executives meeting. These recommendations are based on a gap analysis that compares what evidence will be required to successfully defend a prosecution under the Act with the evidence that can be provided by the present health and safety management system. In this way, cost-effective decisions can be taken based on analysis of both the costs and benefits involved.

Training

3.53 The provision and evaluation of information, instruction and training should also ensure the competence of employees, particularly those involved in risk assessment, and the selection and implementation of the preventive and protective measures. Where necessary, this competence will need to be supported by the provision of health and safety assistance or advice.

List of Relevant Legislation

3.54
- Management of Health and Safety at Work Regulations 1999
- Corporate Manslaughter and Corporate Homicide Act 2007
- Health and Safety at Work, etc Act 1974

Further Information

Publications

HSE Publications

The following are available from *www.hsebooks.com.*
- HSG65 (rev 1997) *Successful Health and Safety Management*

- INDG417 *Leading Health and Safety at Work. Leadership Actions for Directors and Board Members*
- L21 (rev 2000) *Management of Health and Safety at Work. Management of Health and Safety at Work Regulations 1999. Approved Code of Practice and Guidance*

Other Publications

- *Internal Control: Guidance for Directors on the Combined Code*, Institute of Chartered Accountants for England and Wales

Organisations

- Centre for Corporate Accountability
  Web: *www.corporateaccountability.org*
  The Centre for Corporate Accountability is a charitable organisation that monitors worker and public safety, and undertakes research and provides advice on law enforcement and corporate criminal accountability.
- Health and Safety Executive (HSE)
  Web: *www.hse.gov.uk*
  The HSE and the Health and Safety Commission are responsible for the regulation of almost all the risks to health and safety arising from work activity in the UK.
- Institute of Directors (IoD)
  Web: *www.iod.com*
  The IoD provides a professional network for the business community.

General Health and Safety Policy

- A health and safety policy is a document that outlines an organisation's commitment to, and procedures for, health and safety.
- Employers with five or more employees are required to prepare a written statement of their health and safety policy under the Health and Safety at Work, etc Act 1974.
- Employers who have fewer than five employees are exempt from the requirement to have a written policy.
- The health and safety policy should be tailored to the individual company.
- The policy should include a general statement that expresses a commitment from the organisation to their employees' health and safety.
- It should clearly identify who is responsible for what.
- The practical arrangements for health and safety should be included within the policy, with reference to other documentation, eg risk assessments and safe systems of work. The policy must specify how these matters are to be managed.
- Employees should be consulted on the organisation's health and safety policy, rather than just be informed of it.
- The most senior person in the organisation should sign the statement of commitment.
- The policy must be effectively implemented.
- The policy must be communicated to employees in a comprehensible form. The employer must take into account employees with learning difficulties and foreign employees for whom English may be a second language when deciding on the form of the policy.
- Ongoing commitment to the health and safety policy can be secured by promoting it, eg through poster campaigns and suggestion schemes.
- Employers must monitor the effectiveness of the policy and review it, where necessary.
- The health and safety policy should be covered during induction training.
- Records must be kept to document the existence of the policy as part of an overall health and safety management system, in order to provide evidence of legal compliance.

3.55 The preparation of a company health and safety policy is the starting point for managing health and safety in the workplace. Such a policy sets out how the organisation will approach and discharge its duties in relation to the management of occupational health, safety and welfare.

3.56 Where an employer has five or more employees, the policy must be in writing.

Employers' Duties

3.57
- Employers have a duty, under s.2(3) of the Health and Safety at Work, etc Act 1974, (HSWA) to prepare, implement and revise, as necessary, a health and safety policy. Employees must be informed of the policy and of any amendments made to it.

- Employers with fewer than five employees are exempt from the requirement to have a written health and safety policy under the Employers' Health and Safety Policy Statements (Exception) Regulations 1975. However, if an employer operates a number of small establishments, where each establishment employs fewer than five employees but where all form part of the same undertaking and the total number of employees is five or more, the employer is obliged to prepare a written health and safety policy for the whole undertaking.
- Under regulation 4 of the Management of Health and Safety at Work Regulations 1999 (MHSWR), employers have a duty to implement preventative and protective control measures on the basis of the principles specified in schedule 1 to the regulations. According to schedule 1, the policy must incorporate:
  - technology
  - organisation of work
  - working conditions
  - social relationships
  - influence of factors relating to the working environment.
- Under regulation 5 of the MHSWR , the employer must implement appropriate health and safety arrangements. The management system (including the health and safety policy) will need to reflect the complexity of the organisation's activities and working environment. The Approved Code of Practice (ACOP) to the MHSWR refers to the approach taken in the British Standard for health and safety, BS 8800: *Occupational Health and Safety Management Systems Guide*. A successful health and safety management system should include the five elements: planning, organisation, control, monitoring and review.
- For employers with five or more employees, these arrangements must be recorded.
- The Safety Representatives and Safety Committees Regulations 1977 require employers to consult with safety representatives on matters relating to health and safety, including the development of the arrangements section of a company health and safety policy.
- The Health and Safety (Consultation with Employees) Regulations 1996 require employers to consult directly with employees who are not otherwise represented on matters relating to health and safety, which includes the development of the arrangements section of a company health and safety policy.
- Regulation 5 of the Control of Major Accident Hazards Regulations 1999 requires operators to prepare, retain and implement a policy document for preventing major accidents.

Employees' Duties

3.58

- Employees have a duty to take reasonable care of their own health and safety and that of other people who may be affected by their work under the HSWA.
- Under the MHSWR employees must inform their employer of any danger to health and safety posed by a work activity. They must also inform their employer of any shortcomings in the employer's protection arrangements.
- Employees also have a duty to co-operate with the employer's health and safety arrangement under the MHSWR.

In Practice

Benefits of an Effective Health and Safety Policy

3.59   The benefits of having an effective company health and safety policy include the following.

- The company will comply with the relevant legal requirements.
- A commitment to, and competence in, managing health and safety issues will be demonstrated. This, in turn, can have a positive influence on:
  - employment and retention strategies
  - customer and client perceptions
  - the running costs of the business.

Consequences of a Failure to Have a Health and Safety Policy

3.60   It is an offence for an employer to fail to:

- prepare a written statement outlining the organisation's general policy on health and safety
- distribute that statement to employees
- review the organisation's general policy on health and safety.

3.61   Such an offence makes the employer liable, on summary conviction, to a fine not exceeding £20,000.

Tailoring a Health and Safety Policy to an Organisation

3.62   Policy statements do not necessarily need to be long or elaborate. Instead, they must be relevant to the organisation and its circumstances.

3.63   To be effective, whatever is written in the policy must be put into practice. This means that the policy must reflect the company's:

- culture and commitment to health and safety
- organisational structure, roles and responsibilities
- actual systems and procedures that it uses to discharge its responsibilities.

3.64   The true test of a health and safety policy is the actual conditions in the workplace, not how large the policy is or how well it is written. In other words, if you cannot recognise the company when reading the policy, it is highly likely that the policy is not relevant to that organisation.

3.65   Employers should, therefore, avoid the tendency to "clone" policy documents prepared for other organisations, as these will prove to be of little value to the company, its employees, its clients and its suppliers. Indeed, such an approach might prove to be a significant impediment should an enforcing authority, or the courts, have cause to compare the policy with the organisation's practice.

3.66   Only a document that is unique to an organisation can truly reflect its commitment and practical approach to health and safety. This is key in achieving acceptable health and safety standards and reducing accidents and cases of work-related ill health.

Components of a Health and Safety Policy

3.67   Health and safety policy statements usually consist of three parts.
1. A general statement of intent, which is a declaration of the employer's commitment to providing a safe and healthy workplace and a clear direction for the organisation to follow.
2. Details of responsibilities for health and safety throughout the organisation.
3. Details of safe systems of work and/or safe working practices for all work activities.

3.68   While the organisation can make its own choice about the size and format of the health and safety policy, this will largely depend on the size and complexity of the organisation, the nature of its business and the extent of the risks associated with its undertakings.

Preparing the General Statement

3.69   The general statement of policy is usually quite short, often taking up no more that one sheet of A4 paper. Nevertheless, it should meet a number of criteria. The statement should:

- express a clear commitment from the organisation to minimise adverse effects to the health and safety of employees and others
- commit the organisation to complying with all relevant legal requirements
- stipulate compliance by all management personnel with the legal duties and any further requirements relating to occupational health and safety specified in the policy document
- require the compliance of all employees and the commitment to take an active part in maintaining a safe and health-conscious work environment
- specify a commitment to regularly review and, where necessary, revise the policy
- become effective by being signed and dated by senior management
- be communicated to all employees.

3.70   It could further:

- commit to the continuous improvement of the health and safety of employees and others
- oblige the organisation to comply with best practice
- convey the conviction that health and safety protection are not inconsistent with profitability.

Setting Out the Organisational Structure

3.71   It is the responsibility of senior management to specify the organisational and operational structures required for the implementation of its health and safety policy and strategy, as well as the authorities and the associated responsibilities of both line managers and staff functions.

3.72   The organisational structure should identify, in clear terms, the personnel to who managerial and advisory functions are to be assigned. The need to constantly revise the policy following staff turnover can be minimised by referring responsibilities to job titles, rather than jobholders by name. However, where personnel have a primary responsibility — such as occupational health and safety specialists, industrial physicians or safety representatives — it may be more appropriate to refer to them by name.

3.73   The structure must be conducive to implementing the policy and for achieving the targets stated in the policy. Along with the rest of the health and safety policy, the structure should not be seen as set in concrete but subject to review. It should be revised, where necessary, to account for changes in the structure of the organisation or the way in which it seeks to secure its objectives.

3.74 The person with day-to-day responsibility for the health and safety management system should, ideally, report directly to senior management within the organisation on the performance of systems. This will enable senior management to make its own assessment on the policy's effectiveness.

3.75 Regulation 13 of the MHSWR requires specific considerations to be made when an employer entrusts tasks with health and safety implications to employees. In particular, the employer should ensure that those tasks are within the employees' ability, so as not to put themselves, or others, at risk. In other words, employers should take steps to ensure that their employees are competent.

3.76 Competence should be ascertained on the basis of professional qualifications, experience and the physical and mental characteristics that are suited to fulfil the tasks. If not already present when the employee is engaged, training may be required before a jobholder can assume full responsibility for his or her role.

Developing the Arrangements Section

3.77 This part of the policy covers the systems and procedures in place for ensuring employees' health and safety. The health and safety policy statement does not need to record the full details of all procedures. It can refer to other documentation, such as risk assessments, training programmes, emergency instructions, etc. However, the policy statement should record the arrangements and procedures for how these matters are to be managed.

3.78 Core elements to be addressed within the arrangements section of a policy include arrangements for:

- risk assessments
- consultation with employees
- information and instruction to be provided to employees
- supervision of employees
- training, including arrangements for promoting health and safety awareness
- accidents, first aid and ill-health issues
- cases of emergency, eg fire
- providing personal protective equipment (PPE)
- maintaining plant and equipment
- safe handling and use of substances
- monitoring
- machinery maintenance and breakdowns.

3.79 Other elements, such as those arrangements for the management of display screen equipment, noise or working at height, should be added as required, depending on the particular hazards an organisation faces.

Consulting Employees on the Policy

3.80 Acceptance of the policy by employees is crucial to its success. Not only does consultation help to overcome a natural resistance to change, it taps into a potential wealth of experience and knowledge that can improve health and safety arrangements.

3.81 By enabling staff to become architects in the design of solutions, they are empowered to take control and are more likely to "own" the control measures. This approach has the added benefit of increasing peer pressure to comply, which can be an important factor if the policy is to be a success in the long-term.

3.82   The law requires that employees be consulted — not just informed — on matters relating to health and safety. The consultation process can be simplified, encouraged and supported by training employees and by helping them to become organised through the election of safety representatives and the formation of a safety committee.

Securing Senior Level Commitment to the Policy

3.83   The health and safety policy will not be effective without genuine commitment from the most senior person in the organisation. This person should take steps to ensure that health and safety are taken seriously at all levels in the organisation and that the policy is signed and dated to demonstrate management commitment to health and safety in the workplace.

Implementing and Promoting the Policy

3.84   Occupational health and safety is all about protecting people. Unless a health and safety policy is implemented, the effort in developing it will be wasted. Successful implementation of the policy should be seen as a priority for management, in the same way as the launch of a new product or service is a priority. In the absence of sufficient resources, adequate planning and proper management, the implementation will fail. Employers must develop an action plan, assign responsibilities to individuals, agree to deadlines and check progress.

3.85   Special care will need to be taken to ensure that the policy is presented in a way that is understood by employees. While the law requires that the policy be brought to the attention of all employees, simply getting someone to say they have received such information will not be enough to discharge the employer's duty. For example, there may be employees who have a special learning need, such as a difficulty with literacy. For other employees, English might not be their first language.

3.86   Where a need has been identified, further consideration may have to be given to convey parts of the policy to others not directly connected with the organisation. Such persons might include employees of other organisations who may be sharing common workplaces (eg contractors), external bodies (eg public authorities, insurers, visitors) and the general public.

3.87   In large, complex organisations, the health and safety policy and supporting materials can consist of documents of considerable volume. Employees who perceive that there is too much to take in, or that they are being bombarded by irrelevant information, will "turn off" very quickly. To avoid this happening, employers should consider the following points.

- While all employees must see the general statement of policy itself, they may not need to see all of the other documents, especially if they are not relevant to their health, safety or welfare.
- Some hazards carry risks that are higher than others. Introducing the arrangements in a more strategic manner, with priority based on the level of risk, might be a way of reducing overall risk in the short-term.

3.88   Wider participation and ongoing commitment can be secured through the development of an employee handbook, poster campaigns, suggestions schemes, employee-reporting systems for hazards and incidents and incentives for exemplary conduct.

Monitoring the Effectiveness of the Policy

3.89　　Monitoring is an integral part of successful health and safety management; it is the principal means by which employers measure their health and safety performance. The arrangements section of the policy should describe the organisation's approach to this process.

3.90　　Performance can be measured both reactively and actively. Reactive measures will include examination of loss data, such as accident records, claims history, plant and machinery breakdown and repairs. These give an historical perspective and can show not only trends, but also "hot spots" for incidents. Active monitoring (or checking compliance with arrangements, eg by a compliance audit) can be more productive, because, while this approach can also show trends and "hot spots", it has the additional benefits of:

- creating the opportunity to reward success
- being highly visible and therefore a means by which management can "make things matter".

Reviewing the Policy

3.91　　Under s.2(3) of the HSWA and regulation 3 of the MHSWR, employers are required to review and, if necessary, modify their arrangements for managing health and safety. This should occur:

- when there has been significant change in the organisation or its undertakings
- after serious accidents, in cases of ill health or damage to plant or equipment that are attributable to deficiencies in the system
- where the monitoring reports indicate that a review is necessary
- at intervals of not more than one year.

3.92　　Employees must be informed of the changes and receive as much information, instruction and training in them as may be necessary to avoid risks to health and safety.

3.93　　The review should consider the:

- adequacy of the policy and strategy specified in connection with the health and risk management system
- relevance of the strategic objectives derived from them and of the necessary measures in the operational area
- organisation and performance of the management system
- issues of compliance with statutory requirements and other voluntary codes.

3.94　　The review must indicate whether any action needs to be taken to improve the system and this serves as the basis for improvement. The result is a dynamic rather than static approach to the management of health and safety.

Training

3.95　　Adequate training must be provided to all employees where this is required to ensure their own health and safety or the health and safety of others who may be affected by the undertakings of the organisation. Where an employee is deemed at the outset to be competent to perform the tasks assigned to him or her, there might be no need for further training.

Who Might Need Training?

3.96   All those who:
- advise on the content and format of the health and safety policy
- devise organisational structures and arrangements contained in, or referred to by, the policy
- participate in the consultation process
- monitor compliance with the policy
- have day-to-day responsibility for the operation of the health and safety management system.

What Should Training Include?

3.97   Any training should include the:
- importance of the health and safety policy
- strategies for the organisation as a whole and for each individual employee
- relevance of the tasks and responsibility assigned to employees
- potential and real consequences of employees' behaviour for their own health and safety and that of others and for the safety of plant and equipment.

When Should Training Take Place?

3.98   Training should take place when:
- employees commence employment (eg as part of induction training), are transferred or have their job duties or working environment changed
- equipment, machinery and plant, or procedures and processes, are introduced or altered.

3.99   Training should be repeated at the intervals prescribed by law or at appropriate intervals specified by the organisation.

List of Relevant Legislation

3.100
- Railways (Safety Case) Regulations 2000
- Control of Major Accident Hazards Regulations 1999
- Management of Health and Safety at Work Regulations 1999
- Health and Safety (Consultation with Employees) Regulations 1996
- Safety Representatives and Safety Committees Regulations 1977
- Employers' Health and Safety Policy Statements (Exception) Regulations 1975
- Health and Safety at Work, etc Act 1974

Further Information

Publications

HSE Publications

The following are available from *www.hsebooks.co.uk*.
- HSG65 (rev 1997) *Successful Health and Safety Management*
- INDG275 *Managing Health and Safety: Five Steps to Success*

Risk Assessment

- Risk assessments actively consider workplace hazards that could harm employees and others.
- The main elements of an assessment are usually to identify the hazards, decide who is at risk, determine the likely harm, and then evaluate the risk.
- If five or more people are employed, the significant findings of the assessment must be recorded in writing.
- The assessment must be reviewed if there is a significant change in working practices or reason to believe it is no longer valid.
- Assessments tend to consider factors such as likelihood, frequency, duration, severity and extent.
- Protective and preventive measures must be introduced, if required, along with health surveillance and the provision of any information and training for staff.
- Consideration must be given to vulnerable groups, such as young persons, trainees and pregnant workers.
- As well as the general duty to assess risks, more specific risk assessments are required under the various pieces of health and safety legislation.

Employers' Duties

3.101 Employers are required to:
- ensure so far as is reasonably practicable the health, safety and welfare at work of all employees and non-employees as required under the Health and Safety at Work, etc Act 1974 (HSWA) and other legislation; "reasonably practicable" involves striking a balance between risks and costs, in terms of time, inconvenience and financial considerations
- Identify measures that need to be taken to comply with statutory provisions
- record the assessment in writing if five or more people are employed,
- review the assessment if there is a significant change or if there is reason to believe it is no longer valid
- undertake more specific risk assessments under various other legislation.

Employees' Duties

3.102 Employees must:
- where identified by a risk assessment, be trained to ensure the level of risk with regard to a particular hazard can be reduced
- be trained accordingly where certain control measures, such as mechanical aids, are introduced
- have their specific needs considered in a risk assessment where they are deemed potentially vulnerable.

In Practice

Practical Approaches to Risk Assessment

3.103   A risk assessment is a careful examination of what in a workplace or activity could cause harm to people, so as to determine if enough precautions have been taken or if more are needed. A risk assessment must identify significant hazards and evaluate the risks posed by them.

3.104   The Health and Safety Executive (HSE) publication, *Five Steps to Risk Assessment*, outlines the five main steps that all risk assessments should follow.
1. Identify significant hazards in the workplace. Accident and ill-health records, first-aid treatments and incident (near miss) records can help achieve this.
2. Decide who might be harmed, eg employees and non-employees, and how they might be harmed.
3. Evaluate the risks arising from hazards and decide if existing control measures are adequate or if further control measures are required.
4. Record the significant findings if five or more people are employed.
5. Review the assessment from time to time, especially after a significant change or if there is reason to believe it is no longer valid, and revise as necessary.

3.105   Some organisations prefer to work to the following "seven steps approach".
1. Complete an inventory of all sources of hazards. This will form the bedrock of the safety management system, as it will list all equipment, substances and activities that need to be managed. The inventory should be subject to regular review and revision.
2. Identify all hazards. Often each source on the inventory will involve more than one hazard. A forklift truck, for instance, can be a source of many hazards. A useful aid for identifying hazards is to classify them as physical, chemical, biological, ergonomic or psychological.
3. Rate the risks associated with each hazard. By doing so, it is possible to prioritise which needs to be dealt with first. In a simple system, the ratings can be in terms of high, medium and low. In more sophisticated systems, figures will be arrived at through ascribing scores for likelihood and severity, and multiplying them.
4. Determine whether the risk is acceptable or not. This can only be done once the risks have been rated. In general, low risks are equivalent to the risks in everyday life and are therefore acceptable, but high risks require urgent action, as employees could suffer serious injury. Medium risks obviously fall between high and low and while being above the risks in everyday life, do not have the urgency of high risks. The timeframe for dealing with them is therefore longer.
5. Select appropriate control measures. Workplace precautions deal with the actual risk, whereas risk control systems ensure the workplace precautions remain effective.
6. Record the significant findings if five or more people are employed.
7. Review the assessment from time to time, especially after a significant change or if there is reason to believe it is no longer valid, and revise as necessary.

3.106   Organisations that approach risk assessments in a negative way and do the minimum required under the law will fail to reap the considerable benefits. Adopting a proactive approach to risk control, by integrating the risk assessments required under health and safety legislation into a total loss control management framework, will benefit the entire organisation. The more effort put into the risk assessment process, the greater the benefits.

Identifying the Hazard

3.107   Hazards are defined as anything with the potential to cause harm (substances, equipment, activities, etc). The HSE publication, *Five Steps to Risk Assessment*, suggests the assessor should walk around the workplace and "look afresh at what could reasonably be expected to cause harm". A review of relevant accident records may also reveal information about hazards and risks.

3.108   The HSE suggests trivial hazards can be ignored and the focus should be on significant hazards which could result in serious harm or affect several people.

3.109   There are a great many hazards that may be found in the workplace, depending on the type of operations undertaken and the type of equipment used. Typical hazards to be found in many workplaces include:

- slips, trips and falls
- falls from a height
- fire and explosion
- exposure to substances hazardous to health (such as chemicals)
- dangerous moving parts of machinery
- pressure systems
- moving vehicles
- occupational road risks
- manual handling
- noise
- vibration.

3.110   Observation of workplaces and activities is an important part of hazard identification, but it has limitations. Some hazards, such as non-visible radiation, odourless vapours and micro-organisms, are not directly perceptible and even when they are, a certain level of knowledge is often required for them to be identified as hazards. Assessors must therefore be competent and understand the premises, activities and tasks. Observations need to be supported by a structured checklist of questions.

3.111   If task analysis and method study is used in a manufacturing or production process, then job safety analysis may play an important role in hazard identification at each step in the process.

Who is at Risk?

3.112   Having identified the hazards, it is necessary to identify who is at risk. It is not necessary to identify individuals by name but specific groups of employees and others can be referred to, such as production workers, assembly operatives, mix room operatives and maintenance staff.

3.113   Particular attention needs to be given when vulnerable people are identified, eg young workers or new and expectant mothers. Additional controls may be required to reduce the risk to an acceptable level for such employees.

Risk Evaluation

3.114   Risk is the likelihood of a specified harm occurring. Most risk assessments take account of the following.

- Likelihood — the chance of the harm occurring.
- Frequency — how often the chance of the harm happening occurs during the process or activity being assessed.

- Duration — the length of time that the likelihood of harm exists.
- Severity — the likely severity of the harm should it occur. Often this makes use of categories such as those contained in the Reporting of Injuries, Diseases and Dangerous Occurrences Regulations 1995.
- Extent — the extent of the risk depends upon the likelihood of the harm occurring, the potential severity of the harm and those who might be affected by the hazard.

3.115 By considering the extent of each risk, the level and rating of the risk can be determined. Risks can then be ranked into a prioritised hierarchy.

3.116 The HSE publication, *Five Steps to Risk Assessment*, suggests that even after all precautions have been taken, some risk will probably remain. The key is to decide, for each significant hazard, whether this remaining risk is high, medium or low. This calculation should take into account the answers to the following questions.

- Have all legal requirements been satisfied?
- Are generally accepted industry standards in place?
- Have all reasonably practicable measures been taken to keep the workplace safe?

3.117 The various types of risk rating techniques operate on a basic assumption that *risk equals likelihood times severity*, that is, risk equates to the likelihood (of the hazard occurring) times the severity (of the loss). With less sophisticated systems, this calculation is implied in the assessor's subjective judgment of whether the risk is high, medium or low. More sophisticated systems ascribe numbers and levels of probability to likelihood and severity to decide a final risk rating.

3.118 The HSE's publication, *Successful Health and Safety Management*, suggests the adoption of the following points when calculating likelihood and severity.

- Likelihood: high — where it is certain, or near certain, harm will occur; medium — where harm will often occur; and low — where harm will seldom occur.
- Severity: major — death, or major injury or illness, causing long-term disability; serious — injuries or illness causing short-term disability; and slight — all other injuries or illness.

3.119 The results from such an approach can be used as part of a risk level estimator system. The following table, *Risk Level Estimator*, is a suggested estimator from the British Standards Institution's publication, *Guide to Occupational Health and Safety Management Systems*.

Risk Level Estimator

	Slightly harmful	Harmful	Extremely harmful
Highly unlikely	Trivial risk	Tolerable risk	Moderate risk
Unlikely	Tolerable risk	Moderate risk	Substantial risk
Likely	Moderate risk	Substantial risk	Intolerable risk

3.120 It should be noted that the use of intolerable and tolerable in the estimator is suggestive of perception of risk, rather than an exact measurement of risk. The perception of risk can be modified by many factors, including media coverage and trust in those in control of the activity.

3.121 Scoring systems and guide words are often introduced in the assessment process to curb any subjective bias by the assessor when calculations of likelihood and severity are made, as shown in the table, *Likelihood and Severity Guide Words*, below.

Likelihood and Severity Guide Words

Likelihood		Severity	
Rating	Guide words	Rating	Guide words
0	Almost impossible	0	No harm
1	Extremely unlikely	1	Minor harm
2	Unlikely	2	Moderate harm
3	Likely	3	Serious harm
4	Extremely likely	4	Major harm
5	Almost certain	5	Catastrophic

3.122   This model would result in an overall risk rating ranging from 0 to 25.

3.123   The following table, *Risk Assessment: Hazardous Substances in a Motor Vehicle Repair Workshop*, is a simple example using this system — a garage owner has identified hazards in the motor vehicle repair workshop, the type of harm associated with each hazard, those exposed and the risks involved, taking into account existing controls.

Risk Assessment: Hazardous Substances in a Motor Vehicle Repair Workshop

Hazard	Those exposed	Harm	Existing controls	Likeli-hood	Sever-ity	Risk
Hazardous substances (chemicals, oils, diesel and petrol, etc)	Mechanics, those carrying out valet duties	Dermatitis, scrotal cancer, cancer, respiratory problems	Storage in locked metal cupboards, only small amounts in workshop, suitable containers, barrier creams used, face masks provided and worn	1	4	4

3.124   The following points must also be considered.

- Scoring a 0 for either likelihood or severity results in a final 0 outcome, and this may not always appear to be intuitively correct.
- Not all the numbers between 0–25 are achievable and a gap exists between 20 and 25, which is at the high-risk end of the scale and where more discrimination may be required.

3.125   Some systems dispense with the 0 scores and reverse the remaining scores in order to make 1 represent certainty and catastrophic harm and 5 represent extreme unlikelihood and minor harm. Such a system also has the advantage that the risks can then be dealt with in priority order, ie 1, 2, 3, etc.

3.126   Whether or not a number system is used to rank risks, the end result should be a system that clearly indicates the risk level determined and the action that needs to follow. According to the *Guide to Occupational Health and Safety Management Systems*, the approach laid out in the table below, *Risk Level and Action*, can be adopted.

Risk Level and Action

Risk level	Action
Trivial	No action, but keep records.
Tolerable	No additional controls, but monitor existing controls.
Moderate	Cost-effective efforts made to reduce the risk and further assessment.
Substantial	Work should not be started until the risk has been reduced. If the work is already in progress, urgent action should be taken. Considerable resources may need to be allocated.
Intolerable	Work should not be started or continued until the risk has been reduced. If it is not possible, even with unlimited resources, to reduce the risk, then the work must remain prohibited.

Control Measures

3.127 Employers must ensure preventive and protective measures are implemented. After either avoiding the risk altogether or evaluating any remaining risk which cannot be avoided, employers should work towards:

- combating the risk at its source
- adapting the work to the individual
- adapting to technical progress
- replacing the dangerous with the non-dangerous or the less dangerous
- developing a coherent prevention policy which covers technology, organisation of work, working conditions, social relationships and the influence of factors relating to the working environment
- giving collective protective measures priority over individual protective measures
- delivering appropriate instructions to the employees involved.

3.128 The accompanying Approved Code of Practice to the MHWSR states, "Where risks are already controlled in some way, the effectiveness of those controls needs to be considered when assessing the extent of risk which remains. You also need to:

- observe the actual practice; this may differ from the works manual, and the employees concerned or their safety representatives should be consulted
- address what actually happens in the workplace or during the work activity
- take account of existing preventative or precautionary measures; if existing measures are not adequate, ask yourself what more should be done to reduce risk sufficiently."

3.129 The assessor should first ask whether everything has been done that the law requires, and secondly, whether generally accepted industry standards and good practice have been reached. Once this minimum standard has been reached, it is necessary to go further and reduce any remaining risks, so far as is reasonably practicable. An action list needs to be created, which prioritises remaining risks based upon their level and the number of persons exposed to them.

3.130 If additional controls are required, then the following principles, in priority order, need to be adopted wherever possible.
1. Select another option so the work has a lower risk.
2. Prevent access to the hazard through the use of fencing, barriers and guards, etc.
3. Organise the work so exposure to the hazard is reduced.
4. Issue personal protective equipment (PPE) to those involved in the work or those affected.

5. Provide adequate welfare facilities, including washing and first-aid facilities.

3.131 It is not enough to introduce these additional controls without providing effective systems and procedures and giving adequate information, instruction and training to relevant people.

3.132 The design of workplace precautions should also consider human factors. Precautions should be fully integrated into plant and work design procedures so that they satisfy output, quality and health and safety requirements, rather than being perceived as "bolt on" safety requirements.

3.133 The level of risk evaluated by the assessment implies the effectiveness of the existing controls. If additional controls are introduced as a result of a risk assessment, it is important that a reassessment is done to determine the new level of risk and the effectiveness of the new controls.

3.134 It is also important that the reassessment is carried out logically and it is not just assumed that the level of risk is reduced. As risk is calculated through multiplying likelihood by severity, the new controls must either reduce likelihood, severity or both if a reduction in risk is to be achieved.

3.135 Placing barriers or fences to prevent access to dangerous areas, for instance, reduces the likelihood of accidents happening but does nothing to reduce their severity should they occur. Wearing personal protective clothing does nothing to reduce the likelihood of an accident occurring, but reduces the severity of the injury suffered should the accident happen. Prohibiting work with certain electrical equipment in wet conditions may, however, reduce both the likelihood of an accident occurring and the resulting severity.

3.136 Risk control is the process of designing, implementing and maintaining measures that reduce a particular risk, and specific risk control measures for industry must be considered. Most risk control measures tend to adopt one or more of the following.

- Hazard reduction methods — elimination, substitution and redesign, etc.
- Separation methods — height, distance and remote locations, etc.
- Physical barrier methods — around the hazard, around the person or around the location.
- Dose-limitation methods — reduce the dose, number of people exposed to the dose or reduce the time exposed to the dose.

3.137 Risk control measures are also often categorised under the following headings.

- Technical — machine guarding, fencing, ventilation systems, etc that do not have much reliance on people to remain effective but need careful design, installation and maintenance.
- Procedural — systems of work and procedures, etc that need to be carefully designed and implemented, and rely on people following them.
- Behavioural — information and training that relies upon appropriate and effective information and training being provided, as well as it being understood and implemented.

Risk Assessments Concerning Special (Potentially Vulnerable) Groups

3.138 As part of the risk assessment process, consideration must be given to any groups who may be particularly vulnerable. Examples include young people, trainees, volunteers, temporary staff, disabled persons, new or expectant mothers, lone workers, self-employed workers and visitors.

Young Persons

3.139 The full risk assessment will evaluate the work activities identified as potentially harmful in the initial assessment and determine those that present a significant risk to young people.

3.140 These risk assessments should take into account:

- young people's inexperience, lack of perception of danger and immaturity
- the fit-out and layout of their workstations and the workplace
- the nature, degree and duration of any exposure to physical, biological or chemical agents
- the form, range, use and handling of work equipment
- the organisation of work processes and activities
- the health and safety training provided, or intended to be provided, by the employer.

3.141 When deciding whether a significant risk exists, there should be an examination of:

- the presence of any particular hazards
- compliance with prescribed exposure levels, eg lead and ionising radiation
- accident and sickness records
- complaints and information from staff.

3.142 While young persons are generally at no greater risk than other employees in the workplace, there are some defined hazards that employers must take into account. The HSE guidance book, *Young People at Work — A Guide for Employers*, contains examples of physical, biological and chemical agents, as well as various work situations, which employers must consider as part of any risk assessment for young persons.

3.143 Physical agents can cause long-term damage (eg occupational deafness through exposure to noise, or genetic damage through exposure to ionising radiation) and this may have more significant consequences for young people. Physical hazards include:

- temperature extremes
- noise
- vibration (hand/arm and whole body)
- radiation (ionising and non-ionising)
- work in increased atmospheric pressures, eg diving.

Trainees, Work Experience Placements or Volunteers

3.144 There are no specific risk assessment requirements or formats for trainees, work experience placements or volunteers. The risk assessor, however, must be aware of the presence of these people and must allow for them in the risk assessment process. Consideration should be given to the potential lack of experience, different perceptions of risk, lack of knowledge of safety procedures and safe working practices, etc.

Temporary Workers

3.145 Employers must carry out an assessment of the risks posed by the work activities of temporary workers. These assessments should include the risks to temporary workers on-site who may be affected by the employers' work activities.

3.146 The starting point is to identify all possible activities and operations undertaken by temporary workers. Consulting previous temporary workers and other employees can help with the assessment as can consideration of the organisation's general risk assessments.

3.147 It should always be remembered when evaluating the risks and considering the appropriate control measures that temporary workers may be unfamiliar with workplace hazards and are therefore at greater risk.

Disabled Persons

3.148 Less favourable treatment of a disabled person or failure to make a reasonable adjustment can be justified if it would endanger the health and safety of any person, including the disabled person in question. However, health and safety reasons that rely on prejudice or stereotyping of disabled people are no defence.

3.149 Employers should ensure that any action taken in relation to health and safety is proportionate to the risk. There must be a balance between protecting against the risk and restricting disabled people. Disabled people are entitled to take the same risks within the same limits as other people.

3.150 Before using health and safety to justify less favourable treatment, an employer should consider whether a reasonable adjustment could be made.

New or Expectant Mothers

3.151 In order to carry out an accurate risk assessment of a new or expectant mother, employers must understand the many physiological, hormonal and psychological effects of pregnancy and postnatal nursing and the impact they have on the level of risk associated with work. The table below, *New and Expectant Mothers: Risk Factors and Control Measures*, outlines the changes a pregnant woman or nursing mother undergoes and the precautionary measures that can be taken.

New and Expectant Mothers: Risk Factors and Control Measures

Physical/ emotional factors	Work factors	Control measures
Morning sickness, headaches	• Early morning shifts • Exposure to nauseating smells — in some cases this may be an innocuous, ordinary, everyday smell that the pregnant woman suddenly finds intolerable	• Re-organise shifts to avoid early mornings • Avoid duties involving strong/ nauseating smells, eg cleaning up human soiling, laboratory work with strong chemicals

Physical/ emotional factors	Work factors	Control measures
Backache	• Long periods of standing • Moving and handling tasks • Poor posture • Insufficient available working space	• Provide suitable seating where possible or reduce the time spent standing — ensure rotation of work duties to avoid periods of standing or sitting • Assess and control all moving and manual handling activities carried out by the pregnant woman • Re-organise work and/or workplace to avoid poor postures • Ensure adequate space at workstation and for moving around
Hormonal changes	• Manual handling, due to weakened ligaments • Wearing of protective equipment and clothing (PPE), aggravating sensitive breasts and nipples	• Assess and control all moving and manual handling activities carried out by the pregnant woman • Avoid work activities requiring PPE or review and revise any PPE provided
Varicose veins	• Long periods of standing or sitting • Poor posture	• Ensure rotation of work duties to avoid long periods of standing or sitting • Re-organise work and/or workplace to avoid poor posture
Haemorrhoids	• Poor posture • Hot environments	• Re-organise work and/or workplace to avoid poor postures • Avoid or minimise time spent in hot environments • Provide some form of air cooling, if appropriate
Increased visits to toilet	• Work that is difficult to leave, eg production lines, vehicle drivers, etc • Difficult access to, or location of, toilets	• Re-organise work activities and/or workplace to allow necessary visits to toilet

Growing bump.

Physical/ emotional factors	Work factors	Control measures
Increasing size (may also reduce mobility, dexterity and general co-ordination in later stages)	• Moving and manual handling tasks • Display screen work — increasing viewing distance from screen • Protective equipment and clothing (PPE)	• Assess and control all manual handling activities carried out by the pregnant woman • Ensure adequate space at workstation and for moving around • Assess display screen workstation and make necessary changes or re-organise work activities to avoid display screen work • Avoid work activities requiring PPE or review and revise the PPE provided
Changes in blood pressure, tiredness	• Work that is difficult to leave • Long working hours and/or overtime • Evening/night work • Strenuous, physical work	• Provision of rest facilities and organisation of work activities to allow their use, as required • Provision for attending medical examinations • Re-organisation of work to reduce/avoid strenuous activities
Reduced balance	• Working on wet slippery surfaces • Working at height • Work requiring stretching away from the body	• Provision of appropriate anti-slip flooring • Planned preventative maintenance programmes to maintain good condition of flooring • Re-organisation of work activities or workplace to avoid slippery, etc surfaces, working at height or stretching away from body • Provision of suitable ladders/ step ladders
Other factors (psychological effects of stillbirth, abortion, birth of disabled babies, post-natal depression)	• Highly pressurised work • Work involving care of babies, etc • Work involving high levels of concentration and/or life saving decisions	• Provision for leave for counselling or other health-related sessions • Assessment and re-organisation of work activities to fit capabilities of employee • Agree to a rehabilitation plan for the gradual resumption of work activities with the employee and her doctor or occupational health advisor • Avoid work known or shown to cause, or exacerbate, distress

Physical/ emotional factors	Work factors	Control measures
Caesarean births	• Moving and handling • Poor posture • Strenuous work activities	• Agree to a rehabilitation plan for the gradual resumption of work activities with the employee and her doctor or occupational health advisor

3.152 The pregnancy and postnatal periods are "dynamic", that is, the body undergoes constant physiological, hormonal and psychological changes, and the risk assessment process must reflect this. Regular reviews — and, if necessary, revisions — of the risk assessment should take place to pick up any effects of changes as they occur.

3.153 There are some other important points to bear in mind.

• New and expectant mothers are not obliged to inform their employer of their condition or of any associated health issues (although they should be encouraged to do so).

• Many women may not be aware that they are actually pregnant for the first four to six weeks of their pregnancy. The foetus is most susceptible to harm during the first 12 weeks.

• Certain chemicals and infections can be passed on to foetuses through the placenta and to breastfed babies through their mother's milk.

3.154 Given that an employer may not know whether a woman is pregnant or nursing a baby, any control measures implemented as part of the risk assessment must be sufficient to protect these women, regardless of whether or not this is the case.

Lone Workers

3.155 Risks to lone workers can arise because there is no assistance for them (such as with manual handling) or because they are vulnerable to attack by virtue of being alone. The table below, *Hazards and Risks of Lone Working*, gives examples of these risks.

Hazards and Risks of Lone Working

Hazard	Risk to lone worker
Unassisted manual handling	Musculoskeletal injury
Handling cash or valuables, including valuable portable work equipment	Increased risk of being targeted by violent people due to working alone, possibly resulting in physical or mental injury, stress-related ill health, or potential fatality
Driving long distances without adequate rest breaks/change of driver	Increased risk of road traffic accidents/falling asleep at the wheel
Poor working relationships/poor organisational culture	Increased risk of lone workers being bullied or harassed in the absence of witnesses, possibly resulting in stress-related illness or assault

3.156 Control measures should address risks at the source wherever practicable. Employers should also consider measures — such as first aid, recovery measures and counselling — for dealing with lone workers who have experienced violence or stress at work. In this way, an overall preventive and protective strategy can be developed.

3.157 As the next table, *Examples of Control Measures for Lone Working*, shows, a number of precautions can be taken.

Examples of Control Measures for Lone Working

Issue	Examples of possible control measures
Ensuring effective management and supervision	• active supervision of all workers, remotely or indirectly as necessary • effective risk management arrangements • monitoring workers' activities and whereabouts as appropriate when away from base • appropriate levels of support and assistance and prompt response • site visits involving two people to locations, homes or people where services are to be delivered • incident reporting systems and systems for reporting incidents away from base • co-operating with host employers, employment agencies and contractors • monitoring incident records and information provided by community safety officers regarding risks of violence • including home workers and lone mobile workers in display screen equipment (DSE), manual handling, fire and COSHH assessments • periodic site visits and workplace inspections • consultation with lone workers and their representatives • ensuring lone workers are included in staff meetings and communications, wherever they are based
Ensuring a safe system of work	• extra precautions for lone workers carrying out hazardous activities, or specific controls on when, where and how those activities take place if working alone • preventive measures to avoid manual handling injuries, such as equipment at outreach sites to enable lifting operations to be carried out by the lone worker • effective communications systems for lone workers
Providing information, instruction, and training for workers and managers	• develop a lone working policy • permission for lone workers to remove themselves from situations in which they feel unsafe due to threats of violence • raising awareness of the risks to lone workers of stress-related illness and violence at work and what can be done to prevent them • training in use of protective equipment or communication systems designed for lone workers' protection • information about fire instructions and emergency procedures for lone workers away from base • explicit instructions to all workers about prohibited lone working activities

Issue	Examples of possible control measures
Ensuring workplace health, safety and welfare	• avoiding or minimising lone working in unoccupied premises • first aid and welfare provisions for all workers, including lone workers, accessible at all times • including lone workers in fire drills, emergency procedures and fire risk assessments • adequate security and monitoring arrangements for lone workers, including protective barriers and communications systems (with responders) if appropriate
Ensuring safety for remote working (off-site, between sites, in the community)	• effective supervision of lone workers through use of PPE, surveillance and communications systems, checks on lone workers' safe arrival/return, etc if necessary • effective personal safety plans and back-up systems for lone workers with named responders at all necessary times • checks on sites, clients, locations and early warning systems to inform managers and lone workers of any known trouble spots and risks of violence, eg violent clients
Reducing risks of lone working time arrangements	• avoiding the need for lone working at certain times • adjusting start and finish times when working alone • providing extra support, back-up and supervision for lone workers • relocating the work to avoid it being done in isolation • limiting or redistributing overtime and emergency duties, including on-call arrangements • avoiding the need for lone working after hours in empty buildings • avoiding lone working at hazardous times, eg late at night in places with public access or poor security • adjusting working times and/or staffing levels or skill mix • improving lighting and security at times of darkness and in remote areas • ensuring safe access and exit at all times, including hours of darkness

3.158 Lone working should be avoided if there is a risk of violence that cannot be adequately controlled. Depending on the situation, two-person working may be required or additional measures may be needed to provide the necessary support when the lone worker is involved in complex decision-making, problem-solving or conflict resolution.

The Self-employed

3.159 Self-employed people must risk assess their activities, change their methods to eliminate the risks wherever possible, and take precautions to minimise any remaining risks, including providing their own PPE.

3.160 Employers must ensure the health and safety of self-employed people working for them. In addition to this general duty, employers will also need to take account of self-employed workers under other health and safety legislation. This includes the following.

• Work equipment provided for use by self-employed workers must comply with the Provision and Use of Work Equipment Regulations 1998.

• Under the Control of Noise at Work Regulations 2005, hearing protection and training must be provided for self-employed workers that may be affected by noise arising from the host employer's undertaking.

3.161   As an example, an employer might become aware that a self-employed window cleaner working on the premises was not wearing a safety harness while working at height. Self-employed people are responsible for identifying risks to themselves from their activities. This includes providing themselves with and using appropriate PPE. The window cleaner should know that there is a high risk of falling when working at height and should find a safe way of cleaning upper storey windows. If this is not possible, the window cleaner should provide and wear a safety harness.

3.162   Having said that, employers are responsible for the health and safety of non-employees on their site. As the employer is paying for the window cleaner's services, they have a degree of control. The premises should have anchor points for window cleaners if it is not possible to clean windows from the inside without a risk of falling.

3.163   The contract with the window cleaner should require him or her to follow site safety rules and to use PPE where necessary. If the window cleaner persistently fails to wear a safety harness, such a contract would be breached. The employer should then find someone who has a more responsible attitude to health and safety.

Visitors

3.164   If visitors are to be present in the workplace, consideration needs to be given to the risks posed by them as well as those to which they are subjected. It may be necessary to arrange for visitors to be accompanied, provided with PPE, given certain instructions, etc.

Risk Assessments Required by Specific Legislation

3.165   As well as the general duty to assess risks, more specific risk assessments are required under the following.
- Control of Asbestos Regulations 2006
- Control of Noise at Work Regulations 2005
- Control of Vibration at Work Regulations 2005
- Regulatory Reform (Fire Safety) Order 2005
- Control of Substances Hazardous to Health Regulations 2002
- Dangerous Substances and Explosive Atmospheres Regulations 2002
- Control of Lead at Work Regulations 2002
- Health and Safety (Display Screen Equipment) Regulations 1992
- Manual Handling Operations Regulations 1992.

3.166   The risk assessments will centre on the subject of the legislation. However, if all relevant factors have been addressed under the general business risk assessments, then it is not necessary to carry out and record a further risk assessment under the specific legislation (and vice-versa).

More Sophisticated Risk Assessment Techniques

3.167   Hazard identification and risk assessment techniques need to be applied by designers, manufacturers, suppliers, installers and users of articles and substances as well as by employers in relation to the work activities being carried out. The level and complexity of a risk often justifies a simple five-step approach. However, if the risks are high and complex, more sophisticated techniques may be required.

3.168   The techniques range from qualitative, semi-quantitative or quantitative assessments to more specialist methods, such as job safety analyses, hazard and operability studies, failure mode and effect analyses, fault tree analyses and event tree analyses.

Training

3.169 Risk assessments must be completed by competent persons. One aspect of competence involves training. Those carrying out risk assessments need to be trained in general risk assessment techniques and principles as well as in risk assessment procedures. If more than one assessor is to be used, training should include standardisation exercises to ensure similar levels of risk are ascribed in similar situations.

3.170 Risk assessments may identify training needs for other people to ensure the level of risk in relation to the particular hazard can be reduced to an acceptable level. If other control measures are introduced, such as the use of mechanical aids to replace unnecessary manual handling, further training needs may arise.

List of Relevant Legislation

3.171
- Control of Asbestos Regulations 2006
- Control of Noise at Work Regulations 2005
- Control of Vibration at Work Regulations 2005
- Control of Lead at Work Regulations 2002
- Control of Substances Hazardous to Health Regulations 2002
- Dangerous Substances and Explosive Atmospheres Regulations 2002
- Ionising Radiations Regulations 1999
- Management of Health and Safety at Work Regulations 1999
- Maternity (Compulsory Leave) Regulations 1994
- Health and Safety (Display Screen Equipment) Regulations 1992
- Manual Handling Operations Regulations 1992
- Workplace (Health, Safety and Welfare) Regulations 1992
- Health and Safety at Work, etc Act 1974

Further Information

Publications
- *Barefoot Research — A Workers' Manual for Organising on Work Security*, Margaret Keith, James Brophy, Peter Kirby and Ellen Rosskam. International Labour Organisation In-Focus Programme on Socio-Economic Security publication, 2002

- L5 (rev 2005) *The Control of Substances Hazardous to Health Regulations 2002 (as amended). Approved Code of Practice and Guidance*
- INDG163(L) *Five Steps to Risk Assessment*
- HSG183 *5 Steps to Risk Assessment — Case Studies*
- *Fast Guide to Personal Safety at Work*, Suzy Lamplugh Trust publication, product code: G17
- *First Steps to Personal Safety at Work Video and Poster*, Suzy Lamplugh Trust publication, product code: V11
- BS 8800: 2004 *Occupational Health and Safety Management Systems — Guide*
- *Health and Safety Risk Assessment*, Dr Tony Boyle. IOSH Services, Leicester, 2nd Edition.
- HSE Books *Infection Risks to New and Expectant Mothers in the Workplace. A Guide for Employers*
- HSG122 (rev 2002) *New and Expectant Mothers at Work: A Guide for Employers*
- L21 (rev 2000) *Management of Health and Safety at Work. Management of Health and Safety at Work Regulations 1999. Approved Code of Practice and Guidance*
- *Personal Safety for Health Care Workers*, Pauline Bibby. Arena Publications, 1995
- *Personal Safety for Social Workers*, Pauline Bibby. Arena Publications, 1995
- HSG65 (rev 1997) *Successful Health and Safety Management*
- *Working Alone: A Health and Safety Guide on Lone Working for Safety Representatives.* UNISON brochure, London, 2002, stock number: 1750
- INDG73(L) (rev 2005) *Working Alone in Safety*
- EH40 *Workplace Exposure Limits* (revised annually)
- HSG165 (rev 2000) *Young People at Work: A Guide for Employers*

Organisations

- GMB
  Web: *www.gmb.org.uk*
  The GMB is a general union of 700,000 people. Forty per cent of the union's members are women.
- Institution of Occupational Safety and Health (IOSH)
  Web: *www.iosh.co.uk*
  IOSH is Europe's leading body for health and safety professionals and provides guidance on health and safety issues.
- Loss Prevention Council
  Web: *www.redbooklive.com*
  Owned by the Association of British Insurers and Lloyds of London, the council provides a variety of technical services in the field of loss prevention, including research, standard setting, product testing, certification and training.
- Suzy Lamplugh Trust
  Web: *www.suzylamplugh.org*
  The Suzy Lamplugh Trust, a registered charity, is considered a leading authority on personal safety.
- UNISON
  Web: *www.unison.org.uk*
  UNISON is Britain's biggest trade union with over 1.3 million members working in the public services, for private contractors providing public services and the essential utilities. These include frontline staff and managers working full or part time in local authorities, the NHS, the police service, leges and schools, the electricity, gas and water industries, transport and the voluntary sector.

Safe Systems of Work

- A safe system of work is a written procedure detailing how a particular work activity should be carried out in order to minimise the risks (to both employees and non-employees) involved in performing that activity.
- Employers must provide and maintain systems of work that are, as far as is reasonably practicable, safe and without risks to health under the Health and Safety at Work, etc Act 1974.
- The risk assessment process can be used to identify activities that require a safe system of work.
- Safe systems of work are normally adopted for work activities still carrying a residual risk, despite the implementation of control measures. Examples of activities that might require a safe system of work include working at height, maintenance of electrical systems, control of on-site vehicle movements, etc.
- A safe system of work will need to take several factors into account. These include:
  - the work location, equipment and plant to be used
  - staff undertaking and supervising the work
  - the necessary safety precautions
  - the sequence in which the work activity should be carried out.
- Some activities carry such a high residual risk that a more stringent safe system of work might be necessary, such as a permit-to-work system.
- When implementing safe systems of work, employers should ensure that employees are consulted, training is provided prior to implementation and there is an appropriate level of supervision, particularly if systems are in use for the first time.
- Safe systems of work should be monitored and reviewed regularly to make sure they are being followed. This is particularly the case in the event of any accidents, incidents or near misses.
- Employers should keep records of all safe systems of work in a place that is fully accessible to employees.

3.172   A safe system of work is a formal procedure resulting from an examination of any workplace activity in order to identify its hazards and assess its risks. This exercise culminates in the identification of safe methods of work to ensure that the hazards are eliminated or residual risks minimised.

3.173   Safe systems of work were the forerunner of the requirement to carry out risk assessments in the workplace. Many of the elements of formulating a safe system of work duplicate the risk assessment procedure.

Employers' Duties

3.174   The Health and Safety at Work, etc Act 1974 (HSWA) requires employers to:

- ensure, as far as is reasonably practicable, the health, safety and welfare of their employees while at work
- ensure, as far as is reasonably practicable, the health, safety and welfare of non-employees
- provide and maintain systems of work that are, as far as is reasonably practicable, safe and without risks to health

– carry out their activities, as far as is reasonably practicable, in such a way as not to harm the health and safety of those not in their employment.

3.175 The Management of Health and Safety at Work Regulations 1999 (MHSWR) require employers to:
– make an assessment of any risks to the health and safety of their employees while at work
– make a similar assessment of the risks to health and safety of persons not in their employment that may arise as a result of their (ie the employer's) work activities.

Employees' Duties

3.176 The HSWA requires employees to take reasonable care of their own health and safety and that of other people who may be affected by their activities while at work.

3.177 The MHSWR require employees to:
• use machinery, equipment, dangerous substances, transport equipment, means of production or safety devices in accordance with any instruction and training given by the employer
• inform their employer of any danger to health and safety posed by a work activity
• inform their employer of any shortcomings in the employer's protection arrangements.

In Practice

Identifying the Activities That Require Safe Systems of Work

3.178 All work activities will require safe systems of work. However, for many activities, a formal system will not be required. For example, tasks such as operating a PC, sweeping the floor or changing a light-bulb might not require a formal procedure, although they may require a risk assessment and control measures. However, there will be few residual risks involved following the implementation of control measures.

3.179 A formal safe system of work will be required for activities that have been assessed and control measures introduced, but where significant residual risks remain. Examples of such tasks include:
• maintenance of assembly-plant machinery
• window cleaning
• lone working
• vehicle loading-bay activities
• construction work
• working at height
• working in confined spaces
• maintenance of electrical systems and equipment.

Identifying the Risks

3.180   This will be a part of the normal risk assessment process. If possible, where hazards have been identified with a particular activity, any risks should be eliminated or minimised. Where this is not possible, a formal safe system of work should be developed for that activity.

3.181   The residual risks identified through this process will determine the control measures outlined in the safe system of work. For example, if a work activity is to be carried out in close proximity to an excavation site. The hazard, ie the excavation, cannot be eliminated. There would be a risk of persons falling into the excavation site since access to the site is necessary for other work being carried out at the same time. A safe system of work would be necessary to control this risk.

Development of the Safe System of Work

3.182   Having identified the residual risks that need to be controlled with the safe system of work, it is necessary to look at the elements of such a system.

Work Location

3.183   This element will address the physical layout of the workplace and take into account such things as:

- access and egress
- the space available for the activity, allowing for obstructions such as plant and equipment
- hazards such as excavations, low ceilings, overhead power lines
- access hazards such as working at height or working in a confined space
- whether there are adequate means of fire protection
- whether the lighting is suitable or, alternatively, what additional lighting is required
- whether the temperature is suitable for the location and the task
- if there is a suitable provision of welfare facilities.

Equipment and Plant

3.184   Factors to take into account when considering equipment and plant include the following.

- Is it suitable for the task?
- Can it be operated safely in the work environment?
- Are there any noise factors to be taken into account?
- Are the persons allocated to the task trained, and if necessary, certified to use the equipment?
- Has it been maintained to the required standard and is the necessary certification on-site?
- Where is the fuel, ie diesel, petrol or liquefied petroleum gas, to be stored?
- How is the power for the equipment to be safely used?
- Is there adequate security on-site to prevent unauthorised use of equipment?

Materials

3.185   This element includes substances as well as the more traditional materials used for the task. Factors to take into account include the following.

- Is the material suitable for the task?

- Can the material be safely handled manually, or is there a need for mechanical handling?
- Have there been any manual handling assessments carried out for the task?
- Are there facilities for materials to be stored safely?
- Have assessments under the Control of Substances Hazardous to Health Regulations 2002 and/or the Dangerous Substances and Explosive Atmospheres Regulations 2002 been carried out on substances to be used or created (eg dusts)?
- Are there arrangements for the safe disposal of any waste materials?

Personnel

3.186   This is, arguably, the most important factor. Considerations include the following.

- Who is to manage the work?
- Does the work need to be supervised and, if so, by whom?
- Who will be responsible for the various tasks, ie who issues personal protective equipment and who is responsible for safety briefings?
- Are all persons competent for the tasks they are to undertake, eg plant operators?

Safety Precautions

3.187   As a result of all the preliminary personnel considerations, what special safety precautions are needed? For example, consider the following.

- Is there a need to isolate plant/equipment/systems from power sources?
- Is personal protective equipment needed? If so, what type of equipment and to what standard?
- What safety signage is necessary, eg caution or prohibition notices?
- Are there any special instructions or safety briefings necessary before work commences?
- Are emergency procedures in place in the event of a failure of the safe system of work?

Sequence of Operations

3.188   A sequence of operations should be formulated to ensure the safe completion of the activity. For example, electrical equipment must be isolated before work commences.

Example of a Typical Formal Safe System of Work

3.189   This is only an example of what a typical safe system of work should include. Many of the elements are not applicable to more simple activities or for activities in a fixed location, such as a factory. The system will need to be adapted to the particular activity being undertaken.

Example of a Safe System of Work

Activity	Include a description of the work.
Location	Name the location, access and egress arrangements, any hazards posed by the location and any control measures.
Equipment and Plant	List plant and equipment to be used. List any hazards posed by the use of such plant in this environment and the subsequent control measures.
Materials	List materials to be used on the activity and any risks posed by their use. List any chemical substances used or produced, eg dusts and fumes, and refer to assessments conducted under the Control of Substances Hazardous to Health Regulations 2002 (COSHH) and/or the Dangerous Substances and Explosive Atmospheres Regulations 2002 (DSEAR). List any necessary control measures in relation to substances, as well as any manual handling considerations.
Personnel	List key personnel who will perform the activity. For example, who will manage the task? Is there a need for supervision? How many people are needed? What skills do they need?
Safety precautions	Safety precautions should be in addition to those control measures listed under the individual headings above. Included here will be items such as additional personal protective equipment (PPE), safety briefings and the requirement for any permit-to-work systems.
Sequence of operations	This section would list, in chronological order, the elements of the task, together with necessary control measures. It should be a logical sequence, starting with access arrangements and the necessary safety arrangements. It should then describe, in an orderly fashion, the sub-elements of the activity.

3.190   This table could be adapted for use as a form, in order to have a written record of a safe system of work. Alternatively, a slightly more simplified version could be used, covering the location of work, its description, hazards and the safe methods to be adopted.

3.191   A formal, written safe system such as this is sometimes known as a method statement. Many clients ask contractors for method statements before work is carried out on their behalf. Indeed, they are often part of a tendering process and the formulation of a sound safety method statement can be the key to obtaining a contract.

Permit-to-work Systems

3.192   Some work activities carry such high residual risks that they require a more stringent safe system of work, such as a permit-to-work system. Examples include entry into confined spaces and hot work.

Safe Systems of Work Register

3.193   All tasks that have a formal safe system of work should be entered onto a central register. This register must be available to all staff so that they are aware of the safe system of work they should use while carrying out a task.

Implement the Systems

3.194   Successful implementation of safe systems of work will depend on two things — their correct formation and the competence of people using them. Be wary of implementing safe systems of work that are unnecessarily complicated and include measures not strictly required. Such systems will not only lower productivity but the people using them will lose confidence in the system. Once this happens, it may put the whole process into disrepute — with a consequent risk to health and safety.

3.195   The exact procedure carried out to implement safe systems of work will vary according to the type of activity and the organisation. A construction company formulating a method statement for a one-off activity will have to closely monitor the system and make any subsequent changes as that activity is being carried out.

3.196   The implementation of a safe system of work for a new production activity in a factory, on the other hand, can be more measured. As the facility is being built, safe methods of work can be developed by both the manufacturer of the new plant and the employees who will be working at the new plant/on the new activity.

3.197   General points to consider when implementing safe systems of work are to:
- fully involve employers in their creation and implementation — staff need to "buy in" to the system for it to work
- ensure training is provided prior to implementation
- make employees aware of which activities are subject to formal safe systems of work
- ensure that when systems are in use for the first time, there is a level of supervision and expertise available to stop or change the process if it proves unsafe
- ensure written procedures are updated to reflect any necessary changes to the system.

Monitor the Arrangements

3.198   Once the safe systems of work are in place and working, there will be a need to monitor the arrangements. The monitoring should consist of two elements: reactive monitoring and active monitoring.

Reactive Monitoring

3.199   Reactive monitoring involves conducting a review of accidents and near misses while operating the new safe systems. The employer should already have accident-reporting procedures in place and these may well need to be reinforced for this particular purpose. Careful analysis of accident data may result in changes needing to be made to the safe systems of work.

Active Monitoring

3.200   Workplace inspections should initially include a special study of new safe systems of work. Again, as a result of these, changes may be necessary.

Training

All Employees

3.201   An outline of what a safe system of work is should be given to all employees within induction training and general health and safety refresher training.

3.202   This should cover:
- the principles of safe systems of work
- which employee activities are subject to formal safe systems of work, including reference to the safe systems of work register
- employees' individual responsibilities in the working of such systems
- what to do when things go wrong
- how to report concerns with safe systems of work.

Those Who Supervise and Implement Safe Systems of Work

3.203   Such employees should receive the same training as all employees with the addition of:
- a review of the risk assessments that led to the formulation of the safe system of work
- residual risks and how they are to be controlled by the safe system of work
- how the system will work in practice and how the control measures will control the risks
- individual roles within the system
- emergency procedures.

3.204   Technical knowledge, such as that held by qualified engineers, might be necessary to implement some safe systems of work. Tasks such as isolating electrical supplies or some machinery may need specialist knowledge, which could be supplemented by training such as that outlined above.

List of Relevant Legislation

3.205
- Management of Health and Safety at Work Regulations 1999
- Confined Spaces Regulations 1997
- Health and Safety at Work, etc Act 1974

Further Information

Publications

HSE Publications

The following is available from *www.hsebooks.co.uk*.
- HSG65 (rev 1997) *Successful Health and Safety Management*

Step-by-step Guide: How to Provide a Safe System of Work

To provide a safe system of work, employers should take the following steps.

- Review or undertake a risk assessment to identify all activities that require a safe system of work.
- Develop safe systems of work for these activities by taking the following into account:
  - work location
  - equipment and plant
  - materials to be used
  - personnel
  - safety precautions
  - sequence of operations.
- Implement these systems.
- Monitor the arrangements via:
  - active monitoring
  - reactive monitoring.
- Train staff in the safe systems of work.

Employees' Factsheet: Safe systems of work

A safe system of work is a procedure designed to ensure hazards are eliminated and risks are minimised.

If you are carrying out work subject to a formal safe system of work you must:

- not carry out any work unless the safe system is followed
- not carry out any work for which you are not authorised or trained
- take personal responsibility to carry out your own duties as indicated on the safe system of work
- ensure that your activities do not harm yourself or others
- not proceed with the work until you are sure that the precautions required by the system have been completed; this may require you to:
  - use personal protective equipment
  - isolate equipment from sources of power supply
  - put in place temporary supports for structures
  - use barriers, ropes, etc to prevent unauthorised access
- not start work if you are not happy with the safety arrangements (or if work has already commenced, stop work immediately), and report the circumstances to your supervisor
- ensure that the work location/plant/equipment is in safe condition on completion or suspension of the work — if it cannot be made safe, withdraw from service and report to your supervisor.

Safe systems of work have been developed for both your safety and for the safety of those who may be affected by your work. The co-operation of all employees is required to ensure that they are used successfully.

Permits to Work

- A permit-to-work system is a formal written system which specifies the precautions which need to be taken before certain high-risk activities are undertaken.
- Employers are required by the Health and Safety at Work, etc Act 1974 to provide and maintain systems of work that are, as far as reasonably practicable, safe and without risks to health. This includes the implementation of permit-to-work systems where appropriate.
- Activities which require a permit-to-work system will be determined by a risk assessment. A permit-to-work should be considered for all activities where the potential risk is high and cannot be minimised sufficiently by the implementation of control measures.
- Permit-to-work systems are particularly important where failure to implement safety measures could allow serious and immediate risks to health and safety. Examples include working in confined spaces, maintenance of high voltage electrical apparatus and hot work.
- A typical permit to work should include:
  - permit title
  - permit number
  - the location of work
  - plant identification
  - a description of the work to be carried out
  - hazard identification
  - necessary precautions
  - protective equipment
  - authorisation
  - acceptance
  - extension arrangements
  - completion of work arrangements
  - cancellation section.
- It is vital to determine who will be responsible for issuing the permit to work, who will be responsible for putting in place the necessary precautions and who will be responsible for the work that is carried out.
- Contractors working on site are the employer's responsibility. If the employer has permit-to-work systems in place, contractors should use them.
- Records must also be kept of all permits to work.
- Training should be given to all staff, including those who will issue permits and those working under them, before a permit-to-work system is implemented.

3.206   A permit-to-work system is a formal written system used to control high-risk activities. Permit-to-work systems specify the precautions which need to be taken to control the risks. Examples include working in confined spaces, maintenance of high voltage electrical apparatus and hot work. Permit-to-work systems only allow work to begin after safe procedures have been defined and carried out.

Employers' Duties

3.207

- Employers have a general duty to ensure, so far as is reasonably practicable, the health, safety and welfare at work of all employees under the HSWA .
- Employers must provide and maintain systems of work that are, as far as reasonably practicable, safe and without risks to health, under the HSWA and under the Management of Health and Safety at Work Regulations 1999 (MHSWR).
- Employers must carry out their activities, as far as reasonably practicable, in such a way as not to harm the health and safety of those not in their employment, under the HSWA.
- Under the MHSWR, employers must make an assessment of the risks to the health and safety of their employees while at work, and a similar assessment of the risks to the health and safety of persons not in their employment that may arise as a result of their work activities.

Employees' Duties

3.208

- Employees have a duty to take reasonable care of their own health and safety and that of other people who may be affected by their work under the HSWA.
- Employees must use machinery, equipment, dangerous substances, transport equipment, means of production and safety devices in accordance with any instruction and training given by the employer, under the MHSWR .
- Employees must inform their employer of any danger to health and safety posed by a work activity, under MHSWR.
- Employees must also inform their employer of any shortcomings in the employer's protection arrangements under MHSWR.

In Practice

Risk Assessments and Safe Systems of Work

3.209 Risk assessment will identify activities for which formal safe systems of work are necessary.

Which Safe Systems of Work Require Permit-to-work Systems?

3.210 Permit-to-work systems need to be introduced for all activities where the potential risk is high and if risks cannot be eliminated. They are particularly important where failure to implement safety measures could allow serious and immediate risks to health and safety. Examples of activities where permit-to-work systems are necessary include:

- work in confined spaces, such as vessels or sewers
- hot work, such as cutting and welding in premises under refurbishment
- working on high voltage electrical equipment, such as jointing 33,000 volt cables
- maintenance of machinery on production lines, such as power presses
- working at height while using fall arrest systems
- lone working in isolated areas, such as lift motor rooms
- work with asbestos, eg removal of insulation from hot water systems
- work on lifts
- excavation work.

3.211   Many industries, such as chemical and offshore operations, regularly use permit-to-work systems for a host of activities.

3.212   Once the activities which require a permit-to-work system have been established, the details should be entered on a master sheet.

Developing a Suitable Permit-to-work System

3.213   The first consideration is to determine the essential contents of a typical permit-to-work system, which can be tailored to suit any particular activity. Employers must also ensure the system:

- is unambiguous and avoids misleading statements
- identifies all potential hazards
- specifies all necessary isolation of plant and electrical equipment
- clearly determines the personal protective equipment necessary
- clearly identifies responsible persons
- adequately deals with the hand back of plant and equipment after work.

Permit Title

3.214   The title should describe the type of work to be carried out, eg entry into confined space.

Permit Number

3.215   The permit number is a unique reference, for cross-referencing and record purposes.

Location of Work

3.216   There should be clear identification of the work location, eg the exact location of a piece of plant within a factory, rather than the name of the factory.

Plant Identification

3.217   A clear identification of the specific plant will also be necessary, eg when carrying out maintenance on an electrical circuit breaker, identify the particular circuit breaker, rather than just the switchboard.

Description of Work to be Carried Out

3.218 It is important to not only describe the exact work to be carried out, but also to outline the limitations of the work which can be carried out under the permit.

Hazard Identification

3.219 Any residual hazards or additional hazards introduced by the work itself should be identified, eg when working in a confined space, the use of certain plant will introduce fresh hazards.

Necessary Precautions

3.220 The precautions necessary to control the risks should be outlined, such as any isolation required, as well as how the isolation will remain secure. For example, when working on machinery the precautions may specify temporary guarding from other machines, or other parts of that machine, and how guarding will be retained in place, such as locking off.

3.221 If the individual issuing the permit effects such isolation, the permit should specify who is responsible and that person should sign once the procedure has been carried out.

Protective Equipment

3.222 Personal protective equipment, such as respiratory protective equipment, should be specified, as should any barriers, notices or earthing equipment required.

Authorisation

3.223 The signature of the person issuing the permit is necessary to confirm that all safety precautions have been met.

3.224 In some cases, not all the measures can be taken before the issue of the permit. Some isolators, for example, may only be assessable after work has commenced.

Acceptance

3.225 The person in charge of carrying out the work generally signs the acceptance section. It should not be signed until after the person issuing the permit has described the hazards involved and the precautions required. The signature should indicate that the details have been explained to all those who will carry out the work.

3.226 On occasions, the person issuing the permit may be the person carrying out the work, in which case the same process needs to be completed.

Extension Arrangements

3.227 If the work needs to be carried out after the time specified on the permit, any changes of personnel or arrangements should be included. A new time of expiry will be needed.

Completion of Work Arrangements

3.228 The person responsible for the work should sign to acknowledge that the equipment can be returned to service and specify any special precautions which may need to be taken. The person responsible should also confirm that all tools and/or temporary connections have been removed and that the equipment is safe for recommissioning and/or for return to normal service.

Cancellation

3.229 The person issuing the permit signs the cancellation section, which confirms that the plant has been successfully returned to service and that it is no longer safe to carry out work on it. A general permit-to-work form could be used or a more specific permit-to-work form may be required, eg for:

- electrical work
- work in confined spaces
- hot work
- lone work.

Control of Permit-to-work Systems

3.230 An essential element of a permit-to-work system is the management of the system. It will be necessary to determine who will devise the system, who will be responsible for issuing the permit, who will be responsible for putting in place the relevant precautions (if not the person issuing the permit), and who will be the person responsible for the work that is to be carried out.

3.231 Each type of permit will have different control features, however the essentials should be the same.

Who Devises the Permit to Work?

3.232 It is rare for a single person to devise a permit-to-work system, unless the activity is relatively simple. In most cases, a safety advisor or officer will be involved to outline the principles and, eg the means of making apparatus and systems safe are technical and an engineer with knowledge of the task should be involved. For a permit to work on production machinery, for example, a mechanical engineer who understands the principles behind the machinery will need to have input.

3.233 The employees who will, or do, operate the equipment can also make valuable contributions to the process.

3.234 Information from the equipment manufacturer or maintenance manual may be helpful. In practice, the development of a permit-to-work system is normally a team effort.

Who Issues the Permit to Work?

3.235 A competent person, with enough technical knowledge to understand the hazards involved and how to control the risks, should issue the permit to work. The person should have specific training in the operation of permit-to-work systems. Such persons are sometimes known as nominated persons.

3.236 A person nominated to issue permits to work for high voltage electrical equipment, for example, may be a qualified electrical engineer, and a person nominated to issue such permits for hot work on a construction site might be a site manager or works foreman.

Who Puts in Place the Precautions?

3.237 The person who puts in place the precautions needs to be a competent person, working under the direction of the person issuing the permit (if this is not the same person).

3.238   For tasks which have to be carried out from more than one location, or if there is a multitude of tasks that require different skills, a second person will put in place some of the necessary precautions.

3.239   The person issuing a permit to work for a confined space may not have the necessary skill or instrumentation to declare that the atmosphere is safe, hence a second person or organisation may be employed.

Who is Responsible for the Work Carried Out Under the Permit?

3.240   The person responsible for the work carried out under the permit is not always involved in making the work safe, but would normally be competent to carry out the work.

3.241   The person must understand the principles of the permit-to-work system, as he or she has to sign it and explain its contents to staff. The person should also know what to do in an emergency.

3.242   On occasions, the person carrying out the work can also be responsible for issuing the permit. This is more usual for less hazardous tasks, such as hot work.

What About Contractors?

3.243   Contractors working on-site are the employer's responsibility. If the employer has permit-to-work systems in place, contractors should use them. The employer should ensure the contractor's staff are adequately trained and then issue the permit.

3.244   If an employer hires an expert contractor, eg for the disposal of fuel tanks which have contained other hazardous materials, the employer should ensure the contractor is competent and operating a satisfactory permit-to-work procedure of its own. In this example, if the tanks were cut up prior to removal from the site, a hot work permit would be implemented by the employer's own staff prior to the contractor's work.

Implementing Permit-to-work Systems

3.245   Permit-to-work procedures are used to control high-risk activities and it is vital to get it right first time. When the systems are first used, there should be adequate supervision to ensure the process is stopped if it proves to be unsafe. It is sensible to test the procedures, if possible, before they are used in earnest for the first time.

3.246   Employees' views should be sought before permit-to-work systems are implemented. Employees' views on working the systems once they are in place should also be sought.

Monitoring Permit-to-work Systems

3.247   As with most health and safety arrangements, there will be a need for monitoring. The monitoring should consist of two elements.

Reactive Monitoring

3.248   Reactive monitoring should include a review of accidents and near misses while operating the new systems. Those using the permit-to-work systems should be encouraged to report any near misses.

Active Monitoring

3.249 Active monitoring should include workplace inspections while the activity is being carried out.

Training

3.250 Training should be carried out before a permit-to-work system is implemented. All staff, including those who will issue permits and those working under them, should have sufficient, relevant training.

3.251 It should be noted that some of those involved will need to be qualified engineers or have some supplementary training on the control of particular hazards. This will be necessary where technical knowledge is necessary to avoid danger.

3.252 Training specifically for the use of permit-to-work procedures falls into two categories.

All Staff Required to Work Under Permit-to-work Systems

3.253 Training for this group should involve the following.
* A basic understanding of permit-to-work systems.
* Employees' responsibilities under the systems.
* What tasks can only be carried out under a permit.
* What to do in emergency.

3.254 All persons working under a permit-to-work procedure should have a briefing on the safety precautions before work commences.

3.255 The training can be relatively simple, such as a briefing or as part of the induction process. It is recommended that all staff are given a copy of the employee factsheet.

Staff Responsible for Issuing Permits and Putting in Place Precautions and Staff in Charge of Work

3.256 Training for this group should include the following.
* Principles of permit-to-work systems.
* Hazards involved in the particular work.
* Implementation of the necessary precautions, eg means of effecting isolation.
* How to test to ensure it is safe for work to commence, eg testing atmospheres in confined spaces or using live line detectors before work commences on electrical apparatus.
* What to do in an emergency.

List of Relevant Legislation

3.257
- Management of Health and Safety at Work Regulations 1999
- Health and Safety at Work, etc Act 1974

Further Information

Publications

HSE Publications

The following are available from *www.hsebooks.co.uk*.
- HSG65 (rev 1997) *Successful Health and Safety Management*
- HSG250 *Guidance on Permit-to-work Systems: A Guide for the Petroleum, Chemical and Allied Industries*
- HSG253 *The Safe Isolation of Plant and Equipment.*
- INDG98(L) *Permit-to-work Systems*

Step-by-step Guide: How to Manage Permit-to-Work Systems

- Carry out risk assessments of all activities and develop safe systems of work if these are deemed necessary.
- Determine which safe systems of work require permit-to-work systems.
- Develop suitable permit-to-work systems.
- Determine how the system will be managed and who will control it.
- Give training to all personnel involved.
- Implement the system.
- Monitor the function of all permit-to-work systems.

Employees' Factsheet: Permits to Work

Permit-to-work systems save lives — give them proper attention

Many of our work activities pose a high risk to our health and safety, and require rigorous safety precautions. Through risk assessment, we have identified these high-risk tasks and introduced control measures, which include safe systems of work.

A permit-to-work system is a formal written system used to control high-risk activities. A type of safe system of work, permit-to-work systems specify the precautions which need to be taken to control the risks. Only after safe procedures have been defined and acted upon can work begin.

Activities that require permits to work include:

- hot work
- work on high voltage electrical equipment
- work in confined spaces
- work with asbestos
- excavation work
- maintenance of power presses.

If you are carrying out work subject to a permit-to-work system, you must take the following into consideration.

- Do not take part in any work that requires a permit to work unless you are trained to do so or are under direct supervision.
- Take personal responsibility to carry out your own duties as directed by your supervisor or as required by the permit to work.
- Ensure your activities do not harm yourself or others.
- Do not proceed with the work until you have been told that the permit to work is in force and have been told of all of the necessary safety precautions.
- If you are not happy with the safety arrangements, do not start work (or, if work has already commenced, stop work immediately) and report the circumstances to your supervisor.

- In the event of an emergency, follow the emergency procedure and follow the instructions of your supervisor.
- Under no circumstances should you attempt a rescue of any person which will put you in danger. If you have any role in emergencies, you will be trained and authorised to carry out the appropriate action.
- On completion of the work, or suspension of the work, ensure the work location/plant/equipment is in a safe condition. If it cannot be made safe, withdraw it from service and report it to your supervisor.

Behavioural Safety

- Unsafe behaviour through individual acts or omissions is thought to be a contributory factor in 80% of accidents.
- Under the Health and Safety at Work, etc Act 1974, there is an implied duty for employers to ensure safe behaviour through adopting "safe systems of work".
- Employees have a legal duty to act in a safe manner and not misuse any equipment.
- Unsafe behaviour normally occurs through a combination of individual, job and organisational factors.
- Behavioural failures can be down to human error or through deliberate violations.
- Promoting safe behaviour is an important aspect of health and safety management and is an effective risk control measure.
- Behavioural modification models can assist in identifying aspects that may cause unsafe behaviour.
- Behaviour modification can be developed through a range of measures.

3.258   Behaviour is a critical aspect of all activities conducted within every organisation, including health and safety. How safely people behave at work is influenced by the combination of, and the influence between, personal factors, the job and the organisation.

3.259   Behavioural programmes have become popular in the safety domain, as evidence suggests that a high proportion of accidents are caused by unsafe behaviour. It is estimated that up to 80% of accidents may be attributed, at least in part, to the actions or omissions of people due to any one or a combination of the following behaviours:

- a slip or lapse of attention
- a genuine mistake
- deliberately cutting corners
- simple rule-breaking
- environmental factors such as poor maintenance or housekeeping.

3.260   Promoting safe behaviour at work is a critical part of the management of health and safety, because behaviour turns systems and procedures into reality. Good systems on their own do not ensure successful health and safety management. The level of success is determined by how organisations "adopt" their systems.

3.261   Behaviour modification techniques can be used to promote the effective use of risk control strategies and to analyse the "at risk" behaviours to ensure that the risk is minimised.

Employers' Duties

3.262   Under the Health and Safety at Work, etc Act 1974 (HSWA) there is an implied duty to ensure the safe behaviour of employees. Employers must ensure the provision and maintenance of plant and systems of work that are, so far as is reasonably practicable, safe and without risks to health.

3.263 "Systems of work" means the way in which the work is organised and includes, for example, the layout of the workplace, the order in which jobs are carried out, or special precautions that have to be taken before carrying out certain hazardous tasks. This duty therefore means that, for example, a machine itself, and the way it is operated, must both be safe.

3.264 Employers also have an implied duty to ensure appropriate human behaviour under the following regulations.

- Personal Protective Equipment at Work Regulations 1992: under these regulations the employer has a duty to take all reasonable steps to ensure that any personal protective equipment provided to his or her employees is properly used.
- Control of Substances Hazardous to Health Regulations 2002: under these regulations the employer providing any control measure must take all reasonable steps to ensure that it is properly used or applied.
- Control of Asbestos Regulations 2006: under these regulations, the employer providing any control measure must take all reasonable steps to ensure that it is properly used or applied.

Employees' Duties

3.265 Under the HSWA, employees must take reasonable care of their own health and safety and that of other persons who may be affected by their acts or omissions at work.

3.266 Malicious behaviour or horseplay of an obviously dangerous sort is a criminal act. Similarly, an employee is in breach of the law if he or she contravenes an employer's safety policy by knowingly taking risks (eg removing safety equipment). Other contraventions include staff behaving in an unsafe manner by taking unprofessional shortcuts in procedures to save time, or by showing off to impress someone with a dangerous experiment. A manager's or a supervisor's failure might include turning a blind eye to non-observance of safety procedures by those under their control.

3.267 Under the HSWA, it is also an offence for employees, visitors, customers or any members of the public to intentionally or recklessly interfere with anything provided in the interests of health, safety or welfare. Thus, for example, the misuse or abuse of fire extinguishers, first-aid boxes, emergency exits, etc is illegal.

3.268 Employees also have an implied duty to ensure their behaviour is appropriate under the following regulations.

- Management of Health and Safety at Work Regulations 1999: under these regulations, employees are required to use any machinery, equipment, dangerous substance, transport equipment, means of production or safety device provided in accordance with any training and instructions provided.
- Personal Protective Equipment at Work Regulations 1992: under these regulations, employees are required to use any personal protective equipment provided in accordance both with any training and instructions provided.
- Regulatory Reform (Fire Safety) Order 2005: under the Order, employees must take reasonable care for the safety of themselves and of other "relevant persons" who may be affected by their acts or omissions at work.
- Manual Handling Operations Regulations 1992: under these regulations, an employee must make full and proper use of any system of work provided by the employer.

- Control of Substances Hazardous to Health Regulations 2002: under these regulations, employees are required to make full and proper use of any control measure provided.
- Control of Asbestos Regulations 2006: under these regulations, employees are required to make full and proper use of any control measure provided.

In Practice

3.269   Risk control systems are used to make sure that appropriate workplace precautions are implemented and kept in place. As such, behavioural safety intervention can be deemed to be a useful risk control system, as it will minimise risk by reducing the frequency of behaviours that increase risk.

Human Behavioural Failures

3.270   Many accidents are blamed on the actions or omissions of an individual who was directly involved in operational or maintenance work. This response ignores the fundamental failures that led to the accident. These failures are usually rooted deeper in the organisation's design, management and decision-making functions.

3.271   Health and safety behaviours can be divided into the following four main categories.
1. Frontline health and safety behaviours: such as adhering to site rules and procedures as well as specific activities, eg manual handling or the use of personal protective equipment (PPE).
2. Risk control behaviours, eg risk assessing and compliance with emergency procedures.
3. Management actions such as auditing, training, recruitment and purchasing of plant.
4. Leadership and direction, eg demonstrating commitment and prioritising health and safety.

3.272   Current behavioural safety observation and feedback programmes tend to target a limited proportion of critical frontline health and safety behaviours. The main reason for this is that frontline behaviour is easier to observe. As an example, the use of PPE can be observed quite easily in most cases, yet the actual selection of appropriate PPE through risk assessing, along with the recruitment and training of staff and the enforcement of rules for the use of PPE, are not so easy to observe.

3.273   Human behavioural failures can either be down to:
- human error (that is an action or decision which was not intended, which involved a deviation from an accepted standard, and which led to an undesirable outcome)
- a violation (that is a deliberate deviation from a rule or procedure).

3.274   Slips and lapses are the errors that are made by even the most experienced, well trained and highly motivated people. They often result in omitted steps in repair, maintenance, calibration or testing tasks. Lapses cause people to forget to carry out an action, to lose their place in a task or even to forget what they had intended to do.

3.275   Mistakes are a more complex type of human error where a person does the wrong thing believing it to be right. The failure involves the mental processes that control how an individual may plan, assess information, make intentions and judge consequences.

3.276   Violations are any deliberate deviations from rules, procedures, instructions and regulations. The breaching or violating of health and safety rules or procedures is a significant cause of many accidents and injuries at work.

3.277 With a routine violation, breaking the rule or procedure has become a normal way of working. This can be due to:

- the desire to cut corners to save time and energy
- the perception that the rules are too restrictive
- the belief that the rules no longer apply
- a lack of enforcement of the rules.

3.278 Organisational culture and managerial goals and priorities can influence whether health and safety rules are broken. If the wrong messages about health and safety are received, rule breaking can be encouraged. A lack of visible communication from management can be seen as somehow condoning violations of health and safety rules.

3.279 Line managers turning a blind eye, or actively encouraging employees to take short cuts for the sake of production, sometimes further reinforces unsafe behaviour. Unfortunately, this has negative effects that are not always immediately apparent.

- First, employees learn that unsafe behaviour pays.
- Second, it wastes resources as the very behaviours that companies spend a lot of time, money and effort trying to eradicate are reinforced.
- Third, by condoning unsafe behaviour, line managers can be transmitting conflicting messages that undermine employees' confidence in the whole of the management's commitment to safety.

Human Factors

3.280 Behavioural safety is based upon a number of "human factors". The Health and Safety Executive's (HSE) definition of human factors is the "environmental, organisational and job factors, and human and individual characteristics which influence behaviour at work in a way which can affect health and safety". These can be divided into three broad categories.

1. The job: matching the job to the person is more likely to ensure competence in the job and can prove to be an effective contribution to business results. Mismatches between job requirements and people's capabilities provide the potential for human error.
2. The individual: people at work bring to their job personal attitudes, skills, habits and personalities that can be strengths or weaknesses depending on the task demands. Individual characteristics influence behaviour in complex and significant ways.
3. The organisation: organisational factors have the greatest influence on individual and group behaviour. Organisations need to establish their own positive health and safety culture. The culture needs to promote employee involvement and commitment at all levels, emphasising that deviation from established health and safety standards is not acceptable.

Behaviour Modification Model

3.281 Given that a high percentage of workplace accidents are triggered by unsafe behaviour, most people will be aware that reducing accidents and improving safety performance can only be achieved by systematically focusing upon those unsafe behaviours in the workplace.

3.282   The core element of behaviour modification is the following "ABC" model of behaviour.

- Antecedents: the causal event (or trigger) preceding the behaviour. Examples of antecedents include rules, procedures, suitable tools/equipment, information, signage, skills, knowledge, training, etc.
- Behaviour: the observable thing that someone does/does not do.
- Consequence: the outcome of the behaviour for the individual that influences the likelihood that the behaviour will be repeated.

3.283   The ABC analysis enables the identification of the ways that behaviour may be changed, by ensuring the appropriate antecedents are in place and that the consequences support the desired outcome. The overriding tendency is to focus on the individual and to exclude other factors relating to the job, the workplace organisation and environment and the safety climate. However, all of these aspects play a role in determining motivation, attitudes and health and safety-related behaviour at work. The following table, *Example of the ABC Analysis*, shows a simple example based upon the use of PPE.

Example of the ABC Analysis

Antecedents	Behaviour	Consequence
Ear defenders supplied by employer	Wearing ear defenders in noisy environment	Reduced likelihood of hearing damage
Required by employer to wear ear defenders		Less likely to get into trouble with employer
Knowledge of potential damage to hearing if ear defenders not worn		Discomfort of wearing ear defenders
Signs highlight need for use of ear defenders		Unable to hear fire alarms
Noisy environment		
Peers do not wear ear defenders	Not wearing ear defenders in noisy environment	Impaired hearing in the future
Knowledge that rules on use of ear defenders are not enforced		Avoid discomfort of wearing ear defenders
		Able to hear alarms

3.284   Whilst antecedents are necessary to help trigger behaviour, their presence does not guarantee that a particular behaviour will occur or that it will be maintained over a period of time. As a simple example, the presence of safety rules for the use of PPE does not ensure that safe behaviour and the correct use of PPE will occur. To maintain a required behaviour over time also requires significant individual consequence.

3.285   Consequences are defined as the outcome of the behaviour for the individual that influences the likelihood that the behaviour will be repeated. There are three main types of consequence that influence behaviour as follows.

- Positive reinforcement: this includes reward for achievement, recognition, praise and positive feedback.
- Negative reinforcement: this includes avoidance of pain, losses (including financial loss) and penalties/fines.
- Punishment: this includes removal of benefits, disciplinary action, physical injury and feelings of guilt.

3.286   At the individual level, when non-compliance with legislation or safety rules occurs, management traditionally use discipline and punishment in an attempt to rectify the situation. In contrast, management rarely congratulate for correct behaviour, although research shows that positive "reinforcers" are much more powerful than negative ones.

3.287   If people consciously change their behaviour, they also tend to re-adjust their associated attitudes and belief systems to fit the new behaviour. This occurs because people try to reduce any tension caused by a mismatch between their behaviour and attitudes. Behaviour change, therefore, tends to lead to new belief and attitude systems that buttress the new set of behaviours.

3.288   An additional factor that enhances attitude change by focusing on behaviour is the positive reinforcement brought about by peer pressure. If a workgroup adopts the norm that thinking and behaving safely is best for all concerned, the group as a whole will tend to apply social "sanctions" to the individual who deviates from this norm and behaves unsafely. If people wish to remain a part of the social fabric of the workgroup, they soon revert back to the safety norm and behave safely. Importantly, this illustrates the point that workgroups will adopt a collective definition of those behaviours, work practices or tasks that are considered to be risky.

Behaviour Modification

3.289   There is strong research evidence to suggest that behaviour modification techniques can be effective in promoting critical health and safety behaviours, provided that they are implemented effectively. However, to focus solely on changing individual behaviour — without considering necessary changes to how people are organised, managed, motivated or rewarded — can result in treating the symptom only, without addressing the root causes of the unsafe behaviour.

3.290   Behaviour modification can be defined as any intervention directed at changing the behaviour of people carrying out specific workplace tasks to reduce human failures (errors and violations) made in these tasks.

3.291   Behavioural modification programmes, which address safety, typically involve some form of workplace observation of unsafe acts or conditions, with a procedure for follow-up action and a reporting system. The follow-up action can be targeted at the individual, team or organisation, depending on the features of the specific programme.

3.292   There are three core elements of behaviour modification interventions, which are:

* pinpointing of relevant behaviour(s) which contribute or could contribute to accidents
* analysing the behaviour, focusing on the antecedents and consequences, normally by observation, to identify the necessary corrective actions
* evaluation of the behaviour to ascertain whether change has taken place as intended and whether or not the change was due to the intervention of other factors.

3.293   Proactive intervention is obviously more desirable than reactive and as such the process of observation and feedback should be continuous. The three core elements detailed above can be used to form a six-step intervention process.

* Step 1: Establish the desired result or output of the activity or individuals under examination (eg the correct and safe use of PPE).
* Step 2: Specify critical behaviours that influence performance of the area to be improved. Identification of the behaviours can come from the knowledge of the

person involved, past experience, near miss and accident data and should be defined to ensure all parties are looking at the same behaviours.

- Step 3: Ensure that the individual can perform the desired behaviour. If the behaviour is not within their control, it will not be possible to change it.
- Step 4: Conduct an "ABC" analysis on the current and desired behaviour and, where necessary, alter antecedents (for example, change equipment, provide training, improve supervision).
- Step 5: Alter the consequences immediately following desired behaviour to reinforce that behaviour.
- Step 6: Evaluate the impact of altering the consequences on the behaviour and on the desired result (eg by regular follow-up observations).

3.294   One of the most problematic aspects of using behaviour modification to change behaviour is selecting consequences that other people will find reinforcing. What one person finds rewarding or reinforcing may not have the same effect on others. It is therefore important to gain insight into what the person or people whose behaviour you are seeking to change are likely to find reinforcing. The greater the understanding or insight about what is important to the group or person whose behaviour is targeted for change, the easier it is to choose appropriate reinforcers.

3.295   Whilst a focus on changing unsafe behaviour into safe behaviour is appropriate, this should not deflect attention from also analysing why people behave unsafely. To focus solely on changing individual behaviour without considering necessary changes to how people are organised, managed, motivated, rewarded and their physical work environment, tools and equipment, can result in treating the symptom only, without addressing the root causes of unsafe behaviour.

3.296   Reducing human error involves far more than taking disciplinary action against an individual. There are a range of measures that are more effective at control, including design of the job and equipment, procedures and training. Steps to reduce human errors include:

- addressing the conditions and reducing the stressors that increase error frequency
- designing plant and equipment to prevent slips and lapses occurring
- ensuring that effective training takes place
- designing jobs to avoid the need for tasks which involve very complex decisions
- ensuring appropriate levels of supervision
- checking that procedures and instructions are clear, concise, available, up-to-date and accepted by users
- ensuring that errors are avoided when undertaking risk assessments
- reviewing causes of human errors during incident investigations
- monitoring the measures taken to reduce error for their effectiveness.

3.297   To reduce routine violations employers can:

- increase supervision or monitoring to increase the chances of violations being detected
- determine whether there are any unnecessary rules
- make rules and procedures relevant and practical
- explain the reasons behind certain rules or procedures and their relevance
- improve design factors that affect the likelihood of corner cutting
- involve the workforce in drawing up rules to try to increase acceptance.

Barriers to Modifications

3.298   Implementing a behavioural safety system can be fraught with difficulties. Common problems that often arise include the following.

- A lack of workforce buy-in. This is normally due to management imposing the system on the workforce without consultation.
- The observation checklists are not targeting the appropriate accident-causing behaviours.
- Unsafe behaviours have not been defined with sufficient precision.
- The behaviours on the checklists are not acceptable to the workforce as they have been defined without consultation.
- The observation checklists focus on unsafe conditions, not unsafe behaviours.
- Recording people's names, where they were working, what was said to them, and their responses when they are observed as behaving in an unsafe manner. This makes employees unwilling to participate.
- Disciplining people for not behaving safely in accordance with the behavioural items on the observation checklists.
- Safety improvement target-setting meetings not being conducted properly.
- Observations taking place at the same time every day. The timing of each day's observation must be as unpredictable as possible, or else all that might be achieved is that people behave safely only for that particular time period.
- A lack of regular feedback sessions. This creates a lack of workforce buy-in because line management are not perceived as viewing the system as an appropriate weapon to reduce accidents.
- A lack of ongoing support from management as they do not see themselves as a part of the problem, and consequently do not have anything to offer.

List of Relevant Legislation

3.299
- Control of Asbestos Regulations 2006
- Regulatory Reform (Fire Safety) Order 2005
- Control of Substances Hazardous to Health Regulations 2002
- Management of Health and Safety at Work Regulations 1999
- Personal Protective Equipment at Work Regulations 1992
- Manual Handling Operations Regulations 1992
- Health and Safety at Work, etc Act 1974

Further Information

Publications

HSE Publications

The following are available from *www.hsebooks.co.uk*.
- HSG54 (rev 1998) *The Maintenance, Examination and Testing of Local Exhaust Ventilation*
- HSG65 (rev 1997) *Successful Health and Safety Management*

- HSL/2002/25 *Safety Culture: A review of the literature*, Health and Safety Laboratory, Human Factors Group
- OTO 048 *Behaviour Modification Programmes: Establishing Best Practice*, Offshore Technology Report, HSE
- OTO 049 *Safety Culture Maturity Model*, Offshore Technology Report, HSE
- *ACSNI Study Group on Human Factors. Third Report: Organising for Safety*, HSE
- *Contract Research Report 430/2002: Strategies to Promote Safe Behaviour as Part of a Health and Safety Management System*

Other Publications
- *Changing Minds: A Practical Guide for Behavioural Change in the Oil and Gas Industry*, Step Change in Safety

Accident Investigation

- All accidents, incidents and near misses should be investigated to determine the causes and to ensure that a similar accident will not happen again.
- The need to carry out accident investigations is an implied duty under the Management of Health and Safety at Work Regulations 1999.
- The Social Security (Claims and Payments) Regulations 1987 require an employer to take reasonable steps to investigate accidents.
- Safety representatives may examine the causes of accidents at the workplace.
- Inspectors under the Health and Safety at Work, etc Act 1974 may also carry out investigations in the workplace.
- Investigation policies and procedures should be drawn up and made known to all relevant staff.
- Employers should select appropriate staff to carry out investigations and provide them with the necessary training and instruction.
- Suitable equipment and facilities should be provided for investigators to gather evidence, take samples, examine documents and interview persons.
- Investigation reports should be written and records of related procedures should be maintained.

3.300   The investigation of all accidents and incidents that occur in a workplace is an essential part of the proactive management of health and safety. Undertaking investigations of both those accidents that result in injury or worse, as well as near misses, in a systematic and organised way will benefit any organisation. Analysis of and accurate information about previous accidents helps to prevent them recurring.

3.301   The prime objectives of an accident investigation should be to:
- ascertain the facts and sequence of events leading to the accident/incident
- find the causes by establishing any unsafe acts or conditions
- determine the human, organisational and/or job factors that gave rise to the unsafe acts and/or conditions
- take both long-term and short-term measures to prevent a recurrence
- ensure compliance with the law.

3.302   It should be remembered that a Health and Safety Executive inspector may also carry out an investigation of an accident within their enforcement powers.

Employers' Duties

3.303   There is no explicit legal duty to investigate accidents but certain regulations do imply the need to carry out accident investigations.
- The Management of Health and Safety at Work Regulations 1999 imply that investigating the causes of workplace accidents is considered an essential part of good health and safety management and of the risk assessment review process.
- The Social Security (Claims and Payments) Regulations 1987 require an employer to take reasonable steps to investigate the circumstances of every accident that is reported. If there appears to be a discrepancy between the circumstances found by the investigation and those reported, there is a requirement to record those circumstances.

Employees' Duties

3.304

- Employees have a duty to co-operate with employers to enable them to fulfil their statutory duties under the Health and Safety at Work, etc Act 1974. This would include reporting:
  - all dangerous occurrences
  - near misses and accidents, whether or not they resulted in injury, damage or disease.
- Employees are also required to co-operate in an investigation.

In Practice

What Should be Investigated and Why

3.305   Investigation and review should take place for all accidents, reports of diseases, dangerous occurrences and/or near misses where practicable. There is an implied legal obligation to investigate accidents causing injury, dangerous occurrences and occurrences of certain diseases or ill health.

3.306   The investigation process is of value to organisations for the following reasons.

- If acted upon, accurate information and analysis of previous accidents helps to prevent them recurring.
- Prevention of accidents and incidents can bring substantial savings to the organisation, and can lead to increased profits from improvements in efficiency brought about by better morale and motivation of the workforce.
- Subsequent corrective actions can assist in controlling insurance costs.
- It is a way of testing the effectiveness of existing risk assessments (investigation is an essential part of the risk assessment review process) and the validity of the current safety policy.
- It maintains good employee and public relations.

3.307   Near misses should also be investigated. These are incidents where an unplanned event occurs for which there is no resultant injury or damage, but the potential exists for harm to occur if the event occurred under different circumstances.

3.308   The time and effort put into the investigation may vary considerably according to the potential severity of injury and/or damage. It is the potential consequences and the likelihood of the adverse event recurring that should determine the level of investigation, not simply the injury or ill health suffered. Significant incidents will usually require a written report, although there may be no need to document the results in very minor cases. Some form of judgment will determine the extent of the investigation process.

Policy and Procedures

3.309   The employer's safety policy documentation should identify who is responsible for carrying out accident investigations and include the arrangements for the investigation of accidents and incidents. It is important that the procedure specifies the official who must lead the investigation and any other person(s) who must or may be involved in the investigation team. There should be a defined procedure to determine which incidents should be investigated.

Who Should Investigate an Accident?

3.310   Various staff may be involved in the investigation procedure depending on the organisational structure. A team of investigators will often be formed with investigations being led by the health and safety advisor/manager, staff at managerial level or the supervisor in whose area the accident or incident occurred.

3.311   In addition, the skills and knowledge of specialist staff or consultants may be utilised in the investigation process. Such specialists will include electricians, maintenance engineers, mechanical engineers or consultants experienced and skilled in particular processes or activities.

3.312   At least one workforce representative should be involved in the investigation of workplace accidents or incidents.

3.313   All specified staff will require training before they are competent to fulfil their investigation responsibilities.

3.314   The level of involvement of various staff is often dependent upon the organisational arrangements, the type of incident and the outcome of the incident (such as injuries or damage that occurred).

3.315   The following table, *Accident Investigation and Who Becomes Involved When*, is a guideline as to when a specific person becomes involved in the investigation based upon an increasing scale of seriousness.

Accident Investigation and Who Becomes Involved When

Staff at supervisory level	• When an incident is reported to them by an employee under their supervision, which the employee believes indicates the presence of any danger to persons, plant or equipment.
Staff at managerial level	• When an incident occurs within the manager's area of responsibility involving the failure of or damage to any part of the premises, plant, equipment, tool or substance. • When an incident occurs in which an employee or other person within the manager's area of responsibility has suffered death or injury. • When an incident occurs within the manager's area of responsibility which could have led to the death or injury of persons or to the failure/damage of any company property.
Health and safety advisor/ manager	• Incidents to be reported to the enforcement authority. • Incidents involving the death of, or personal injury to, anyone doing anything with or in relation to any activity carried out by the company. • Incidents which a department manager believes could have led to the death of, or personal injury to, any person.

Staff at supervisory level	• When an incident is reported to them by an employee under their supervision, which the employee believes indicates the presence of any danger to persons, plant or equipment.
Specialists and consultants	• When specific skills, knowledge or experience is required to carry out an effective investigation.
Staff representative	• Any incident in which a member of staff that they represent is involved.

Investigation Equipment

3.316 No specific guidance sets out what equipment will be required to carry out an accident investigation but a typical list includes:

- photographic equipment
- portable lights (for when electrical power has to be switched off and for poorly lit areas)
- sketchpads, pencils and measuring equipment
- record-keeping equipment such as notepads or recording and filming equipment.
- collection equipment for sample taking such as paper bags, cartons and jars that can be sealed
- tools for cleaning spillages and/or debris.

3.317 All equipment should be maintained in good order with suitable records kept of any maintenance. Investigation staff should be made aware of its location.

Gathering Information Following an Accident

3.318 In deciding on the amount of resources to commit to any investigation, it is helpful at an early stage to review the relevant risk assessments in the light of the accident or incident. For example, it may be quite apparent which risk factors within the earlier assessment should be focused on in any further investigation, or the discovery of a mistake in the assessment may save time in investigating why certain measures had failed.

3.319 The investigator(s) should keep an open mind and not be unduly influenced by what should have happened as it is important to determine what actually happened. It is important to remember that apportioning blame is not an objective of the investigation. This may arise as part of the investigation findings, but should not be emphasised at this stage.

3.320 The earlier an investigation begins, the less chance there is of evidence being destroyed and the scene of the accident being disturbed. It will not always be possible to interview all witnesses immediately after an event, but there is great merit in completing the information-gathering process as soon as possible after an accident has taken place.

3.321 It is vital that the scene of an accident is left undisturbed until the investigation has been completed or at least until all of the physical evidence has been gathered and accurately recorded.

3.322 During the carrying out of investigations, conditions may be less than ideal, with debris on the floor and other unprotected hazards present. For reasons of safety, therefore, only the absolute minimum number of people should be allowed into the accident scene area. They must be made aware of the unique circumstances that exist during the very important period of time immediately after the occurrence of an accident.

3.323 The following flow chart highlights the normal activities to be undertaken in an investigation.

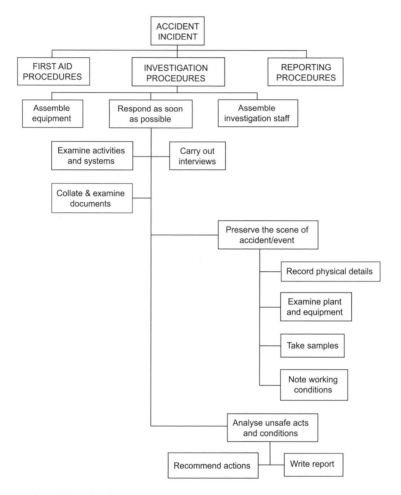

Information Required

3.324 The information required during an accident investigation will include:

- location, time and date of the incident
- details of persons involved, including any witnesses
- details of injuries and ill health
- damage to plant and equipment
- work activities performed at the time of the incident
- control measures and systems of work employed
- working conditions at the time of the incident (eg ground conditions, weather, lighting and heating)
- the sequence of events leading to the incident
- organisational arrangements such as supervision, staff training and work demands (eg production targets)
- the maintenance and cleaning procedures adopted
- materials and substances involved

- safety equipment that was employed.

3.325   To collect this information the investigator will need to:
- carry out a visual examination of the scene of the accident or incident
- carry out a visual examination of tools and equipment involved
- take samples from substances or materials involved
- inspect relevant documentation
- interview the injured person, witnesses or others who may have relevant information.

3.326   Photographs, sketches and plans are a useful method of recording the physical evidence and conditions at the location. Samples may also be taken and equipment removed for further investigation and examination.

Relevant Documentation

3.327   There are many pieces of documentation that may be helpful in accident investigations. The following list indicates some of the more obvious ones.
- Risk assessments of the work carried out at the time of the accident.
- Training records for the work being done.
- Safe working procedures or safe operating procedures relating to the activity.
- Method statements (if applicable).
- Any special arrangements in place, such as permits to work or emergency safety procedures.
- Commissioning, repair and maintenance records for any machinery or equipment being used at the time of the accident.
- Clock cards or other time-recording records.
- Records confirming the issue of stationery/consumables/equipment to person(s) involved in the accident.
- A computer audit trail to pinpoint specific timings relevant to the accident.
- Telephone records (where available) indicating calls made from particular extensions (especially useful to establish the time the accident was reported).

Investigation Interviews

3.328   When performing an investigation interview, the following three guiding principles should be followed.
1. Be sure of the purpose of the interview. When interviewing an individual, determine what aspects of the investigation they will be able to assist with and structure the interview questions to ensure that the nature and amount of information they provide is relevant.
2. Keep an open mind. Assumptions as to the cause of any accident should be avoided.
3. Get the person to talk. The interviewer must be sensitive to the interviewee's mood and appreciate the pressures that they may feel during a formal interview. If individuals feel they are going to be blamed, it may be more difficult to get an accurate account from them.

3.329   In the interview investigators should:
- be gentle and show concern
- avoid allocating blame
- explain clearly to the witness the nature of the interview
- establish the facts surrounding the accident, for example find out:
  - what normally happens

- what procedures are in place
- who is responsible for them
- establish the sequence of events on the day of the accident
- not lead the witness or make assumptions
- start the questioning with a general, easy, open question (eg "Please could you tell me what happened on the day of the accident?")
- follow up by asking a more detailed question relating to a specific part of the answer (eg "Could you tell me a little more about the way the machinery in question functions?")
- probe the answer to check factual details (eg "So was the noise that you describe normal?")
- then ask more about specific detail (eg "Was the guard fitted to the machine?")
- summarise and seek agreement (eg "So it was normal for two people to operate the machine, but on that day you were on your own, the machine started making a funny noise and one of the guards was missing — is that right?")
- start the sequence again but relating to a different topic.

3.330   The following should also be kept in mind when interviewing.
- Interview the injured person, any witnesses or any other person who may have relevant knowledge and/or information.
- Interviews need to be carried out as soon as possible after the incident to ensure accuracy.
- The interviews should be separate and as private as possible, although if it is conducted at the scene of the accident it can assist the witnesses' memory.
- The witnesses should be encouraged to talk and explain rather than be asked questions likely to elicit a yes/no response.
- During the interview the witnesses should be put at ease, using prompting, rather than leading questions.
- Investigators should confirm their understanding by summarising key points at appropriate times. This is valuable to ensure accuracy, shows interest and concern and will encourage witnesses to give further information.
- The interview should end on a positive note by, for example, thanking any witness and giving encouragement.
- The interview should also be left open so that a witness can come back to the investigator if he or she thinks of any further information; or if the investigator needs to go back to cross check information with the witness from other sources.

Determining the Accident/Incident Causes

3.331   By careful analysis of the information collected, the investigator (or team) will be able to identify the unsafe acts and/or unsafe conditions which caused the accident. These are sometimes called the "primary" or "immediate" causes.

3.332   According to the Health and Safety Executive (HSE), immediate causes can be placed into four sectors as follows:
(1) *Place or premises where the incident occurred.* Causes under this heading will include:
- inadequate access and egress
- workplaces that are unsuitable (for example due to lack of space) or are being used incorrectly
- poor work environment and ergonomics
- poor segregation of people from hazards
- lack of warning signs and information.

(2) *Plant, equipment and substances.* Causes under this heading will include:
- use of unsuitable plant, equipment and substances
- poor maintenance of plant and equipment
- improper use and poor guarding of plant and equipment
- misuse and poor storage of substances and materials
- incorrect or lack of personal protective equipment.

(3) *Process and procedures.* Causes under this heading will include:
- safe working procedures not being in place or out of date or inadequate
- lack of supervision of procedures
- lack of training in procedures and processes.

(4) *People involved.* Causes under this heading include:
- use of unsuitable staff
- use of poorly trained and supervised staff
- deliberate violation of procedures by those involved
- lapse due to fatigue, poor motivation, distraction, pressure of work, etc.

Secondary Causes

3.333   Unsafe acts and conditions will often have an underlying or a root cause. These are sometimes called the secondary causes. These can be grouped under the following eight headings.

(1) Control
- Was there a lack of supervision and monitoring?
- Were people held accountable for their performance?
- Were contractors controlled?

(2) Co-operation
- Were staff and their representatives involved in ensuring health and safety?
- Was information shared amongst those involved in the accident?

(3) Communication
- Were duties and responsibilities set out and understood?
- Was information passed on in respect of health and safety?
- Were written safe procedures available? How good was internal communication?

(4) Competence
- Were those involved competent?
- Was suitable safety training provided?
- Was training effectively delivered?
- Was the competence of contractors checked?

(5) Design
- Were the workplace, equipment and controls well designed and set out properly?

(6) Implementation
- Were suitable and sufficient plant, equipment and materials available?
- Was suitable labour available?
- Were cleaning and maintenance arrangements adequate?
- Were there adequate means to report defects, near-misses, safety concerns, etc?
- Was there adequate monitoring and health surveillance?

(7) Risk assessment
- Were adequate assessments carried out?

- Were controls in place as a result of the assessment?

(8) Management

- Was there a written safety policy?
- Were senior management committed to health and safety?
- Were adequate resources given to health and safety?

3.334 The use of an investigation checklist may assist in answering these questions.

Remedial Action Following Accident Investigation

3.335 Actions should be taken to remedy all of the identified deficiencies.

3.336 When remedial action is required to prevent recurrence, staff should be fully consulted on any issues that will impact on the activities taking place. Information, instruction and training in any additional control measures, systems of work or protective equipment will have to be considered, along with the potential costs of the remedial action.

3.337 It is essential that progress on the identified remedies is closely monitored to ensure that they do not get unnecessarily delayed or even forgotten. There should be a follow-up review to ensure that the actions taken are effective and do not create other unforeseen hazards.

3.338 Records should be kept of all investigations and any existing remedial action.

Report of Accident Investigation Findings

3.339 The amount of detail required in a report depends upon the severity of the outcome, and the use made of the investigation and report.

3.340 The report should contain:

- time, date and location of the accident/incident
- a summary of what happened
- a summary of events leading up to the accident
- information collected during the investigation
- details of those injured, those who assisted and witnesses
- details of the outcome of the accident (ie injury, loss or damage)
- conclusions including the causes of the event and probability of recurrence
- recommendations and costing of remedial actions
- supporting material (photographs and sketches)
- the date of the investigation
- the signature of the person carrying out the investigation.

3.341 Additional information may be requested to facilitate notifications within and outside the company (eg relatives, the HSE and insurers).

3.342 The results of the investigation should be widely circulated to ensure that there is no risk of a recurrence of a similar incident in other areas of the operation. Copies of the investigation findings may need to be circulated to:

- managers, supervisors, employees and other departments who have similar equipment or processes
- maintenance or engineering departments who may have to carry out repairs and/or modifications

- planning or production control departments who may have to change job instruction or control documentation
- personnel/training departments who may need to implement new or refresher training
- the safety department for inclusion in statistical reports and review of safety procedures
- the department responsible for keeping incident records, completing statutory reports and notifying the organisation's insurers
- safety representatives and safety committee members
- the employee or employees who were involved in the accident
- the employer's insurer.

3.343   The accident investigation policy should specify who is to receive copies of the report. The investigation team will determine who else needs to receive copies or other information relevant to the incident.

3.344   In the main, the findings will be communicated in writing but in certain cases it can be verbal, ie briefings for all other employees.

Investigations by Safety Representatives

3.345   A safety representative appointed by a recognised trade union may:
- examine the causes of accidents at the workplace
- inspect the part of the workplace where a notifiable accident or dangerous occurrence has occurred or notifiable disease has been contracted
- extend their inspections to other parts of the workplace if these other parts are relevant to the accident, dangerous occurrence or disease.

3.346   It is often desirable to ensure that employees have some form of involvement in the investigation of accidents. This may be achieved by allowing the safety representative to participate in the investigation process.

Investigations by Inspectors

3.347   An enforcement authority inspector may:
- carry out an examination and investigation
- direct that the premises or any part of them, or anything on the premises, should be left undisturbed for the purpose of any examination or investigation
- take measurements, photographs and recordings
- take samples of any articles or substances
- dismantle and/or test any article or substance found in any premises
- secure possession of any article or substance for use as evidence
- require any persons to give any information relevant to an investigation
- require the production of any books or documents
- ask to be afforded such facilities and assistance as are necessary.

3.348   If an enforcement officer has carried out a separate accident investigation, it may be appropriate to let them know the outcome of the company's own investigation. However, legal advice should be sought before disclosing this information.

Training

3.349   The training for accident investigation needs to be relevant to the organisation concerned and reflect its policy and procedures.

3.350   The training provided to those who will carry out an investigation should cover:

- the purpose of an investigation, ie to ascertain the facts to prevent recurrence, rather than to apportion blame
- the accident and near-miss investigation policy and procedures
- roles and responsibilities of those expected to carry out investigations
- the equipment available and its correct use
- the information that needs to be gathered and recorded following an accident
- interview techniques
- report-writing techniques.

3.351   A record of staff who are trained to carry out accident investigations should be maintained.

List of Relevant Legislation

3.352
- Management of Health and Safety at Work Regulations 1999
- Reporting of Injuries, Diseases and Dangerous Occurrences Regulations 1995
- Social Security (Claims and Payments) Regulations 1987
- Health and Safety (First-Aid) Regulations 1981
- Safety Representative and Safety Committee Regulations 1977
- Health and Safety at Work, etc Act 1974

Further Information

Publications

The following are available from *www.hsebooks.co.uk*.
- HSG245 *Investigating Accidents and Incidents: A Workbook for Employers, Unions, Safety Representatives and Safety Professionals*
- L87 (rev 1996) *Safety Representatives and Safety Committees*

Organisations
- Royal Society for the Prevention of Accidents (RoSPA)
  Web: *www.rospa.com*
  RoSPA is a registered charity that provides information, advice, resources and training in order to promote safety and prevent accidents.

Consultation With Employees

- All employers are required to consult with employees on health and safety arrangements.
- In a unionised workplace, employers must consult with the union safety representative under the Safety Representatives and Safety Committees Regulations 1977.
- In a non-unionised workplace, employers must either consult with employees directly or through a representative of employee safety under the Health and Safety (Consultation with Employees) Regulations 1996.
- Consultation is not the same as providing information. It involves:
  - inviting feedback
  - listening to the views of employees
  - taking viewpoints into account before making decisions.
- Employers should consult on:
  - any new measures that might affect health and safety
  - the appointment of competent persons
  - any information that must be provided under health and safety law
  - health and safety training
  - the health and safety implications of new technologies.
- Employers must provide representatives with relevant information, facilities and reasonable assistance to fulfil their duties.
- Representatives are allowed paid time off to fulfil their duties.
- Union safety representatives will usually have their training arranged by the relevant union.
- Employers may have to arrange training for representatives of employee safety in non-unionised workplaces.

3.353   Consultation with employees on arrangements for health and safety is a legal requirement in both unionised and non-unionised workplaces. Effective consultation can make a significant contribution to a positive health and safety culture within the workplace.

3.354   A proactive approach will assist in meeting legal requirements, and has the added potential for reducing accidents and increasing efficiency.

3.355   The Health and Safety Executive (HSE) places emphasis on *involving* employees. According to the HSE involvement means "active participation where the workforce and their representatives participate in the key elements of health and safety management such as setting targets and reviewing performance".

Employers' Duties

3.356

- Under the Health and Safety at Work, etc Act 1974 (HSWA), the employer is required to consult any safety representative appointed by a recognised independent trade union. The Act also places a duty on the employer to establish a safety committee, if requested to do by a safety representative.
- Under the Safety Representatives and Safety Committees Regulations 1977 (as amended by the Management of Health and Safety at Work Regulations 1999),

employers must consult any recognised trade union safety representative on health and safety arrangements. In particular, employers should consult safety representatives on:

- the introduction of any measure that will affect the health and safety of employees
- arrangements for appointing persons to assist the employer in complying with legislation, and to assist in emergency procedures
- the provision of information as required under health and safety legislation
- any planning and organisation of training required to be provided to employees under health and safety legislation
- the health and safety consequences of introducing new technologies into the employees' workplace.

- In non-unionised workplaces, the Health and Safety (Consultation with Employees) Regulations 1996 require employers to consult with employees directly, or through nominated representatives of employee safety, on arrangements for health and safety. This includes:
  - supplying any information representatives might need to participate in consultation
  - providing appropriate and reasonable training to representatives
  - giving paid time off for representatives to perform their functions and attend training.

Employees' Duties

3.357   There are no specific legal duties placed on employees acting as safety representatives under the Safety Representatives and Safety Committees Regulations 1977 or representatives of employee safety under the Health and Safety (Consultation with Employees) Regulations 1996.

3.358   Such representatives do not incur criminal or civil liability for any act or omission whilst performing their representative duties. However, like all employees, representatives have a duty to co-operate with their employer in relation to health and safety.

- Under the HSWA, employees must take reasonable care of their own health and safety and that of others.
- Under the Management of Health and Safety at Work Regulations 1999, all employees, including safety representatives, must:
  - use machinery, equipment, dangerous substances, transport equipment, means of production or safety devices provided by their employer in accordance with any training given
  - inform their employer of any work situation they reasonably consider to represent a serious and immediate danger to health and safety.
- Under the Safety Representatives and Safety Committees Regulations 1977 trade unions are required to inform the employer of the groups of employees represented by the safety representative.

In Practice

Difference Between Unionised and Non-unionised Workplaces

3.359   If the workforce is represented by a recognised trade union, the union may appoint a safety representative from among a group or groups of workers. The elected person's main function is to represent employees in consultation with employers on health and safety.

3.360   If there is not a recognised union representing employees, then the employer is still legally required to consult employees on health and safety. This can be carried out with each employee directly, or via one or more nominated representatives of employee safety.

3.361   It is important to clarify the terminology used. A representative of employee safety is someone elected under the Health and Safety (Consultation with Employees) Regulations 1996. A safety representative is someone appointed by a trade union under the Safety Representatives and Safety Committees Regulations 1977.

3.362   A significant difference between the two pieces of legislation relates to training. Where a safety representative is appointed by a trade union, the union will usually arrange whatever health and safety training is necessary. The responsibility for meeting the training needs of a representative of employee safety rests with the employer.

The Difference Between Informing and Consulting

3.363   An employer is already required by law to provide employees with information about:
- the health and safety risks identified by risk assessments
- the protective and preventive measures designed to ensure their health and safety at work
- emergency procedures for the organisation
- who is the competent person for health and safety
- any risks highlighted by another employer in the same workplace arising from that employer's business.

3.364   The crucial aspect of consultation is that employers are not just required to pass on information, but also to:
- actively invite feedback from employees
- listen to the views of employees
- take these views into account before any decision is taken.

3.365   Time must be built in to allow proper consultation to take place before a decision is made on any issue that might affect the health and safety of employees.

Union Safety Representatives

3.366   Union safety representatives must be members of the recognised union for their workplace. They must have been employed by the employer or have been in similar employment for at least two years.

3.367 Union safety representatives must also be able to keep up with any legislative and technological developments applicable to their workplace. It is vital they understand hazards and control measures associated with the work activities of the employees they represent. This is of paramount importance where the industry is potentially high-risk (eg demolition, steel erection, etc).

Functions of a Union Safety Representative

3.368 Union safety representatives have a number of functions. They can:

- consult with employers on health and safety matters
- investigate and make appropriate representations on hazards, dangerous occurrences and accidents in the workplace they represent
- raise issues relating to general health and safety matters
- carry out three-monthly (or if necessary more frequent) inspections of the workplace
- consult with enforcing inspectors and be made party to any relevant enforcement-related information
- attend safety committee meetings.

What Should Representatives be Consulted On?

3.369 Employers must consult with representatives on:

- the introduction of any new measures which may affect the health and safety of employees
- the appointment of competent people to assist the employer in complying with health and safety laws and with implementing emergency procedures
- any information that must be given to employees under health and safety law
- the planning and organisation of any health and safety issues
- the health and safety consequences of introducing new technologies into the workplace.

Information Employers Must Make Available

3.370 Safety representatives, upon request, are entitled to see and receive copies of any relevant health and safety documents relating to their workplace, including plans of proposed changes. Such documents may include:

- accident statistics
- accident reports
- cases of ill health
- reports of dangerous occurrences
- monitoring procedures.

3.371 Information which breaches national security, is involved in legal proceedings or breaks personal confidentiality, etc need not be made available.

Assistance Employers Must Provide

3.372 Employers must provide reasonable facilities and assistance for the safety representatives to perform their duties. This could include:

- providing office space
- secretarial support

- time away from their normal work activities.

Time Off

3.373   Safety representatives are legally entitled to paid time off (during working hours) for performing their duties and attending any training associated with those duties. If an employer refused time off with pay, the representative could take the complaint to an employment tribunal. If the complaint were proven, the employer would have to pay compensation.

Safety Committees

3.374   The employer must establish a safety committee if it is requested by two or more trade union safety representatives. The committee must be set up within three months of the request. Details of membership and work areas covered must be posted around the workplace. The committee should be independent of both management and safety representatives.

Membership of Safety Committees

3.375   There are no definite rules on committee membership, although it should be compact and representative of the whole workforce (both employees and management). The number of management members should not exceed the number of safety representatives, but should include line managers and supervisors.

3.376   Specialists, eg works managers, personnel managers, etc may be invited to join the committee or may attend individual meetings as necessary.

3.377   Attendance at meetings should be considered part of the members' normal work. Meetings should be held as often as necessary, planned well in advance and made known to the workforce. The meetings should be minuted, with copies given to each member and distributed around the workplace.

Functions of Safety Committees

3.378   Safety committees should have the following objectives and functions:
- study accident statistics and trends to develop reports for management
- examine safety audit reports
- analyse enforcement reports and establish a link with the enforcing officers
- consider safety representative reports
- develop, introduce and monitor safety rules and safe systems of work
- appraise safety training
- monitor the effectiveness of health and safety communication in the workplace.

3.379   Managers should ensure the committee has full and proper authority and should consider any points raised.

Non-unionised Consultation with Employees

3.380   In non-unionised workplaces, employers may consult with their employees either directly or through elected representatives of employee safety. In very small workplaces, direct consultation with employees may be more beneficial.

3.381   Self-employed people and non-employees, eg agency staff, volunteers, etc, do not have to be consulted. However, including them in consultation is good practice, particularly if they are working long-term at the employer's workplace. Trainees on work experience are considered to be employees and must therefore be consulted.

3.382   Consultation methods will vary. Examples include:

- health and safety committees
- newsletters
- notice boards
- employee surveys.

Functions of a Representative of Employee Safety

3.383   A representative of employee safety is entitled to:
- raise with the employer any general matters affecting the health and safety of the employees he or she represents
- highlight to the employer any potential hazards and dangerous occurrences at the workplace that affect the employees that he or she represents
- represent the interests of employees in any consultations at the workplace or with the enforcing authorities.

3.384   Representatives of employee safety should be consulted on the same matters as union safety representatives.

3.385   The employer must inform employees of the names of representatives and when consultation with these representatives stops, eg if the representative leaves the company.

Information Employers Must Make Available

3.386   Employers must provide any information necessary for employees or their representatives to effectively participate in consultation on health and safety. This information includes:
- likely hazards and risks associated with the work
- risks that might arise from proposed changes to the work
- implemented and proposed control measures and safe working practices.

3.387   In addition, representatives of employee safety should be provided with information on reportable accidents in relation to the group of employees they represent.

3.388   Employers do not have to provide information if:
- there are legal proceedings involved
- it would breach national security
- personal confidentiality would be broken
- it would harm the employer's undertaking.

Training, Time Off and Facilities

3.389   In order to fulfil their duties and responsibilities, representatives of employee safety must be:
- appropriately trained
- allowed paid time off from their regular work for training, canvassing in elections, etc
- provided with any reasonable facilities
- paid for any reasonable expenses, eg for travelling, training, etc.

Electing Representatives of Employee Safety

3.390   The representatives of employee safety must be elected from within the group of employees they represent. There is no guidance on the length of office for representatives of employee safety. Where there is a rapidly changing workforce, a representative may need to be elected more frequently in order to continue to remain the choice of those workers.

3.391   There is no limit on the number of representatives elected. The number selected should take into account the:

* size of the workforce
* different activities and/or shift work undertaken
* nature of the work.

3.392   All of the above points should be clarified and made known before an election is held.

Employee Involvement

3.393   In the workplace, to ensure the successful organisation of health and safety, the co-operation of employees and communication with them is fundamental. HSG65: *Successful Health and Safety Management* states that "participation by employees supports risk control by encouraging their ownership of health and safety policies. Pooling knowledge and experience through participation, commitment and involvement means that health and safety really becomes everybody's business."

3.394   The Health and Safety Commission (HSC) has stated that "an organisation's greatest asset is its workforce. Employees are often best able to spot issues and bring about real improvements. We need to expand the base of employee involvement in health and safety management to cover the whole workforce."

3.395   The *HSC Statement on Worker Involvement and Consultation* makes the case for worker involvement and consultation and highlights what a collaborative approach between partners can achieve. To be effective, the following principles should be applied.

* Value the contribution employees can make.
* Actively seek the view of employees.
* Involve employees as equal partners.
* Involve employees in all areas of health and safety management.
* Nurture, support and sustain involvement.
* Be prepared to adapt and change current practices and procedures.

Training

3.396   Where a safety representative is appointed by a trade union, the particular union will usually arrange whatever health and safety training is necessary for the individual. The responsibility for identifying and meeting training needs for the representative of employee safety rests with the employer.

Health and Safety Training for Representatives of Employee Safety

3.397   The training needs for representatives of employee safety will vary widely from one organisation to another, and probably from one individual to another. Training needs should reflect the particular individual's previous knowledge and experience, and the extent of their role.

3.398   It is obviously important that any representative undertakes the same health and safety training that is offered to those that he or she represents. Additionally, a representative is likely to require more detailed training on:

- the legal requirements relating to health and safety at work and, in particular, any specific aspects that relate to the group of workers he or she represents
- the type and extent of hazards within the workplace, and the controls that are put in place to minimise the risks
- the employer's health and safety policy, and the arrangements in place to fulfil the policy commitments.

3.399   In most cases, representatives of employee safety will need training in the skills to enable them to fulfil their function as two-way communicators. Additionally, the representative may be involved with any or all of the following, each of which may generate specific training needs:

- promoting workplace health and safety initiatives
- helping to develop the organisation's health and safety policy
- taking part in accident and incident investigations
- participating in safety audits
- helping in plant, equipment and premises inspections
- preparation of safe working procedures
- membership of safety committees
- improving communication about health and safety
- evaluating the understanding of health and safety issues amongst colleagues
- identifying training needs
- maintaining competence through further training and self-development.

Appropriate Training Methods for Representatives of Employee Safety

3.400   Once training needs have been established there are a number of options available, including:

- in-company courses that can be delivered at convenient times and locations by a specialist training provider
- training by other employees within the organisation
- courses offered by trade associations, educational establishments, etc
- courses offered by trade unions for safety representatives, where the union is agreeable (although it is important to realise that the role of a union safety representative may be more extensive than that of a non-union representative and therefore the course may not be appropriate)
- distance learning.

3.401   Any training that is modular, or well-spaced over a period of time, is often likely to be more productive than an initial, very intensive block of training.

3.402   The employer is obliged to meet both the costs of training and any reasonable travel/subsistence costs. The employer is also obliged to provide reasonable time off with pay, during working hours, for relevant training.

List of Relevant Legislation

3.403
- Management of Health and Safety at Work Regulations 1999
- Health and Safety (Consultation with Employees) Regulations 1996
- Safety Representatives and Safety Committees Regulations 1977
- Health and Safety at Work, etc Act 1974

Further Information

Publications

The following are available from *www.hsebooks.co.uk*.
- HSG217 *Involving Employees in Health and Safety. Forming Partnerships in the Chemical Industry*
- INDG232(L) *Consulting Employees on Health and Safety: A Guide to the Law*
- L87 (rev 1996) *Safety Representatives and Safety Committees*
- L95 *A Guide to the Health and Safety (Consultation with Employees) Regulations 1996*

Occupational Health: Principles

- Employers must address occupational health, as well as safety in the workplace under the Management of Health and Safety at Work Regulations 1999.
- Of the 35 million working days lost through occupational ill health and injury in 2004/05, the Health and Safety Executive (HSE) estimates that 28 million working days were lost due to ill health.
- The effective management of occupational health and the avoidance of occupational ill health save business money in the short and longer term.
- Occupational health is involved with:
  - aiding employees in their return to work after illness
  - assisting the disabled to access work
  - managing work-related aspects of illness with multiple causations
  - monitoring employees' health and the effects of work on health as well as health on work.
- Employers may need to obtain specialist advice to enable them to effectively assess and manage the occupational health risks within their business. Such advice may come from competent persons within the organisation, occupational health professionals, etc.
- When considering employing an occupational health service provider, it is important to establish the professional qualifications of the provider for the job, eg of occupational health nurses/doctors, ergonomists, therapists, etc.
- The exact services provided will depend on the risks, the numbers of personnel involved, and the nature of the business.
- Medical information is deemed to be confidential to the individual and their medical advisor, and employers do not have an automatic right to know an employee's medical diagnosis or treatment regime.

3.404   Occupational health addresses:

- the effects of work on health and the prevention of occupational disease

- the effects of health on work — assessing the fitness of the job to the worker, not just the fitness of the worker for the job

- rehabilitation and return to work after illness, injury or other absence

- assisting the disabled to access work, stay in work and return to work after absence

- managing work-related aspects of illness with multiple causations, eg heart disease, back pain, etc and helping employees make informed choices about lifestyle issues.

3.405   The Health and Safety at Work, etc Act 1974 (HSWA), subsequent regulations and other legislation place a duty on employers to safeguard the health and well-being of people at work, and those who may be affected by the work, eg visitors and contractors. There is no specific requirement in UK law for an employer to buy in or provide occupational health services. Instead, the Management of Health and Safety at Work Regulations 1999 (MHSWR) require employers to appoint competent persons to enable them to fulfil their statutory responsibilities. While larger organisations may have such expertise available in-house, smaller organisations are likely to need to look outside for competent support.

Employers' Duties

3.406

- Employers have a general duty to ensure, so far as is reasonably practicable, the health and safety at work of all employees under the HSWA.

- Under the MHSWR, employers must assess the risks to the health of their employees of all aspects of work.

- Employers must also assess the risk to the health of persons not in their employment arising out of the work being undertaken.

- Employers must, before they employ a young person under the age of 18, undertake a specific risk assessment in relation to the health risks to which that young person will be exposed in the course of their work.

- Where more than five people are employed, the significant findings of the risk assessment must be recorded.

- Employers must take appropriate steps, following the risk assessments, to reduce the risks to the health of their employees as far as is reasonably practicable, ie implement appropriate risk control measures.

- Employers must inform their employees, and others affected by their work, of the findings of the risk assessments and of the steps being taken to reduce the risks to their health at work.

- Employers must provide suitable training and information to their employees to enable them to comply with the risk control measures being implemented.

- Employers must monitor the implementation of risk control measures and manage non-compliance to maintain the risks to employee health at the lowest practicable level.

- Employers must provide appropriate health surveillance where the risk assessment identifies a need.

- Employers must appoint one or more competent persons to assist them in carrying out the risk assessments and undertaking health surveillance.

3.407 Risk assessments must be:

- suitable and sufficient — they must look at all potential health risks and have anticipated all reasonably foreseeable factors

- carried out by a competent person who has an:
  - understanding of all relevant legislation, regulations and guidance
  - understanding of the work being undertaken and its possible impact on employee health
  - awareness of individual capabilities and limitations
  - ability to recognise particular risks, both to individuals and to groups of employees
  - ability to identify health surveillance needs
  - ability to recommend reasonably practicable solutions.

- kept up to date, reviewed regularly and revised where there has been a significant change (whether of personnel or in the work processes), or in the light of experience.

Employees' Duties

3.408   Under the HSWA, employees must:

- comply with the employer's arrangements to ensure their health at work — this includes using equipment or carrying out work activities according to the training given, and complying with health surveillance arrangements
- inform their employer of any situation which represents a serious and imminent danger to health in the workplace
- inform their employer of any situation that represents a shortcoming in the employer's arrangements for the protection of employee health — this would include a change in their personal health/circumstances such that their health at work may be adversely affected, eg where a woman becomes pregnant, and the risks to her health and that of her baby need to be reassessed.

In Practice

3.409   All elements of occupational health need to be considered together, not in isolation.

Effects of Work on Health and the Prevention of Occupational Disease

3.410   The effects of work on health and the prevention of occupational disease cover:

- sudden damage to health — typically as a result of an accident or injury in the workplace or exposure to high levels of a toxic or irritant substance
- long-term ill health — as a result of exposure to a health hazard over a long period of time, eg lung disease as a result of exposure to dusts or fibres.

3.411   In practice, employers need to consider:

- identifying the hazards to health in the workplace, including physical and mental health hazards
- the control measures in place to reduce, so far as is practicable, the risk of injury to employees from any aspect of work, ie what employees do, what tools, equipment or substances they use to do their work, and how they carry out their work activities. Examples might include:
  - setting up a work area to minimise the amount of reaching required, thereby reducing the risk of upper limb problems in the long-term
  - substituting a potentially hazardous substance for a less toxic alternative
  - implementing health surveillance as an additional control measure to monitor the effects of work on health.

Effects of Health on Work

3.412   The assessment of job-fit — how suitable the job is to the worker, as well as how suitable the worker is to the job — should form an essential element of recruitment and human resources practice.

3.413   Employers need to consider:

- the physical and mental health demands of the job — what the employee will be exposed to in terms of physical demand, eg stamina, load-carrying; and mental pressures, eg speed of work, response times, knowledge and skills needed
- whether the job carries any specific risk to employees with particular health problems and, if so, what special arrangements need to be made to assess the health of employees before employment
- informing employees and prospective employees of the demands of the job, of any specific risks where identified, and of any mandatory health assessments
- providing adequate and appropriate training on employment, and updating at appropriate intervals to maintain the best possible job-fit.

Rehabilitation and Return to Work After Illness, Injury or Other Absence

3.414   The earlier and the more actively an absence from work is managed, the more likely it is that the employee will return promptly.

3.415   Prolonged absences from work, ie greater than four consecutive weeks, are associated with significant loss of personnel, with some research suggesting that, after six consecutive weeks' unplanned absence, there is no more than a 50% chance of the employee returning to their job.

3.416   In practice, employers need to:

- maintain regular contact with the employee, understanding the reason for absence, and working towards a prompt and safe return to work
- identify any modifications to the job on either a temporary or permanent basis that will facilitate return to work and their ability to continue in work
- obtain adequate information on the effects of the illness, etc in relation to the employee's ability to return to their job — without breaching medical confidentiality
- take action, where appropriate, to reduce the risks to the employee and others, of the incident which led to the absence, from recurring.

Assisting the Disabled to Access Work

3.417   The Government is keen to assist employers in the employment of disabled people, and the local Access to Work team (contacted through the local Job Centre) offers assistance to employers in identifying suitable jobs for people with a disability, and in the recruitment and placement of disabled people. Much of their assistance is free. Funding is also available in many cases to assist the employer to modify the workplace or install specialist equipment to enable a disabled person to work.

3.418   In practice, employers should:

- obtain expert advice from the Access to Work team or an occupational health provider on the employment of disabled people, whether for a new appointment or because an existing employee has become disabled
- work with the disabled employee to clarify what modifications might be needed to enable them to undertake the work activity
- use the risk assessment process to identify both the health risks to the individual and the control measures necessary to ensure their health in work
- provide appropriate support and training for the disabled person and their work colleagues to maintain their health in work.

Managing Work-related Aspects of Illness with Multiple Causations

3.419   Managing work-related aspects of illness with multiple causes almost always requires the involvement of specialist health advisors, eg:

- occupational health professionals
- ergonomists
- experts in health education.

3.420   The focus of the specialist involvement should be the management of the individual in relation to work, whether at a preventive level or when the health problem is affecting ability to work.

3.421   Employers seeking to prevent or reduce the risk of employees developing such illnesses, eg back pain, upper limb disorders or heart disease, will benefit from accessing information from sources such as:

- the Health and Safety Executive (HSE)
- professional journals
- trade unions
- the Department of Work and Pensions.

Costs of Occupational Ill Health

3.422   Of the 30 million working days lost through occupational ill health and injury in 2005/06, the HSE estimates that 24 million working days were lost due to ill health and 2 million people were suffering from work-related illness.

3.423   Most companies cannot fully account for the costs of ill health — sick pay is just one element of the equation, and while it may be possible to measure the amount spent on staff replacement costs, it is much more difficult to put a cost on the reduced productivity of other workers either because they are supporting the replacement employee or because they too are working below par because of ill health.

3.424   Companies that introduce occupational health schemes find it difficult to justify the cost-benefit analysis, particularly in the short-term, because the cost of occupational ill heath is hard to quantify. In the longer-term, efficient management of absences and quicker returns to work, the reduction in the risk of claims for occupational injury or disease, and the improved performance and productivity of well people with a good job-fit all offset the expenditure on service provision.

Occupational Health Support

3.425   Both HSE and local authorities welcome the opportunity to work proactively with employers and employees. It is far more cost-effective to co-operate to prevent ill health.

3.426   In practice, what most employers seek is sector-specific guidance on practical measures to reduce employee exposure to health hazards and ways of helping employees with health problems to continue working. They also need information they can give their employees about ways to keep healthy. The HSE and local authorities are well placed to provide this guidance.

3.427   Appropriate and relevant advice and guidance may also be obtained from:

- technicians
- engineers
- suppliers of goods, materials and equipment

- trade associations
- trade unions, including safety representatives
- professional bodies, eg Institution of Occupational Safety and Health (IOSH).

3.428 Material safety data sheets provide written information on the health hazards associated with the use of a particular material or substance. Manufacturers' brochures and handbooks also provide information on the safe use of supplied goods. Local business forums, Business Links and other local business development agencies offer employers informal support, advice and information from colleagues on managing occupational health issues at work. Local authority enforcing officers, eg environmental health officers, are also important sources of free advice and support for employers.

3.429 The HSE is a valuable and free source of advice for companies seeking occupational health support, providing a wide range of leaflets and guidance for employers on the identification and management of occupational health risks within the workplace. HSE personnel, such as inspectors, employment medical advisors and employment nursing advisors, actively encourage employers to use their expertise proactively rather than wait for disaster to overtake them.

3.430 Many businesses neither need nor can easily afford full-time on-site occupational health services, and the trend is for commercial occupational health service providers to offer a variety of services that include on-site work and remote support provided by telephone, e-mail, fax, etc.

Occupational Health Qualifications

3.431 Doctors and nurses with specialist professional qualifications in occupational health provide most occupational health services. Some services are led by other health professionals, eg ergonomists and therapists. The key issue for any employer considering employing an occupational health service provider is to establish the professional qualifications of the provider.

3.432 Most general practitioners (GPs) have no experience, training or qualifications in occupational health and are not best placed to give occupational health advice or provide occupational health services. There are, however, several training courses available including the following.

- Diploma in Occupational Medicine — an entry-level examined course intended for GPs or those exploring an interest in occupational health to provide insight into the discipline.
- AFOM — Associate of the Faculty of Occupational Medicine — denotes successful completion of a registered training course for doctors intending to work in occupational health.
- MFOM — Member of the Faculty of Occupational Medicine, which is an AFOM plus a dissertation/thesis — those with the MFOM accreditation are entitled to have their names included on the Specialist Register of the General Medical Council.

3.433 A proportion of nurses with occupational health qualifications will hold a Certificate in Occupational Health Nursing. This basic course has been superseded by diploma and degree courses, with most of those recently qualified in occupational health nursing holding a bachelor's degree. Depending on the university, the degree may be a BSc or a BA with occupational health in the expanded title.

Identifying and Commissioning an Occupational Health Service Provider

3.434 The HSE website and local offices can provide companies with the names of occupational health service providers, but it is up to the employer to choose the provider. Searching the Internet under the term "occupational health services" or "occupational health provider" will give employers lists of both large and small providers to choose from.

3.435　National occupational health providers will have staff in locations across the country, and are well placed to provide services to companies in one location or with several locations. Small or single-handed service providers may only be able to operate within a local geographical area.

3.436　All reputable occupational health companies will offer to visit a company free of charge and discuss what services might be appropriate before providing a formal proposal for the provision of services. They will treat information shared about occupational hazards and risks in confidence, and are highly likely to want to include a short tour of the premises in their visit so they can make an assessment of the likely, or known, occupational health risks.

3.437　It is reasonable for an employer to commission an occupational health provider to undertake an audit or detailed occupational health risk assessment separate from a contract to provide services. Most occupational health providers will recommend an assessment as part of their proposal, unless there is good reason to believe that the assessment has recently been done to such a professional standard that no further assessment is required. The employer requires the provider to give the best possible advice regarding effective risk reduction and control.

3.438　The provider will want to undertake the assessment to ensure they are giving the employer appropriate, defendable professional advice. The audit or occupational health risk assessment will also identify the priorities for service provision. This will assist the employer in the allocation of funds for the service, therefore demonstrating a commitment to effective risk management.

3.439　Contracts for occupational health services are commonly let for one year, with the option to extend for a further period of one or more years. Larger organisations may put out formal tenders for services — many organisations simply request proposals, followed by presentations from short-listed suppliers. Some agreed form of service monitoring should be implemented as part of the set-up process, eg monthly reporting of activity or quarterly audit against agreed service specification or standards.

Key Elements of Occupational Health Service Provision

3.440　The exact services provided will depend on the:

- health risks
- number of personnel involved
- nature of the business.

3.441　Key elements of occupational health service provision can include the following.

Pre-employment Screening

3.442　Pre-employment screening includes the vetting, by an appropriately qualified person, of a completed health questionnaire. The purpose is to establish, so far as is possible, that the person is fit for the job they are applying for and have no health conditions that might be worsened by the work.

3.443　The questionnaire will normally be tailored to reflect the occupational hazards and risks within the business. Vetting commonly takes place at the provider's offices rather than requiring the company to cover the cost of having the nurse on-site to review completed forms.

Pre-employment Examination

3.444   Pre-employment examinations, by a nurse or doctor, of prospective employees are normally only undertaken when there is a health condition noted on the questionnaire that requires further investigation or where the occupational health hazards are such that only by examination can fitness for work be established. Pre-employment examinations usually take place on-site or may, in some cases, take place at the provider's offices.

On-employment Examination

3.445   Health examinations, by a nurse or doctor, of new employees are required when health surveillance is needed following the occupational health risk assessment. The examinations provide baseline data, eg hearing tests or lung function tests, against which future health surveillance records are assessed. On-employment examinations almost invariably take place on work premises.

Periodic Health Surveillance

3.446   Periodic health surveillance includes specific tests by a nurse, doctor or technician for employees exposed to specific health hazards for which surveillance is required. Examples include:
- mill workers having regular lung function tests due to the risk of developing occupational asthma
- chemical workers having skin assessments due to the risk of occupational dermatitis.

3.447   Periodic health surveillance almost always takes place on work premises to minimise downtime from work.

Workplace Risk Assessments

3.448   Workplace risk assessments, either for an individual or group, undertaken by an occupational health specialist may be in response to:
- a particular individual risk, eg very tall or very short employees
- an employee with a health condition, eg back pain
- a change in the process requiring a detailed occupational health risk assessment for a group of employees.

Absence Management

3.449   Absence management assists the employer to manage an individual with either multiple short-term absences or a single long-term absence from work. The occupational health provider obtains and interprets medical information, advising both employer and employee on the impact of health on work, and on modifications to assist return to work or improved attendance. Long-term absences can often be managed from the occupational health provider's offices with attendance on-site for a workplace risk assessment or return to work assessment.

Health Assessment

3.450   Health assessments include screenings of well employees and providing advice on maintaining health in general and in relation to work. Health assessments may, in some cases, include vaccinations for employees exposed to particular health hazards.

Training

3.451 An occupational health provider can provide training for managers and employees on health issues. Training sessions can range from short toolbox talks to half-day or day seminars and can cover:

- stress management
- safe manual handling
- correct wearing of personal protective equipment
- first aid.

Employee Assistance and Counselling Programmes

3.452 Employee assistance and counselling programmes can include telephone helplines and one-to-one counselling support for employees needing help to cope with pressures, stress or other demands. Telephone helplines are normally freephone numbers or low cost. One-to-one counselling is normally arranged with a local counsellor at their premises.

Manager's Helpline

3.453 Most providers offer a telephone advice service or helpline for employers as part of a service package, particularly if there is not a daily on-site presence. This provides managers with rapid access to specialist advice on any occupational health matter and support in dealing with health-related issues at local level.

Reports

3.454 All providers should deliver regular reports to the employer on service activity. Often these reports are provided on a monthly or quarterly basis, alongside invoices. Employers should also encourage the provider to give additional information, eg trend analysis or perceptions of areas of increased or additional occupational health risk, and be willing to act on it.

Confidentiality and Occupational Health

3.455 Medical information is deemed to be confidential to the individual and their medical advisor, and employers do not have an automatic right to know an employee's medical diagnosis or treatment regime.

3.456 In many cases, an employee will volunteer the information to their manager or the diagnosis will be written on the sick note provided by the GP, but employers do not have the right to see any medical information about an employee. The Employment Practices Data Protection Code covers information about workers' health, and sets out in what circumstances and by whom health information can be accessed under the Data Protection Act 1998.

3.457 In essence, no one who is not a healthcare professional, or working to the standards of confidentiality required by the healthcare professional codes of conduct, has the right to see employees' medical information, including:

- health questionnaires
- health records
- occupational health records

- GP or other medical reports.

3.458   Information about an employee gathered under health and safety legislation, and specifically under the Control of Substances Hazardous to Health Regulations 2002 (COSHH) has to be held in such a way that the employer has a record of the surveillance and its outcomes and recommendations, but not confidential medical information.

3.459   Occupational health providers are aware of the confidentiality of medical information, but are equally aware of their professional requirement to provide information that helps managers do their job.

3.460   All occupational health reports and recommendations should clearly spell out:

- if there is a medical condition affecting the individual's ability to do their job
- the impact the condition has on their ability to do their job, eg they cannot climb stairs but they can walk for 50m on the flat; they are unsafe to work alone but can be expected to perform to normal standards at their desk-based job; or they have a progressive condition but are capable of certain tasks, etc
- the length of likely incapacity or the need for further treatment and how performance is likely to be affected
- what modifications to their job are recommended as a consequence of the medical condition and how long these are likely to be needed
- whether the condition is permanent or temporary, and whether the employee would be regarded as having a disability under the Disability Discrimination Act 1995
- whether the individual satisfies the criteria for termination of employment or ill health retirement on the grounds of incapacity.

Co-operation and Occupational Health

3.461   There is always some overlap between safety and occupational health, eg both may undertake risk assessments, but they are separate disciplines with a professional expectation that they will work co-operatively for the benefit of the employer and employees.

3.462   In larger organisations, the safety and occupational health functions often share the same reporting structure. In some organisations, the safety function will report through operational management and the occupational health function through human resources. The important requirement is that the two functions work together with line management and the human resource function to address health and safety across the organisation.

3.463   Like safety management, occupational health is an advisory function. The occupational health providers advise management on safe working practices or appropriate surveillance programmes and they recommend actions, but they do not have executive authority within the company. It is the task of managers to manage and to implement or reject the recommendations of occupational health professionals. Managers always have the option to reject advice, but it is rare for a provider to make a recommendation without considering the impact on the business and consulting with all parties to reach workable solutions.

Training

3.464   Line managers and supervisors should have sufficient training and instruction to be competent to carry out risk assessment and to identify occupational health hazards. Employees must be provided with the necessary information, instruction and training to enable them to co-operate in reducing the risk to their health.

3.465 The National Examination Board in Occupational Safety and Health (NEBOSH) offers certificate and diploma courses at a large number of centres nationwide. The IOSH offers a wide range of occupational health and safety training. Open courses attract delegates from a range of organisations. In-house courses mean that material can be tailored to the occupational hazards and risks within the organisation.

3.466 Many occupational health providers will develop and deliver specific training programmes for employees. These may include training a few employees in, for example, skin examination, so they can undertake frequent skin surveillance of employees rather than leave the assessment for an annual health surveillance check, by which time the employee might have a serious health problem.

List of Relevant Legislation

3.467
- Control of Noise at Work Regulations 2005
- Control of Vibration at Work Regulations 2005
- Disability Discrimination Act 1995 (Amendment) Regulations 2003
- Control of Substances Hazardous to Health Regulations 2002
- Management of Health and Safety at Work Regulations 1999
- Data Protection Act 1998
- Disability Discrimination Act 1995
- Manual Handling Operations Regulations 1992
- Health and Safety at Work, etc Act 1974

Further Information

Publications

HSE Publications

The following is available from *www.hsebooks.co.uk*.
- HSG65 (rev 1997) *Successful Health and Safety Management*

Other Publications
- *Occupational Hygiene*, Croner Publications
- *Management of Health Risks*, Croner Publications

Organisations

- British Occupational Hygiene Society (BOHS)
  Web: *www.bohs.org*
  The BOHS seeks to promote and protect occupational and environmental health and hygiene and offers training in occupational hygiene and related subjects.
- National Examination Board in Occupational Safety and Health (NEBOSH)
  Web: *www.nebosh.org.uk*
  Founded in 1979, NEBOSH is an independent awarding body.
- Institution of Occupational Safety and Health (IOSH)
  Web: *www.iosh.co.uk*
  IOSH is Europe's leading body for health and safety professionals and provides guidance on health and safety issues.
- Trades Union Congress (TUC)
  Web: *www.tuc.org.uk*
  The TUC describes itself as "the voice of Britain at work". With 71 affiliated unions representing nearly 7 million working people from all walks of life, it campaigns for a fair deal at work and for social justice at home and abroad.
- Chartered Institute of Personnel and Development (CIPD)
  Web: *www.cipd.org.uk*
  The CIPD is a professional body for those involved in the management and development of people.

Chapter 4

Contingency Planning

Emergency Planning

- How an organisation responds to an emergency will hold sway with a jury that is deciding whether or not a gross management failing has taken place.
- The Corporate Manslaughter and Corporate Homicide Act 2007 (the Act) does not impose a duty of care on the emergency services to the victim when they are responding to a life-threatening incident.
- The King's Cross Underground station fire, the capsizing of the Herald of Free Enterprise at Zeebrugge and the fire on the Piper Alpha North Sea platform illustrate how emergency procedures have been found wanting during fatal incidents.
- If an organisation's emergency procedures are good enough to prevent an incident becoming a fatality, the company cannot be prosecuted under the Act.
- For the vast majority of businesses, their emergency procedures need mainly to address fire precautions and first aid.
- Planning for emergencies should encompass a wide range of potential accidents, incidents and scenarios.
- Identifying hazards in the workplace is vital to implementing successful emergency procedures.
- Specific hazards will need specific procedures in place in the event of an emergency.
- Chemical hazards are covered by specific legislation.
- Planning should encompass consideration of the necessary internal and external resources needed.
- All emergency procedures should be integrated into an overall emergency plan.
- Emergency planning should consider the aftermath of an emergency, eg measures to achieve a swift return to normal working.
- Once the plan has been prepared, it is vital to inform and train staff who may be on the premises.

4.1 The lack of suitable emergency plans has frequently caused companies loss of competent staff and/or damage to property with costs of restitution. In addition to the threat of prosecution for corporate manslaughter, the disruption caused is likely to impact on productivity and profitability and any adverse publicity may also have a negative effect.

Employers' Duties

Corporate Manslaughter and Corporate Homicide Act 2007

4.2 The Corporate Manslaughter and Corporate Homicide Act 2007 (the Act) places senior managers and organisations at risk of prosecution if their gross management failings lead to the death of an employee or a member of the public to whom a duty of care is owed. The legislation states that there has to be a relevant duty of care owed by the organisation in the law of negligence to the deceased and a gross breach of that relevant duty of care leading to that person's death.

4.3   When considering whether or not a gross breach has taken place, the Act requires juries to consider, among other matters:

- failure to comply with any relevant health and safety legislation and, where this occurs, the seriousness of the failure and the risk of death it posed
- attitudes, policies, systems or accepted practices likely to have encouraged the failure to comply with the relevant health and safety legislation, or led to a tolerance of this failure
- any relevant health and safety guidance
- any other matters they consider relevant.

4.4   Therefore, how an organisation prepares for an emergency can directly impact on how liable it is under the Act.

Specific Health and Safety Legislation

4.5   The Health and Safety at Work, etc Act 1974 (HSWA) requires employers to ensure "so far as is reasonably practicable" the health, safety and welfare of their employees and other persons who may be affected by their work. This includes sub-contractors and the general public.

4.6   Under the Management of Health and Safety at Work Regulations 1999 (MHSWR), employers must:

- undertake suitable and sufficient assessments of the risks to employees and non-employees
- implement procedures for serious and imminent danger and for danger areas
- establish and implement procedures
- nominate competent persons to implement evacuation procedures (eg fire marshals)
- liaise with external services for first aid, emergency medical care and rescue work.

4.7   Under the Regulatory Reform (Fire Safety) Order 2005, employers must:

- carry out a fire risk assessment identifying possible dangers and risks
- consider who may be especially at risk
- eliminate or reduce the risk from fire as far as is reasonably possible and provide general fire precautions (including fire detection and fire alarms, if appropriate) to deal with any possible risk left
- take other measures to make sure there is protection if flammable or explosive materials are used or stored
- create a plan to deal with any emergency and, in most cases, keep a record of the findings
- review the findings when necessary.

4.8   Under the Health and Safety (First Aid) Regulations 1981, employers must:

- provide equipment and facilities for enabling first aid to be rendered to employees; in most workplaces, this includes provision of trained first aiders
- inform employees of the arrangements that have been made.

4.9   The Control of Major Accident Hazards Regulations 1999 (COMAH) require that operators "take all measures necessary to prevent major accidents and limit their consequences to persons and the environment".

Employees' Duties

4.10   The HSWA states that employees must take reasonable care for the safety of themselves and of other persons who may be affected by their acts or omissions. They should co-operate with their employers and others in carrying out their statutory obligations. There are no specific duties on employees in respect of emergency planning.

4.11   Self-employed persons should provide appropriate equipment to render first aid to themselves while at work.

In Practice

Reasons for Emergency Preparedness

4.12   The Corporate Manslaughter and Corporate Homicide Act 2007 (the Act) places senior managers and organisations at risk of prosecution if their gross management failings lead to the death of an employee or a member of the public to whom a duty of care is owed. The legislation states that there has to be a relevant duty of care owed by the organisation in the law of negligence to the deceased and a gross breach of that relevant duty of care leading to that person's death.

4.13   When considering whether or not a gross breach has taken place, the Act requires juries to consider, among other matters:

* failure to comply with any relevant health and safety legislation and, where this occurs, the seriousness of the failure and the risk of death it posed
* attitudes, policies, systems or accepted practices likely to have encouraged the failure to comply with the relevant health and safety legislation, or led to a tolerance of this failure
* any relevant health and safety guidance
* any other matters they consider relevant.

4.14   Therefore, how an organisation responds to an emergency will hold sway with a jury when deciding whether or not a gross management failing has taken place.

4.15   As with most occupational health and safety matters, the reasons for taking action are combinations of both financial and moral factors, together with statutory duties. Planning for emergencies and training staff in the implementation of a plan and procedures will:

* reduce the time taken to respond to an incident
* assist the organisation in meeting its legal and moral responsibilities
* enable rapid recovery from any incident and assist with business continuity
* help mitigate any losses such as lost business, insurance premium increases, damage to property and goods, etc
* reduce exposure to liability, both criminal and civil
* improve the public image of the organisation.

Ambit of the Legislation

Emergency Services and the Act

4.16   Section 6 of the Act does not impose a duty of care on the emergency services to the victim when they are responding to a life-threatening incident. For example, if someone is trapped in a building by a fire and the response of the fire and rescue authority fails to save the person, that incident lies outside the scope of this legislation. Rescue operations involving NHS personnel, the coastguard and the Royal National Lifeboat Institution are similarly exempted.

4.17   However, if the fire engine responding to an incident had not been adequately maintained, and was shown to have caused the vehicle to be involved in a road traffic accident killing one of the crew, then a charge of corporate manslaughter might be brought against the fire authority.

4.18   As the implementation date of most provisions of the Act was 6 April 2008, it cannot be used in the case of the deaths of four part-time firefighters in a warehouse fire in Warwickshire in 2007, where questions were raised about the wisdom of the decision to send the men into the building.

4.19   While matters relating to the organisation and management of medical services fall within the scope of the Act, the eventual interpretation of this by the courts is difficult to predict.

Examples of Poor Contingency Planning

4.20   The King's Cross Underground station fire, the capsizing of the Herald of Free Enterprise at Zeebrugge, and the fire on the Piper Alpha North Sea platform are all cases where better emergency response could have, to some extent, mitigated the death toll.

4.21   While the initiating events, and the responsibility for them, were probably of greater significance, the purpose of contingency planning is to recognise that sometimes things go wrong (for whatever reason) and to put in place procedures to minimise the chance of fatalities.

4.22   The following examples illustrate how emergency procedures have been found wanting during fatal incidents. The emergencies have all arisen due to shortcomings in the management of the companies' normal activities, although deficiencies in their emergency procedures have also been identified.

King's Cross Underground Station Fire

4.23   At King's Cross, the probable cause of the fire was a discarded cigarette falling onto detritus that had accumulated under an escalator. In response to this, smoking on the Underground was banned (long before the smoking ban was introduced for health reasons in all public buildings) and a programme of improvements to escalators at many stations was also carried out.

4.24   The official report on the incident also found many deficiencies in the emergency procedures. A fire was a foreseeable occurrence (in fact there had been several), and adequate plans should have been developed to evacuate passengers safely. This, in particular, needed trained staff to implement.

4.25   In total there were 157 recommendations, which included the following.
- Station instructions for emergencies and closure must be agreed with the London Fire Brigade and used in training station staff.
- Fire hydrants and cabinets must be marked with outrigger signs.

- A rendezvous point for the emergency services and a staff assembly point must be agreed and marked.
- Station evacuation plans should include evacuation by train.
- Water fog equipment must be regularly tested and staff trained in its use.
- In agreement with the London Fire Brigade, London Underground shall produce and maintain up-to-date station plans and place them in boxes it has provided at locations agreed or specified by the London Fire Brigade.
- Every two years, all management and supervisory staff shall receive refresher training in controlling station emergencies and the use of fire and communications equipment.
- Every six months, fire and safety training must be provided for non-supervisory staff and booking clerks. Staff must be given site familiarisation training before they are permitted to take part in the running of the station.
- Instructions to the staff as to the calling of the fire brigade shall be re-drafted in plain English.

4.26   There were many shortcomings in emergency preparedness. Under legislation current at the time, a "controlling mind" had to be identified for a charge of manslaughter to be brought. However, the complications of a large organisation meant that this was impossible. Under the Act, this will not be necessary and the organisation rather than an individual could be prosecuted.

Herald of Free Enterprise

4.27   In the case of the Herald of Free Enterprise, there was a huge death toll despite the fact that the ship capsized within sight of the harbour and lay on her side rather than sinking. The disaster was caused by the ship sailing with the bow doors open, and the reasons behind this would have been sufficient for a charge of corporate manslaughter had the Act been in place at the time.

4.28   Plans for abandoning ship should have been in place and rehearsed. Further, while their total effectiveness cannot be guaranteed, particularly in bad weather, the official report stated that not a single lifeboat was launched on the night of the disaster.

4.29   The scale of the tragedy was due to rapid capsizing as soon as the sea flooded onto the car deck and this was a consequence of the ship's design. This flaw had never been properly considered, and even the best evacuation plans would have been severely tested under these circumstances.

Piper Alpha Platform

4.30   A report by Lord Cullen investigating the Piper Alpha platform fire concluded that the immediate cause of the fire was a leakage of flammable gas, and this was as a result of major failures in the design and operation of safety systems. The automatic deluge system had been deactivated and no message was given over the public address system.

4.31   The limitations of the emergency plans may also owe much to the design of the rig rather than their execution, with men trapped in the accommodation block. The Cullen report drew attention to basic failures to show all newcomers the location of their lifeboats, and that evacuation drills and exercises were not carried out with the required frequency or in the required way.

Industrial Accidents

4.32   There are various Health and Safety Executive (HSE) reports on a number of industrial accidents in the chemical industry indicating shortcomings in emergency arrangements.

4.33   An explosion causing fatalities occurred at the site of Hickson and Welsh in Castleford, killing four workers in the control room. A fifth victim was a young office worker. The incident occurred at lunchtime when it was unclear which members of staff had left the site. There was a delay before it became known to the emergency services precisely where to search for the fifth person, who, when located, had been overcome by smoke. The smoke had spread above a false ceiling and through breaches in the fire-resisting construction. She died later in hospital.

4.34   One of the "lessons" identified in the report produced by the HSE states: "When exercising their on-site emergency plans, companies should ensure that roll call information on missing persons is passed immediately, accurately and directly to the senior fire officer in charge. Roll call procedures should be practised routinely to ensure that they are effective when carried out at all periods of the working day."

4.35   The company was convicted of an offence under the HSWA.

Developing Emergency Procedures under the Act

4.36   No matter what regulations have been contravened leading to an incident, if an organisation's emergency procedures are good enough to prevent an incident becoming a fatality, the company cannot be prosecuted under the Act.

4.37   If a fatality does occur, the organisation's procedures will be put under the microscope, and any positives might just swing the balance when the decision on whether to prosecute under this Act (or alternatively under some less serious regulation) is made.

Management of Health and Safety at Work Regulations

4.38   The general requirement for emergency procedures is found in the MHSWR. Regulation 8, which concerns procedures for serious and imminent danger and for danger areas, requires employers to establish and implement procedures and to nominate competent persons to implement evacuation procedures (eg fire marshals).

4.39   Regulation 9 requires employers to liaise with external services for first aid, emergency medical care and rescue work. The accompanying Approved Code of Practice (ACOP) indicates the content of the procedures including:
- the nature of the risk and how to respond to it
- the additional responsibilities of any employees who have specific tasks to perform in the event of an emergency
- the role, responsibilities and authority of the competent people nominated to implement the detailed actions
- any requirements laid on employers by health and safety regulations covering specific emergency situations
- details of when and how the procedures are to be activated so that employees can proceed in good time to a place of safety.

Developing an Emergency Plan

4.40   In the smallest organisations, the emergency plan can be very simple and prepared internally, using common sense with observations of what is done elsewhere, readily available advice from various organisations and perhaps some basic health and safety training.

4.41 In high-risk organisations, the planning may require expert consultants, and liaison with not only emergency services but also neighbours. Even so, simplicity and user-friendliness should be retained; in an emergency nobody has time to study complex procedures.

4.42 Consideration must be given to setting up a control centre, and to who will take charge — including during shift work when senior management must first be called from home. Equipment may be needed, not only for fire fighting, but also for protecting people and the environment.

4.43 The stages in developing emergency plans are as follows.

- Carry out a risk assessment to identify threats.
- Develop a general strategy allowing for what resources can be made available.
- Prepare specific procedures for principal scenarios.
- Co-ordinate procedures into a common framework that will be adaptable to all situations.
- Validate and test the plans.
- Review and revise the plans.

4.44 When developing emergency plans, several principles should be kept in mind. Namely, the plan should:

- respond to the incident and not the cause of the incident
- be integrated into the organisational structure and management systems
- be flexible to handle any incident
- include co-operation and co-ordination with other organisations and agencies
- identify and provide the necessary resources to ensure recovery and give an estimate of recovery time
- take account of the core and critical functions required to ensure recovery
- have the support of senior management.

Risk Assessment

4.45 The range of events that may be taken into account by contingency planning is vast. The starting point for any planning process will be the risk assessment, to determine the most foreseeable and likely events that may threaten the organisation. Risk assessment will certainly aid in the planning process.

4.46 Anticipating the effect of emergencies on an organisation and devising a response may also include other risk management techniques, eg:

- impact analysis to estimate the costs to the organisation
- a vulnerability study to determine the parts of the organisation that are most vulnerable to disaster
- a threat scenario to assess the type of contingency most likely to affect the organisation.

4.47 Procedures should be developed to deal with a full range of scenarios, but they should focus on those scenarios that are assessed to be of the highest risk.

Identifying Hazards

4.48 The first stage of any risk assessment is the identification of hazards. In the case of emergency planning, this is often expressed in terms of an analysis of threats.

Factors which lead to an incident might be internal or external. The table below, *Emergency Threats*, lists some possible hazards and causes.

Emergency Threats

Scenario	Internal Cause	External Cause
Fire	Faulty electrical equipment	Lightning strike
Flood	Overflow of tank	Heavy rain
Chemical pollution	Contamination by leakage of liquid chemical from storage tank	Toxic chemical gas cloud from adjoining premises
Militant action	Industrial action by employees	Protest action by pressure group
Disease	Legionella bacteria in water system	Introduced by livestock

4.49 The response to a scenario might well be the same, irrespective of whether the causative factor is internal or external. However, to avoid having to make the responses in the first place, emergency planners should always consider whether everything possible has been done to prevent the incident happening. For example, while procedures will be necessary in case of fire, adequate maintenance procedures of electrical equipment and lightning conductors should be in place to reduce the likelihood of fire.

Risk Management

4.50 When risks have been assessed there will be choices to be made as to the management strategy to deal with them. Insurance will play a large part in the plans of many organisations, complementing the emergency procedures. Insurance might go beyond cover for property damage and personal injury and incorporate cover for loss of productivity. Some organisations also subscribe to schemes whereby they have an option on a suite of offices to which they can relocate if necessary, or schemes that provide them with alternative IT facilities if their own fail.

Procedures for Principal Scenarios

Business Crises

4.51 For the vast majority of businesses, their emergency procedures need mainly to address fire precautions and first aid. However, emergency planning is not simply about evacuating premises if a fire breaks out.

4.52 The range of scenarios that have affected businesses in recent years include:

- terrorist incidents
- computer viruses
- petrol shortages
- transport accidents
- severe weather causing flooding, power loss, etc
- war
- protests such as public marches and demonstrations
- foot and mouth disease.

4.53 Some of these occurrences fall into what might be described as business crises. Many of the actions needed to recover from them are similar to the actions needed when handling the aftermath of a fire or flood. Workplace emergency planning should focus primarily on emergencies that:

- threaten the safety of employees
- can cause damage to the workplace
- despoil the environment.

4.54   In all cases, plans should deal with restoring normality as well as "putting out the fire".

First Aid

4.55   The Health and Safety (First-aid) Regulations 1981 and accompanying ACOP require that a risk assessment is carried out to determine what first-aid facilities are appropriate in the circumstances.

4.56   Some small premises, especially if near to medical facilities, may need nothing more than an appointed person to take control of the situation if someone needs assistance. Larger premises and high-risk activities are likely to require at least one trained first aider present at all times, including cover for absences, shift-working, etc. Where specific risks are identified, first aiders may need additional training, eg in the use of antidotes for phenol or hydrogen fluoride contamination.

4.57   On the basis of this, the appropriate resources should be provided. Selected personnel should be trained and first-aid boxes (as a minimum measure) provided. Locations of first-aid boxes should be clearly marked. All employees must be informed of the arrangements made.

4.58   All incidents and illnesses requiring first-aid treatment should be recorded in a book, indicating:

- the date, time and place of the incident
- the name of the person treated
- the work being undertaken by the victim at the time of injury
- the nature of the injury
- the treatment applied
- whether the person returned to work/was sent home/was sent to hospital/was advised to consult a doctor
- the name and signature of the first aider.

4.59   This record might be combined with the record to be kept in the statutory accident book. Procedures should make clear how it is made known which first aiders are on duty and how they can be contacted.

Fire Procedures

4.60   Since the introduction of the Regulatory Reform (Fire Safety) Order 2005, there is a responsibility on employers to undertake a fire risk assessment. For some higher-risk premises, this was previously done with the assistance of the fire authority. The fire risk assessment is a good basis for reviewing or preparing emergency procedures.

4.61   The basic elements of a fire evacuation procedure are as follows.

- In larger premises the means of raising alarm will be by an installed system, perhaps triggered by smoke or heat detectors or manually activated. In some workplaces, this will include a warning system for deaf and hard of hearing persons. In smaller organisations, the alarm might be raised by shouting a warning or using a horn on a canister of compressed air.

- The fire brigade must be contacted. Some alarm systems will do this automatically, otherwise procedures must specify who is responsible for this action.
- Only persons who have been trained in the use of hand-held fire extinguishers should attempt to tackle the fire and even then only if the fire is small and safe to tackle.
- All employees, contractors and visitors should leave the premises by designated escape routes, without using lifts, turnstiles or revolving doors. These persons may be helped by the fire wardens and may be asked to assist in the evacuation of disabled people.
- Industrial processes might need to be shut down if it is possible to do so without jeopardising personal safety. Such actions should be stipulated in procedures and covered in training.
- Nobody should stop to collect personal belongings.
- Windows and doors should be closed. In particular, fire doors delay the spread of smoke and fire and are vital for maintaining a safe means of escape from the building.
- Employees and contractors should quickly make their way to their designated assembly points for registration. The procedures should define how registration is to be carried out and by whom. There should be a list against which to check names. It will be possible to account for visitors in premises where visitors have been signed in, however, in buildings to which the public has free access, reliance for this must be placed on checking by fire wardens and the searching of the building by the fire brigade.
- Details of any missing persons should be reported to the employer and to the fire brigade.
- If an incident is likely to be protracted, evacuees should be allowed to go to an alternative building and consideration should be given to their personal needs.
- Re-entry to the premises should only take place when authorised.

Bomb Threats

4.62   The increase in terrorism in recent years has dictated that most organisations now require procedures to deal with the possibility of explosive devices being planted on their premises, or of packages being delivered that contain explosive devices or chemical/biological agents.

4.63   If a telephone call is received indicating that a bomb has been planted, every effort should be made to obtain as much information as possible for a decision to be made on what action to take. A standard form should be circulated to anyone who receives outside calls to their workstation, indicating how to proceed.

4.64   Any such call should be immediately reported to the police. How the police respond will depend on a number of factors, such as the current level of alert and the type of premises involved. It should not be expected that, if a building has been evacuated, the police will go in to see whether everything is safe. They will contact the army bomb disposal team if they perceive the risk as high, eg if the warning message contains a pre-notified code word.

4.65   If a telephoned bomb threat is received, there are three options.
1. Evacuate the premises.
2. Search the premises, but only evacuate if something suspicious is found.
3. Do nothing.

Evacuating the Premises

4.66   Immediate evacuation is rarely appropriate unless the location of the device is specified and there is an indication that it will explode imminently. However, if the employer decides that this option is appropriate, the list below suggests a typical sequence of reasonable actions. This list also indicates some differences between bomb threat and fire evacuations.

- The alarm should be sounded. Ideally this should be distinguishable from the fire alarm as different actions are required.
- The police should be informed of the bomb threat.
- All persons should leave the premises, taking their personal belongings with them, eg bags, cases and clothes.
- All doors and windows should be closed for fire evacuations, but should be left open for bomb threat evacuations. Closing the windows restricts the supply of oxygen to the fire, whereas opening them dissipates the blast effect from an explosion.
- Lifts must not be used in fire evacuations but may be used in bomb threat evacuations.
- The safe distances from danger must be greater in the event of bomb threat evacuations than in fire evacuations. The assembly point should be behind another building. It is also possible that refuges (safe havens) within other buildings are designated as an alternative to external assembly points.
- The designated bomb wardens should carry out a search of their zones for any suspect packages and should report as each area is clear. If a suspected item is discovered, the police will notify the bomb disposal team.

Searching the Premises

4.67 One reason for not evacuating a building is that if the location of the explosive device is not known, persons outside the building could be at greater risk than those indoors, eg if there is a car bomb. Furthermore, if the building is evacuated, nobody can search for the bomb, whereas the most effective check is by the regular occupants of the building, as they are most likely to spot something unusual.

4.68 Obtaining co-operation in these circumstances is only likely to be successful if the procedure has been determined in advance with full consultation. Often "bomb wardens" are appointed from willing volunteers.

Taking No Action

4.69 The only justification for doing nothing is if there is very good reason for believing that the bomb threat is a hoax.

Other Suspect Packages

4.70 Warnings are not always given when bombs have been planted by terrorists. Therefore, procedures are required for dealing with any suspect item that is discovered. Abandoned items of luggage at locations such as airports are a frequent source of alerts. Depending on the circumstances, threat level, etc, it might be appropriate to isolate the item whilst an attempt is made to trace its owner rather than evacuate the building immediately.

Mail Rooms

4.71 Mail rooms are a particular concern, being the likely point of entry for packages containing explosive devices or chemical/biological agents. Such devices are usually triggered only on opening the item, so isolating the item is usually the most appropriate initial step. Items should not be immersed in water, as this may well short out an electrical triggering device.

4.72   Organisations perceived as being at high risk will probably acquire some screening equipment and check all incoming mail. Otherwise, staff dealing with mail should be advised to be alert for:

- protruding wires
- grease marks
- a smell similar to marzipan
- heaviness relative to size/uneven weight distribution
- excessive fastening of the package
- packages addressed to a specific person, crudely hand-written
- unfamiliar postmark/no name of sender.

Chemical Incidents

4.73   Companies working with chemicals will need emergency procedures to deal with appropriate scenarios, such as shelter to avoid exposure to escapes of toxic gases. The Control of Substances Hazardous to Health Regulations 2002 (COSHH) set out the requirements for dealing with accidents, incidents and emergencies, expanding on the general requirements in the MHSWR. Similar requirements are also found in the Dangerous Substances and Explosive Atmospheres Regulations 2002, which are concerned with the flammability and explosivity of chemicals and combustible dusts.

4.74   For those companies with inventories exceeding the thresholds in the COMAH, the emergency planning requirements are even more onerous, including, for top-tier sites, an off-site emergency plan prepared by the local emergency planning authority.

4.75   Guidance produced by the HSE for COMAH sites may also prove useful to other companies, as it describes the general issues and topics such as training and testing, initiation and review, in addition to the specific requirements of COMAH.

4.76   In general, procedures for dealing with chemical emergencies need to address the following.

- Appropriate types of fire extinguishants. Most fire brigades have only limited stocks of foam, so companies storing flammable liquids in bulk might need to hold some foam concentrate themselves.
- Availability of containment measures (absorbents, bunds, booms, etc) to protect the environment. This should include containment for water run-off from fire-fighting if it is contaminated with chemicals.
- Air monitoring to determine level of contamination.
- Personal protective equipment (PPE), including respiratory protective equipment, required by responders.
- Means of raising an alert, including whether there is a need for a different sounding alarm from those for fire or bomb threat. For sites with major accident hazard potential, a public warning system might be required to alert the neighbourhood, in which case, residents will need to be informed in advance about the response required.
- Assembly points up-wind of any release of toxic materials, or safe havens within buildings.
- Access to safety data sheets.
- Treatment of affected persons. Local hospitals might need to be advised of the chemicals present and given data on antidotes, etc.
- Inventories and location plans for chemical storage.

4.77   Companies despatching dangerous chemicals will also need to have a procedure for dealing with reports of incidents during transport.

Flooding

4.78   Not all emergency situations are man-made, and flooding (though it can occur from overflowing tanks or burst pipes) is most often a consequence of inclement weather. Naturally, premises in low-lying areas are predominantly those at risk.

4.79   When determining the likelihood of flooding, it is recommended that the history of flooding in the area is researched along with the geographical details of the area. A number of questions can be asked.

- Has the property or surrounding land ever flooded in the past?
- Have neighbouring properties ever flooded?
- Is the property in a floodplain?
- Have flood warnings ever been issued for the area in which the property is located?
- Is the property close to streams, rivers, drainage ditches?
- Are there any major water mains near to or under the premises?
- Is the property in a hollow or low-lying ground?
- Is the property protected by any flood defences?
- Are there issues in relation to groundwater overflow?

4.80   Measures that might be taken to avoid ingress of floodwater include:

- barriers created with sandbags, etc
- sealing gaps around doors and blocking air vents
- preventing backflow from sewers by blocking drains (a sandbag in a toilet is particularly effective).

4.81   Measures to minimise damage include:

- isolating electricity supply (and not restoring it until after it has been checked by an electrician)
- moving items upstairs or to higher ground
- weighting down articles that could float.

Integration of Emergency Procedures

4.82   The procedures required for dealing with various types of incidents should be brought together within an overall emergency plan. This ensures a co-ordinated and effective response irrespective of the nature of an event. A structure for command and control needs to be established. Also, the procedures for various incidents should be made to dovetail with the response of the public emergency services and other organisations that might be involved in the response to an incident. For the plan to be effective, it is important that the organisation knows when and how to implement it.

4.83   To ensure flexibility, criteria should be set to state when implementation needs to take place. It must be remembered that emergencies can occur at any time, not just in working hours and, as such, consideration must be given to who can implement the plan.

4.84   The type of action taken will also be influenced by the amount of time given between warnings and an actual emergency occurring. The correct response to the emergency in the first instance can greatly help to mitigate the long-term consequences of the incident. Planning for possible losses and then having in place procedures to carry out salvage work, damage control and assessing the organisational requirements to ensure recovery are vital.

4.85   The overall emergency plan should designate who has the authority to activate various steps and who from the organisation will have control of the response. It is helpful if tabards are worn by persons taking certain roles so that they are easily recognisable, eg the person delegated to conduct the roll call at the assembly point.

4.86   Larger organisations will have an emergency centre, from where the response will be co-ordinated by the person described in the table below, *Respective Duties of Incident Controllers*, as the "site main controller". This will reduce the burden on the person at the forward control point (the "site incident controller"). The location of the control centre should be chosen to be of low vulnerability.

Respective Duties of Incident Controllers

Site Main Controller:	Site Incident Controller:
• based in emergency control centre • receives situation reports from site incident controller (or nominee) • calls up external resources • activates crisis management procedure • informs company headquarters • contacts relatives of injured persons • issues press statements and information to neighbours • arranges relief of personnel if an incident is protracted. In extreme cases it might be necessary to arrange for some senior staff to be sent home to rest so that they can return later and take over from their colleagues.	• located near scene of incident • assesses situation • orders evacuation • calls up internal resources • keeps control centre informed of situation (probably through a designated nominee) • ensures that casualties are receiving assistance • confirms all personnel are accounted for • liaises with emergency services officers at forward control.

Note:
These lists are not exhaustive and need to be adapted to the requirements of specific organisations.

Importance of Communication

4.87   Good communication is always critical in handling emergencies. This applies to communication at the time of the emergency and to communication beforehand. Consultation should take place with organisations such as the emergency services. It is important that site emergency procedures dovetail with those of external responders. When the fire or ambulance service is called, someone should be designated to intercept them on arrival, brief them and direct them to the appropriate location.

4.88   Emergency procedures should take into account the different levels of staffing that apply during shift work. There should be arrangements for contacting key personnel out of normal working hours.

Consideration of Available Resources

4.89   Good emergency procedures take into account the necessary resources and where these are to be provided.

4.90 Several resources should be made available, as follows.

- Plans of site and buildings showing utility supplies with isolation points, drains, etc.
- Telephones — it might be necessary to have dedicated lines for certain purposes as switchboards can easily become overloaded.
- Other communication equipment.
- Fire-fighting equipment.
- First-aid supplies, stretcher.
- Chair for evacuation of physically disabled persons.
- Chemical containment equipment, eg drain covers, bunds, booms, drums.
- Means to cordon off an area including warning signs.
- PPE, breathing apparatus.
- Equipment for flooding, eg sandbags, pumps.
- Tabards or arms bands for key personnel so they are readily recognised.

When the Emergency is Over

4.91 The emergency plan should include dealing with the aftermath of an incident and may take account of:

- the checks which have to be carried out before a building can be reoccupied
- preservation of evidence
- clean-up, salvage, waste disposal
- stand-down of responders, debriefing
- damage assessment
- information to staff (those present in the workplace, those deployed elsewhere and those off-duty at the time) and safety representatives
- reporting to authorities such as the HSE or Environment Agency
- advising insurers
- counselling of affected persons
- investigation of the incident
- public relations
- environmental restoration.

Is the Emergency Plan Easy to Find and Use?

4.92 Consideration should be given regarding how the plan is to be presented. Though it needs to be comprehensive, the plan should be kept as simple as possible. A contents list will help readers to find the appropriate section quickly. If the plan is only available in electronic format, it might not be accessible in an emergency if the power supply fails. If issued in hard copy, consideration should be given as to how it will be updated. Summaries or checklists for quick reference are useful, eg laminated cards that people can keep in their pockets or can be kept with emergency equipment.

4.93 The plan should incorporate information needed quickly in an emergency, such as telephone numbers for key contacts. These are usually in an appendix that can be easily updated without re-issuing the entire plan.

Information and Training

4.94 Once the plan has been prepared, informing and training staff and others who may come on the premises is vital. Drills and exercises must be conducted, initially to validate the plan and to familiarise everyone with it, but thereafter a regular schedule of tests should be carried out to ensure everything is kept up to date. The incident reports investigating disasters illustrate how often this is lacking.

Training

4.95 All employees should be given sufficient information and be trained in what to do in the event of an emergency. Drills and exercises are useful in this respect to ensure that everyone is familiar with the procedures in place. Many employees and contractors will only require familiarisation with evacuation procedures and first-aid arrangements. They should be informed about these in an induction course. They should participate in a fire drill at least once annually.

4.96 Certain employees might receive specific training (eg as first aiders) in using fire extinguishers, or on how to wear chemical protective suits. The training needs for all responders in the emergency procedures should be analysed and a programme set up that will give them the opportunity to participate in exercises from time to time. These will involve a certain amount of simulation, or perhaps "table-top" exercises. Virtual reality exercises are used for simulating the stressful conditions that can be encountered by senior personnel managing a major incident.

4.97 Training should also be considered for any person who might be required as a spokesperson for the organisation and have to face questions in front of a television camera. Representatives of the local media might be invited to participate in an emergency exercise and carry out a mock interview. Well-run training exercises build the confidence of the participants and develop their teamwork skills.

List of Relevant Legislation

4.98
- Regulatory Reform (Fire Safety) Order 2005
- Control of Substances Hazardous to Health Regulations 2002
- Dangerous Substances and Explosive Atmospheres Regulations 2002
- Control of Major Accident Hazards Regulations 1999
- Management of Health and Safety at Work Regulations 1999
- Health and Safety (First-aid) Regulations 1981
- Corporate Manslaughter and Corporate Homicide Act 2007
- Health and Safety at Work, etc Act 1974

Further Information

Publications

HSE Publications

The following are available from *www.hsebooks.co.uk*.
- HSG191 *Emergency Planning for Major Accidents*

- L5 (rev 2005) *The Control of Substances Hazardous to Health Regulations 2002 (as amended). Approved Code of Practice and Guidance*
- L21 (rev 2000) *Management of Health and Safety at Work. Management of Health and Safety at Work Regulations 1999. Approved Code of Practice and Guidance*
- L74 *First Aid at Work: The Health and Safety (First-aid) Regulations 1981: Approved Code of Practice*
- L138 *Dangerous Substances and Explosive Atmospheres. Approved Code of Practice and Guidance. Dangerous Substances and Explosive Atmospheres Regulations 2002*

Stationery Office Publications

The following is available from *www.tso.co.uk*.
- *Fire Safety — An Employer's Guide*
- *Investigation into the King's Cross Underground Fire*, 1988, D Fennell
- *The Public Inquiry into the Piper Alpha Disaster*, 1990, WD Cullen
- *The Fire at Hickson and Welsh Ltd*, 1994

Other Publications

- *The Contingency Planning Disaster Recovery Guide* is available to view at *www.contingency-planning-disaster-recovery-guide.co.uk*

Organisations

- Centre for Corporate Accountability
  Web: *www.corporateaccountability.org*
  The Centre for Corporate Accountability is a charitable organisation that monitors worker and public safety, and undertakes research and provides advice on law enforcement and corporate criminal accountability.
- Civil Contingencies Secretariat
  Web: *www.ukresilience.info*
  The Civil Contingencies Secretariat supports the Home Secretary and works to build the UK's resilience and ability to manage the consequences of major emergencies.
- Emergency Planning Society
  Web: *www.the-eps.org*
  The Emergency Planning Society is a member-led organisation for professionals dealing with emergency planning and crisis and disaster management.
- Health and Safety Executive (HSE)
  Web: *www.hse.gov.uk*
  The HSE and the Health and Safety Commission are responsible for the regulation of almost all the risks to health and safety arising from work activity in the UK.
- National Chemical Emergency Centre (NCEC)
  Web: *www.the-ncec.com*
  The NCEC provides advice for chemical health and safety compliance and emergencies.
- Society of Industrial Emergency Service Officers (SIESO)
  Web: *www.sieso.org.uk*
  The SIESO provides a forum for sharing ideas, experience and practices for avoiding industrial and commercial accidents and improving the planning and management of responses.

Step-by-step Guide: How to Plan for Emergencies

- Identify all incidents that can give rise to an emergency.
- Consider whether anything can be done to reduce the likelihood of incidents happening or to lessen their effects.
- Consider what internal resources are presently available to respond to incidents.
- Consider what external resources can be called upon to mitigate the effects of incidents.
- Decide what further resources are required and make arrangements for them to be obtained.
- Develop procedures to deal with accidents, incidents and emergencies and also to deal with the consequences of these events. Consult with others involved.
- Validate and test the procedures.
- Provide the necessary information, instruction and training to all personnel who might be affected by the emergency and to those who are required to respond.
- Regularly review and update the procedures.

Employees' Factsheet: Emergency Planning

What you should do if you discover a fire

- Do not attempt to extinguish the fire yourself unless you have received portable fire extinguisher training and are a company fire warden or member of an emergency squad. Even if you are a fire warden, your main duty is to signal the existence of a fire and evacuate, so only tackle the fire if it is small.
- Close windows, if this can be done swiftly and without jeopardising your safe evacuation.
- Leave the area quickly, closing the door.
- Raise the alarm at the earliest possible opportunity by triggering a manual call point.
- You should then follow the emergency evacuation procedures for fire alarms.

What you should do on hearing the fire alarm

- Turn off any electrical equipment that you are using, if this can be done swiftly and without jeopardising your safe evacuation.
- Close windows, if this can be done swiftly and without jeopardising your safe evacuation.
- Do not stop to collect your personal belongings.
- Close doors as you leave your workplace.
- Leave the building by the nearest available fire exit, unless advised otherwise by a company fire warden.
- Do not try to use the lifts, access control gates, escalators or revolving doors to leave the building, but remain in the designated stairwells.

- If you are asked to help with the evacuation of a disabled colleague or visitor by a fire warden, please do so with the minimum of delay.
- You should immediately report to the designated fire assembly point outside the premises and ensure that the fire warden for your work zone registers your presence.
- Do not re-enter the premises unless given permission by a manager.

What you should do on hearing the bomb threat alarm

- Turn off any electrical equipment that you are using, if this can be done swiftly and without jeopardising your safe evacuation.
- Open windows, if this can be done swiftly and without jeopardising your safe evacuation.
- Collect your personal belongings, particularly cases, bags and coats, with a minimum of delay. The company bomb wardens will search all work zones and they will not want to be delayed by suspicious packages.
- Leave open all doors as you leave your workplace.
- Do not use your mobile phone or text communicator during the evacuation, as this could trigger an explosive device immediately.
- Leave the building by the nearest available fire exit, unless advised otherwise by a company fire warden.
- Do not try to use the access control gates, escalators or revolving doors to leave the building, but remain in the designated stairwells. The company may continue to operate one lift to assist with the evacuation of disabled or elderly persons.
- If you are asked by a fire warden to help with the evacuation of a disabled colleague, please do so with the minimum of delay.
- Report to the designated bomb threat assembly point outside the premises and ensure that the fire warden for your work zone has registered your presence.
- Do not re-enter the premises unless given permission by a manager.

Crisis Management

- Following a serious incident, an appropriate response often amounts to common sense and the need to prepare in advance for what might happen.
- Dealing with any tragedy or similar crisis is essentially a matter of following the rules of crisis management, which should be linked to an emergency preparedness plan. This, in turn, should be closely aligned to any business continuity plan.
- Any organisation should maintain and regularly review its business continuity management (BCM) policy, strategies, plans and solutions on a regular basis, in line with the risks it faces and the probable consequences that might follow any crisis.
- An exercise programme rehearsing what to do before an incident occurs should form a part of business continuity management.
- In any crisis situation there has to be a simple and quickly formed structure to confirm what has just happened, control the immediate and post response, contain the spread of physical damage and to communicate events to all stakeholders.
- People not forming the core of any crisis management team should not feel obliged to communicate if they have nothing direct to contribute, or feel left out if their opinion is not sought immediately after the incident.
- Not giving enough due diligence to emotional well-being can result in health and attendance being gravely affected, morale plummeting, an increase in the number of accidents, and a decrease in productivity and performance.
- Reporting accidents and ill health at work is a legal requirement.
- When talking to the press following a fatal accident, supply reporters with a holding statement that expresses sympathy, understanding and a willingness to support any Health and Safety Executive enquiry.
- Employees should have sufficient information and training to be able to deal with the consequences of a tragedy.

4.99   Following a serious incident, an appropriate response often amounts to common sense and the need to prepare in advance for what might happen. This does not just apply to sudden events in factories, farms or warehouses; 6000 people die each year in the UK from work-related cancers alone.

4.100   For instance, consider the following selected cases that occurred in London within just 12 months during 2006.

- Cheryl Moss, a nurse, died when she was stabbed 72 times while she took a cigarette break behind St George's Hospital in Hornchurch, East London.
- Roger Gill fell from a stepladder and died, while repairing a door in the Bank of England.
- Anastasis Poumburis was fatally injured when he fell while cutting down trees at a community centre.
- Peter Juszczyz, a Polish labourer, drowned when he fell into a trench full of water. He was employed by the householder.
- Ferdinand De la Cruz was crushed to death by a tenpin bowling machine he was trying to clean.
- Andrew McGoldrick died after being electrocuted when plugging in his guitar before a pub gig on a Saturday night.
- John Cloke, a crane operator from Guildford, died when his 165ft crane collapsed onto a block of flats.

4.101   In addition to being part of an effective health and safety management system, it makes sense to know how to cope with the consequences and people affected should a tragedy occur in the workplace.

Employers' Duties

4.102 The Health and Safety at Work, etc Act 1974 (HSWA) requires employers to ensure "so far as is reasonably practicable" the health, safety and welfare of their employees and other persons who may be affected by their work. This includes sub-contractors and the general public.

4.103 The Reporting of Injuries, Diseases and Dangerous Occurrences Regulations 1995 (RIDDOR) require the specified responsible person, usually an employer, to report certain defined work-related events to the enforcing authority. The enforcing authority will either be the Health and Safety Executive (HSE) or the local authority. Accidents or incidents to be reported include:

- all fatalities
- accidents resulting in any of the specified major injuries
- certain defined, work-related diseases
- accidents resulting in employees being absent from work for more than three days
- certain dangerous occurrences, such as when a building collapses or a gas explosion occurs.

Employees' Duties

4.104 The HSWA states that employees must take reasonable care for the safety of themselves and of other persons who may be affected by their acts or omissions. They should co-operate with their employers and others in carrying out their statutory obligations.

In Practice

4.105 Every year in the UK there are about 180 fatal industrial accidents to employees, 60 to self-employed workers and 400 to members of the public. The chances of a workplace fatality occurring is not as remote as might be thought.

4.106 Consider being called to a serious accident in the workplace where a new member of staff was badly hurt while operating a heavy machine. His fellow workers did what they could to apply first aid to serious wounds and otherwise comfort him. An ambulance was called, but he was pronounced dead on arrival at the nearby hospital. The police arrived about an hour ago, took statements and sealed off the immediate area where the accident occurred. The HSE is now on the telephone, as are the press, the wife of the deceased employee and a number of important clients.

4.107 While just as traumatised as everyone else, as a board director or senior manager it is crucial to make some very important and sober decisions quickly. The right actions taken now can reduce the number of employees suffering from post-traumatic stress, maintain key operations, minimise disruption to cash flow, reduce the likelihood of prosecution and safeguard the organisation's reputation.

Incidents that Might Result in Distress

4.108   It is not just gruesome industrial accidents that might occur and leave workforces disturbed. Other possibilities that might result in employee distress include the following.

- Suicide.
- A terrorist attack close to work, or en route.
- Medical emergency such as heart attack or stroke.
- Physical fighting or other violence.
- Natural disaster such as severe weather.
- Spousal/partner abuse that spills over to the workplace.
- Attacks by outraged vendors or customers.
- Armed robbery.
- Rape.
- Bullying/harassment.
- Mentally-disordered behaviour from employees or others.
- Chronic fatigue syndrome.
- An event directly caused by drug/alcohol abuse.

Dealing with a Crisis

4.109   Following many serious events, it is sometimes possible to take advantage of the opportunity of increased levels of communication that develop immediately following a crisis to help develop a unified team and solidify relationships. Over the long term, ongoing improvements in company-wide communication will help to decrease the possibility of post-traumatic stress interfering with the well-being of the workforce.

4.110   Dealing with any tragedy or similar crisis is essentially a matter of following the rules of crisis management, which should be linked to an emergency preparedness plan. This, in turn, should be closely aligned to any business continuity plan.

Business Continuity

4.111   Business continuity has recently advanced well beyond IT disaster recovery to embrace the entire workplace and the organisation's key assets — people. In addition, business continuity is progressively being seen as a cornerstone of corporate resilience which can be enhanced for those people who are more likely to become first responders.

4.112   British Standard 25999 is a useful code of practice on business continuity management setting out how to prepare business continuity plans.

Business Continuity Management Policy

4.113   Any organisation should maintain and regularly review its business continuity management (BCM) policy, strategies, plans and solutions on a regular basis in line with the risks it faces and the probable consequences that might follow any crisis.

Business Continuity Management Key Activities

4.114   However BCM is resourced, there are key activities that should be carried out both initially and on an ongoing basis. These include:

- defining the scope, roles and responsibilities for BCM
- conducting risk assessments to identify threats and mitigate them
- appointing an appropriate person to specifically consider the welfare of employees both at the time and following any tragedy
- keeping the BCM programme up to date through good practice
- administering an exercise programme to rehearse what to do before an event occurs
- establishing and monitoring change management and succession management regimes
- reviewing the crisis management actions to be applied during the acute phase of any tragedy/crisis/disaster.

4.115   Reviewing crisis management actions is vital in any scenario where someone has been seriously hurt or has died. This includes not only in the workplace, but also en route to work, or anything connected with work.

4.116   The line between work and home is seldom clear and has nothing in common with how inanimate systems work, such as IT. BCM is therefore not just about recovering systems and procedures, it is also about recovering employees. This is where prompt crisis management procedures are crucial.

Crisis Management

4.117   Crisis management is one of the most vital parts of preparing to deal with any catastrophe. If applied diligently and on time it might even obviate the need to trigger BCM since all crises will require crisis management to identify and resolve the problems, but not all will need BCM.

4.118   In very serious cases when the build-up of damaging events — such as a fatality at work — rapidly passes a certain point (normally designated as crossing the border of "business as usual"), a state of chaos often erupts that will need an even more rapid response to counter the event. This response should focus on the speedy transition from routine to crisis management styles commensurate with the immediate problem and what will happen afterwards.

4.119   Equally important is the return to normality at the most appropriate opportunity, which is the second priority for crisis management. However, what passes for normality after a serious incident will sometimes be different to what life was like before, especially for those that are deeply affected by what has happened.

Those Affected by a Crisis

4.120   After a tragedy, the situation for any of those people might be better classified as a "new normal". The list of people affected by any dramatic event includes anyone:

- physically injured
- who went to help
- who feels they should have helped
- for whom this incident triggers distressing memories
- not involved but who could have been, had something not occurred to change their plans.

Avoiding the Spread of Rumours and False Allegations in a Crisis

4.121   Often, organisations do not necessarily take the wrong actions in terms of crisis management, but are late to do the right ones, by which time the crisis itself sets the pace and the company might end up losing control of events rather than managing the situation and stopping the spread of rumours and false allegations.

4.122   In any crisis situation there has to be a simple and quickly-formed structure to:

- confirm what has just happened
- control the immediate and post response
- contain the spread of physical damage
- communicate, not just to staff, but to all stakeholders.

4.123   This is the stage where demands for urgent decisions will be at their highest, yet accurate information about what is going on now and what might happen in due course will be very low. A crisis management team that is quickly set up can look at "quick time" events such as:

- establishing what actually took place
- preventing it happening again
- providing a car to take next of kin to hospital
- appointing someone to be in constant touch with relatives
- preparing to meet with police/health and safety officials
- preparing to respond properly to all media enquires
- arranging for the most senior person in the organisation to visit the relatives of the deceased
- going to the workforce to listen to staff concerns and deal sensitively with all questions.

How a Crisis Management Team should Respond

4.124   A crisis manager or crisis management team should respond to an incident by answering five urgent questions.
1. What is known about the incident?
2. What is not known about the incident?
3. What would ideally like to be known?
4. How can this be determined?
5. What time is available?

4.125   From the answers to such basic questions, a more accurate picture of events should emerge. However, a crisis management structure needs to be owned, rehearsed and updated as an extension of routine management so it can quickly be called up and adjusted according to anticipated requirements. It also fits comfortably with enterprise risk management to ensure that a uniform approach to risk identification, measurement and treatment is utilized across the entire organisation.

4.126   By adopting this proactive approach to managing risk and crises, organisations can move from a "silo" management approach to a deeper integration of its various businesses to:

- start the alarm as soon as possible following an incident
- arrange a pan-company response without delay.

4.127   In addition, members of any crisis management team should:

- know exactly what their roles involve in advance
- have the means to be rapidly contacted
- have a set of agreed tools/protocols to help assimilate what is going on

- have access to rehearsed decision-making structures/diagrams
- have the ability to give accurate and measurable directions
- have a back-up in place if they are not available
- be the supreme executive layer at the commencement of any crisis response
- have an agreed quorum
- operate in a high-risk/no-blame culture to encourage rather than deter prompt decision making
- have direct linkage to any business continuity/emergency procedures plan
- have immediate access to legal, HR, welfare, business, finance, IT and media advice (often as core team members)
- have the ability to prepare a media holding statement within 30 minutes.

4.128   People not forming the core of any crisis management team should not feel obliged to communicate if they have nothing direct to contribute, or feel left out if their opinion is not sought at this stage.

Dealing with Stress or Trauma

4.129   It is important to take care of employees' personal and emotional well-being following any workplace trauma. Days, weeks, months or even years after a tragedy takes place at work, it is possible to suffer from the emotional aftermath of an incident.

4.130   Not giving enough due diligence to emotional well-being can result in health and attendance being gravely affected, morale plummeting, an increase in the number of accidents, and a decrease in productivity and performance. Often, all it takes is a birthday, inquest, court case, TV programme or some anniversary to jog memories and, for many people, to relive the original crisis they were involved in or that they witnessed. Directors and managers must lead by example in this respect by paying attention to their own health, both physical and emotional, and talk about what happened. This is where help from a trained and competent professional is vital.

4.131   Dr Anne Eyre is one of the UK's leading experts in this area. She offers the following advice.

"Much of my training and consultancy focuses on highlighting strategies for enhancing resilience in first responders and others involved in emergency management. I try to focus on resilience as a positive quality in people rather than looking for vulnerability, or over-exaggerating the likely extent of traumatic stress and exceptional disorders such as Post-Traumatic Stress Disorder (PTSD). I emphasise the role of both individual and organisational factors in determining levels of resilience and well-being in organisations — before, during and after disaster strikes."

4.132   Eyre is keen to emphasise that resilience is not the same as saying "we are all (and should be) strong all of the time". For her it is about acknowledging that to be human means that sometimes people are strong and sometimes they are vulnerable. The practical implications of this are not just about having policies and procedures for stress management and having good, effective occupational health systems in place, but also about building an environment that fosters and recognises resilience holistically. Those that get this right before disaster hits usually cope better during and after the event.

Awareness, Training and Education

4.133   The key is to make sure that most people are able to cope, especially if conditions enhancing resilience and coping skills are present and put in place. Although one of the major obstacles can be the attitudes and behaviour of personnel themselves — namely the perpetuation of the myth that it is a sign of weakness to seek help — and the view that psychological help is only for people with a mental illness.

4.134 Awareness-raising, training and education can make a significant difference. If personnel can understand the factors influencing stress and resilience — both general occupational stress and the sorts of normal reactions after critical or traumatic events — they can take preparatory and preventive measures to reduce harm.

Post-incident Investigations

4.135 David Tredrea is another specialist in the area of PTSD who raises the issue of post-incident investigations.

"You might need a few liaison officers if the crisis is substantial and those liaison officers will also need special support. If there are to be investigations by the police, health and safety authority, environmental health and other regulatory or interested bodies, there will be inevitable delays about reports. Gagging orders may be placed for very long periods and there are risks of subterfuge within the company if it is felt that matters are not being handled transparently and fairly."

4.136 He suggests the following approach.
- Do not jump to conclusions without reliable evidence or other data.
- Do not make promises that cannot be kept.
- Do not relax too soon in case the worst is yet to come.
- Do not avoid responsibility.
- Do not talk loosely about any confidential matters that should remain out of the media domain.
- Do not forget to look after personal well-being and other essential needs.
- Do not hog the limelight to avoid criticism of ego issues.
- Do not try and hide anything from investigatory authorities (eg the HSE).

The Health and Safety Executive

4.137 One of the residual stress factors can sometimes be the "threat" of an HSE investigation. The Health and Safety Commission (HSC) is responsible for health and safety regulation in the UK. The HSE and local government are the enforcing authorities who work in support of the HSC.

RIDDOR

4.138 It is useful to be aware of the RIDDOR which state a legal duty to report the following.
- Work-related deaths.
- Major injuries.
- Over three-day injuries.
- Work-related diseases.
- Dangerous occurrences (near-miss accidents).

4.139 Incidents can be reported by calling the HSE Incident Contact Centre (ICC) on 0845 300 99 23.

4.140 The following people are legally required to make reports.
- Employers.
- Self-employed people.

- People in control of premises.

4.141　Reporting accidents and ill health at work is a legal requirement. The information enables the HSE and local authorities to identify where and how risks arise and to investigate serious accidents. The HSE can also provide help and advice on how to reduce injury and ill health in the workplace.

4.142　The responsible person, usually the employer or person in control of the premises, must report all incidents and keep appropriate records. The ICC consultant will pose questions and take down appropriate details and the resulting report will be passed on to the relevant enforcing authority. In due course, the ICC will send a copy of the information recorded which should be filed appropriately — this meets the RIDDOR requirement to keep records of all reportable incidents.

Criminal Procedure and Investigation Act 1996

4.143　The Criminal Procedure and Investigation Act 1996 requires that "all reasonable lines of enquiry are pursued" in the course of any HSE investigation. Implicit in this phrase is the requirement that investigators should pursue lines of enquiry that could also assist the defence. This is clearly a move away from the normal investigation process in which the investigator primarily looks for evidence to support the prosecution case. It requires the investigator to be a "finder of fact".

Health and Safety at Work, etc Act 1974

4.144　Under the HSWA, an inspector may, at any reasonable time (or, in a situation which in his opinion is or may be dangerous, at any time), enter any premises which he has reason to believe is necessary for him to enter for the purpose of carrying out his duties under the HSWA.

4.145　The HSWA requires employers to ensure "so far as is reasonably practicable" the health, safety and welfare of their employees and other persons who may be affected by their work. This includes sub-contractors and the general public. The term "reasonably practicable" has been interpreted in law to mean that an employer is entitled to take into account the cost of any measure he may be considering, against the consequences of the risk involved. The HSWA also covers the duties of employees at work who must take reasonable care for the safety of themselves and of other persons who may be affected by their acts or omissions. They should co-operate with their employers and others in carrying out their statutory obligations.

Dealing with the Media

4.146　One of the first rules when facing the press following a fatal accident is to appear sincere and honest and, if facing a camera, wear a black tie. Be in a position to supply reporters with a holding statement that expresses sympathy, understanding and a willingness to support any HSE enquiry. Consider issuing a photo of whoever is ultimately in charge of the organisation and/or site looking genuinely concerned. There have been cases where these simple steps did not happen and, as a result, the company's reputation has suffered.

4.147　Any media response should be realistic, exercised and documented. The following points should be considered

- An incident communications strategy must be established. A press holding statement might have to be ready in 30 minutes otherwise speculation will fill in for facts.

- The organisation's preferred interface with the media should be defined. Reporters and journalists do not want to speak to spin doctors or third-party agencies; they want a senior figure who can appear honest and make sense of what is going on.
- A guideline or template for the drafting of a statement should be provided to the media at the earliest practicable opportunity following the initial incident.
- Appropriate numbers of trained, competent, spokespeople should be nominated and authorised to release information to the media. Ideally, an elected group of suitable trained executives should always be contactable and a decision should be made taken in advance on what any manager might say, for example, if "door-stepped" by a reporter. Saying "no comment" is not a good idea.
- In some cases it may be appropriate to:
  - provide supporting detail in a separate document
  - establish an appropriate number of competent, trained people to answer telephone enquiries from the press
  - prepare background material about the organisation and its operations (this information should be pre-agreed for release and especially mindful if any "gagging orders" have been imposed)
  - ensure that all media information is made available without undue delay.

Interview Techniques

4.148 The following should be considered during an interview.

- Key messages should be prepared in advance to incorporate into the interview.
- Following a death, a black tie/dark jacket should be worn.
- The whole issue need not be addressed in one answer.
- Interviewees should look directly into the camera lens.
- A sound bite of around two sentences will usually be what is sought and messages should be prepared accordingly.
- Key messages should be repeated.

Training

4.149 Ensure that employees have sufficient information and training to be able to deal with the consequences of a tragedy. For example, do they need to respond to the media, and if so how should a response be prepared?

4.150 Provide sufficient information and training to employees in the event of their suffering with post-traumatic stress disorder.

List of Relevant Legislation

4.151

- Management of Health and Safety at Work Regulations 1999
- Reporting of Injuries, Diseases and Dangerous Occurrences Regulations 1995
- Corporate Manslaughter and Corporate Homicide Act 2007
- Health and Safety at Work, etc Act 1974

Further Information

Publications

British Standards Publications

The following are available from *www.bsi-global.com.*
- BS 25999–1: 2006 *Business Continuity Management. Code of Practice*
- BS 25999–2: 2007 *Specification for Business Continuity Management*

Organisations

- Business Continuity Institute (BCI)
  Web: *www.thebci.org*
  The BCI was established in 1994 to enable members to obtain guidance and support from fellow business continuity practitioners.
- Centre for Corporate Accountability
  Web: *www.corporateaccountability.org*
  The Centre for Corporate Accountability is a charitable organisation that monitors worker and public safety, and undertakes research and provides advice on law enforcement and corporate criminal accountability.
- Health and Safety Executive (HSE)
  Web: *www.hse.gov.uk*
  The HSE and the Health and Safety Commission are responsible for the regulation of almost all the risks to health and safety arising from work activity in the UK.

Step-by-step Guide: How to Respond Immediately Following a Tragedy

- Establish what actually took place by answering five key questions.
  - What is known about the incident?
  - What is not known about the incident?
  - What would ideally like to be known?
  - How can this be determined?
  - What time is available?
- Prevent the incident from happening again.
- Provide a car to take next of kin to hospital.
- Appoint someone to be in constant touch with relatives.
- Prepare to meet with police/health and safety officials.
- Prepare to respond properly to all media enquiries
  - prepare in advance key messages to incorporate into the interview
  - appear sincere and honest and, if facing the camera, wear a black tie
  - be in a position to supply reporters with a holding statement that expresses sympathy, understanding and a willingness to support any HSE enquiry
  - consider issuing a photo of whoever is ultimately in charge of the organisation/site looking genuinely concerned
  - do not feel the need to address the whole issue in one answer
  - look directly into the camera lens
  - repeat key messages
  - ensure any media response is realistic, exercised and documented
  - provide supporting detail in a separate document
  - establish an appropriate number of competent, trained people to answer telephone enquiries from the press
  - prepare background material about the organisation and its operations.
- Arrange for the most senior person in the organisation to visit the relatives of the deceased.
- Listen to staff concerns and deal sensitively with all questions.

Step-by-step Guide: How to Arrange a Business Continuity Management Plan

- Define the scope, roles and responsibilities for business continuity management. A crisis management team should:
  - know exactly what their roles involve in advance
  - have the means to be rapidly contacted
  - have a set of agreed tools/protocols to help assimilate what is going on
  - have access to rehearsed decision-making structures/diagrams
  - have the ability to give accurate and measurable directions
  - have a back-up in place if they are not available
  - be the supreme executive layer at the commencement of any crisis response
  - have an agreed quorum
  - operate in a high-risk/no-blame culture to encourage rather than deter prompt decision making

- have direct linkage to any business continuity/emergency procedures plan
- have immediate access to legal, HR, welfare, business, finance, IT and media advice (often as core team members)
- have the ability to prepare a media holding statement within 30 minutes.

• Conduct risk assessments to identify threats and mitigate them.

• Appoint an appropriate person to specifically consider the welfare of employees both at the time and following any tragedy.

• Keep the business continuity management programme up to date through good practice.

• Administer an exercise programme to rehearse what to do before it happens.

• Establish and monitor change management and succession management regimes.

• Review the crisis management actions to be applied during the acute phase of any tragedy/crisis/disaster.

Employees' Factsheet: Crisis Management

Dealing with the Media

If not part of the crisis management team, do not feel obliged to communicate with the media.

Otherwise:

• prepare key messages in advance to incorporate into the interview

• do not wear a white shirt without a jacket; following a death, wear a black tie/dark jacket

• do not feel the need to address the whole issue in one answer

• look directly into the camera lens

• bear in mind that a sound bite of around two sentences is usually what is sought and prepare messages accordingly

• repeat key messages.

Corporate Social Responsibility

- Corporate social responsibility (CSR) is concerned with treating the stakeholders of the organisation in an ethical or in a responsible manner.
- The three aspects of CSR are social, economic and environmental.
- The main drivers for CSR are compliance with legislation, enhanced reputation and the benefit to the environment.
- Facilities managers can contribute across all areas to enhance an organisation's CSR, promoting the reputation of the organisation.
- Establishing links between public sector, charity organisations and commercial organisations in a community project is a method of engaging in the social aspect of CSR for the organisation.
- A comparison of CSR approaches by organisations can be achieved through the Business in the Community (BITC) Index of Corporate Responsibility.
- The current high level of interest in CSR has led to a wealth of initiatives, guidance and regulations.

4.152   Corporate social responsibility (CSR) can be defined as an organisation's commitment to operating in a responsible manner. CSR comprises commitments to economic, social and environmental issues.

4.153   CSR is becoming an increasingly important issue for the Government, professional institutes and the business community in general. Organisations need to communicate with government bodies, investors, customers, employees, business partners and local communities, and recognise their interests when preparing a CSR policy.

4.154   Key CSR issues include:
- responsible sourcing
- human rights
- governance
- environmental management
- stakeholder engagement
- labour standards
- employee and community relations
- social equity.

Employer's Duties

Corporate Manslaughter and Corporate Homicide Act 2007

4.155   CSR is the acknowledgement by companies that they should be accountable not only for their financial performance, but also for the impact of their activities on society and/or the environment. This obviously includes deaths at the workplace.

4.156   In order to avoid prosecution under the Corporate Manslaughter and Corporate Homicide Act 2007, it is essential that evidence can be obtained, when required, that demonstrates that effective health and safety management systems are in place and that those occupying senior management positions are both competent and fully committed to health and safety in the workplace. Organisations with a positive attitude to health and safety will be doing this already and will have nothing further to do to ensure compliance.

In Practice

Company Policies

4.157 CSR embraces all aspects of an organisation as it encompasses many things, including supply chain practices, employee relations, health and safety, public protection and marketing practices.

Drivers

4.158 There are numerous business drivers which stimulate an organisation to develop CSR policies and working practices. These include:

- complying with legislation
- enhancing their reputation
- benefiting the environment
- enhancing health, safety and welfare of staff and customers
- doing the "right thing"
- meeting client requirements
- reducing waste
- meeting customer expectations and demands
- having a competitive edge
- having a stronger financial outlook
- improving quality of workplace
- taking advantage of government initiatives
- championing innovation
- improving staff retention and recruitment.

Definitions

4.159 Corporate social responsibility — CSR is concerned with treating the stakeholders of the organisation ethically or in a responsible manner. "Ethically or responsibly" means treating the key stakeholders in a manner deemed acceptable in civilised societies. "Social" includes economic and environmental responsibility. Stakeholders exist both within a firm and outside of it. The wider aim of social responsibility is to create high standards of living for people inside and outside the corporation while preserving its profitability.

4.160 Corporate citizenship — this is about business taking greater account of its social, environmental and financial activities.

4.161 Corporate governance — this is concerned with holding the balance between economic and social goals and between individual and communal goals. The corporate governance framework is there to encourage the efficient use of resources and equally to require accountability for the stewardship of those resources. The aim is to align as closely as possible the interests of individuals, corporations and society.

4.162 Corporate sustainability — this aligns an organisation's products and services with stakeholder expectations, thereby adding economic, environmental and social value.

4.163 Ethics — this is the science of morals in human conduct.

4.164 Ethical accounting — this is the process through which the company takes up a dialogue with major stakeholders to report on past activities with a view to shaping future ones.

4.165 Ethical auditing — this is regular, complete and documented measurements of compliance with the company's published policies and procedures.

4.166 Ethical bookkeeping — this is systematic, reliable maintenance of accessible records for corporate activities which reflect on its conduct and behaviour.

4.167 Reputation assurance — this covers a number of common global principles for the business environment assembled to provide quantitative and trend information.

4.168 Social reporting — this includes non-financial data covering staff issues, community economic developments, stakeholder involvement and can include voluntarism and environmental performance.

4.169 Sustainable development — this includes environmental impact measurement, improvements, monitoring and reporting.

Initiatives and Regulations

4.170 The current level of interest in CSR has led to a wealth of initiatives, guidance and regulations as shown in the table below, *Initiatives, Guidance and Regulations*.

Initiatives, Guidance and Regulations

Sector	Initiatives/guidance/regulations
Reporting, auditing and planning	The Association of Chartered Certified Accountants (ACCA) environmental, social and sustainability reporting, ISO 14001 standard for environmental management systems, Corporate Impact Reporting initiative, The Natural Step, Environmental Information Regulations, Freedom of Information Regulations, operational reporting in companies OFR, annual reporting and accounts, Sarbanes-Oxley regulations, the *Turnbull Report*, FTSE4Good
Environmental regulations	Environmental Protection Act 1990 (EPA), the Environmental Liability Directive and the Waste Electronic and Electrical Equipment Regulations
Other initiatives relating to the environment	Carbon Trust, carbon trading, DBERR initiative to expand use of sustainable energy in buildings, fuel cell demonstration project

Sector	Initiatives/guidance/regulations
Health and safety	Health and Safety at Work, etc Act 1974, Control of Asbestos Regulations 2006, Electricity at Work Regulations 1989, Regulatory Reform (Fire Safety) Order 2005, fire risk assessments, L8: Legionnaires' Disease, environmental health, transport of dangerous goods, Construction (Design and Management) Regulations 2007
Corporate manslaughter	Corporate Manslaughter and Corporate Homicide Act 2007
Building operation	Building Act and Building Regulations 2000, building logbooks, Energy Performance of Buildings Directive, EcoHomes
Human resources	Investors in People, skills cards, Better Payment Practice Campaign, Disability Discrimination Act 1995/2005
Ethical business	Ethical Trading Initiative, Fairtrade and Tradecraft certified products, supply chain management, forest stewardship council, Sullivan's Principles, marine stewardship council
Other sector specific	NHS Improving Working Lives Healthcare Commission Standards

Benefits of CSR

4.171   The benefits of adopting a CSR approach to business include:
• increased awareness and trust in the organisation by the stakeholder
• improved stakeholder relations and overall image
• improved reputation in the marketplace
• increased brand value
• protection of the organisation's operating space, through enhanced reputation and reduced risk
• an increasingly sustainable future with long-term financial viability
• being an attractive investment to others
• improved relationships in the supply chain
• meeting customers expectations
• enhanced customer loyalty
• employing environmentally and ethically-sound processes and procedures
• complying with relevant legislation
• recruiting and retaining responsive and motivated employees
• attracting new suppliers with similar policies
• reduced operational risks
• good corporate governance in particular with regard to taxation, reporting and other fiscal measures
• increased operational efficiency through resource productivity.

Community

4.172   Establishing links between public sector, charity organisations and commercial organisations in a community project is a method of engaging in the social aspect of CSR for an organisation. Ideally, the best community initiatives have:
• direct contact with the local community: public, animals, plants, weather, fresh air, etc

- an experience of "how I made a difference"
- an element of team challenge
- the chance to try something new.

4.173 The benefits for the organisation through its employees taking part in a CSR initiative include:

- increased sense of loyalty
- increased sense of pride in the company
- renewed sense of achievement.

4.174 Examples of social initiatives that could be organised include:

- working with a local community to renovate their public garden, paint their nursery school or build a playground
- working with a youth centre to fit out a theatre for amateur productions, teaching children a new language or build a computer room
- working with a third world community to set up an Internet café , build an irrigation system or have a party
- working with an animal/conservation organisation to repair trails, clean up habitats, monitor and care for wildlife.

4.175 CSR requires the systematic appraisal of social, ethical and environmental impacts by an organisation. The adoption of a CSR policy by an organisation will be driven primarily by stakeholder and business interests, although there are many legislative requirements affecting the three aspects of CSR.

4.176 An organisation may decide to look at the various standards and their marketplace to judge what its CSR objectives may be and what resources may be required to meet them.

Benchmarking CSR

4.177 A comparison of CSR approaches by organisations can be achieved through the Business in the Community (BITC) Index of Corporate Responsibility. The BITC Index allows invited companies to report on their management of CSR. It also allows them to compare management processes and performance with others in their sector. The BITC Index investigates four key areas.
1. Community.
2. Environment.
3. Marketplace.
4. Workplace.

4.178 It also looks at performance across a range of social and environmental issues. Significantly, the BITC Index also allows companies to demonstrate to their various stakeholders how they are taking a lead in promoting public reporting and increasing transparency in business performance.

Standards

AA1000

4.179 Known as AccountAbility 1000, these process standards are designed to assist an organisation in the definition of goals and targets, the measurement of progress made against these targets, the auditing and reporting of performance, and feedback mechanisms. The standard is intended to provide the basis for improving the sustainability performance of organisations in any sector, including the public sector and civil society, of any size and in any region. The Institute of Social and Ethical AccountAbility has developed these standards.

SA8000 2001

4.180   The most respected standard in the field of social accountability is Social Accountability International's (SAI) SA8000 2001 standard. This was developed in 1997 and is the widest recognised standard globally. The British Standards Institution (BSI) is accredited by the SAI to deliver assessments to SA8000 and, as the leading global management systems provider, is in a unique position to assess organisations from a wide range of sectors and countries.

4.181   The elements in the standard are as follows.

- Child labour — no workers under the age of 15, minimum lowered to 14 for countries operating under the ILO Convention 138 developing country exception; remediation of any child found to be working.
- Forced labour — no forced labour, including prison or debt bondage labour, no lodging of deposits or identity papers by employers or outside recruiters.
- Health and safety — provide a safe and healthy work environment, take steps to prevent injuries; regular health and safety worker training, system to detect threats to health and safety; access to bathrooms and portable water.
- Freedom of association and right to collective bargaining — respect the right to form and join trade unions and bargain collectively; where law prohibits these freedoms, facilitate parallel means of association and bargaining.
- Discrimination — no discrimination based on race, caste, origin, religion, disability, gender, sexual orientation, union or political affiliation, or age; no sexual harassment.
- Discipline — no corporal punishment, mental or physical coercion or verbal abuse.
- Working hours — comply with the applicable law but no more than 48 hours per week with at least one day off for every 7-day period. Voluntary overtime paid at a premium rate and not to exceed 12 hours per week on a regular basis; overtime may be mandatory if part of a collective bargaining agreement.
- Compensation — wages paid for a standard work week must meet the legal and industry standards and be sufficient to meet the basic need of workers and their families; no disciplinary deductions.
- Management systems — facilities seeking to gain and maintain certification must go beyond simple compliance to integrate the standard into their management systems and practices.

ISO 14001

4.182   ISO 14001 is a series of voluntary standards and guideline reference documents which include:

- environmental management systems
- eco-labelling
- life cycle assessment
- environmental auditing
- environmental performance evaluation
- environmental aspects in product standards.

BS 8555: 2003 Environmental Management Systems

4.183   This British Standard (BS) provides guidance to all organisations on the phased implementation, maintenance and improvement of a formal environmental management system (EMS). It outlines an implementation process that can be undertaken in up to six separate phases and allows for phased acknowledgment of progress towards full EMS implementation. It also includes advice on the integration and use of environmental performance evaluation techniques during the implementation process and the co-ordination of an EMS with other management systems.

4.184 BS 8555: 2003 will help all organisations improve their environmental performance and their supply chain relationships with the following guidance.

- The description of a six-phase incremental approach to implementing an EMS using environmental performance evaluation.
- The provision of information to organisations on environmental performance management and the use of environmental performance indicators.
- The help for organisations to satisfy the environmental criteria increasingly being set in contract tenders by new and existing major clients
- The use by organisations who may wish to self-declare or seek voluntary phased recognition throughout the implementation process.

BS 8900: Guidance for Managing Sustainable Development

4.185 This standard will help organisations towards effective management of their impact on society and the environment, along the route to enhanced organisational performance and success. BS 8900 is designed to help organisations to develop an approach to sustainable development that will continue to evolve and adapt to meet new and continuing challenges and demands. It offers practical advice with which to make a meaningful contribution to sustainable development. This includes:

- providing a framework so organisations can take a structured approach to sustainable development by considering the social, environmental and economic impacts of their organisation's activities.
- being applicable to all organisations, in terms of size, type, etc including civil societies and trade unions.
- making it easier for organisations to adjust to changing social expectations.
- helping organisations to connect existing technical, social and environmental standards, both formal (eg ISO 14001 series of standards) and private (eg the AA1000 standards).
- offering a maturity pathway for the development of the management of sustainable development issues and impacts.
- providing organisations' stakeholders with a useful tool to assess and engage in improving organisational performance.
- contributing to international level dialogue in the international standard on social responsibility, currently under development.

EMAS

4.186 The EU Eco-management and Audit Scheme (EMAS) is a management tool for companies and other organisations to evaluate, report and improve their environmental performance. The scheme has been available for participation by companies since 1995 (Council Regulation (EEC) No. 1836/93 of 29 June 1993) and was originally restricted to companies in industrial sectors.

4.187 EMAS has been open to all economic sectors, including public and private services in the EU and the European Free Trade Association (EFTA) — Iceland, Liechtenstein, Norway and Switzerland. EMAS is a powerful standard because it:

- integrates EN/ISO 14001 as the EMS

- allows the EMAS logo to be used by successful organisations to signal EMAS registration
- considers the indirect effects of an organisation's processes on its environmental performance.

4.188 EMAS requires a statement on environmental performance to achieve registration, and this can be part of a CSR report. EMAS also requires an environmental policy to be in existence within the organisation, fully supported by senior management, and outlining the policies of the company, not only to the staff but to the general public and other stakeholders. The policy needs to clarify compliance with environmental regulations that may affect the organisation and stress a commitment to continuous improvement. Emphasis has been placed on policy as this provides the direction for the remainder of the management system.

ISO 26000

4.189 The International Standards Organization (ISO) is developing an international standard providing guidelines for social responsibility. The guidance standard will be published in 2010 as ISO 26000 and be voluntary to use. It will not include requirements and will thus not be a certification standard.

4.190 The need for organisations in both public and private sectors to behave in a socially responsible way is becoming a generalised requirement of society. The standard will promote respect and responsibility and it will give common guidance on concepts, definitions and methods of evaluation.

Legislation

EU Accounts Modernisation Directive 2003/51/EC

4.191 This requires large UK companies to provide a business review within the directors' report which includes information on environmental matters which may significantly affect a company's performance.

Pollution Prevention and Control Act 1999

4.192 Pollution prevention and control is a regime for controlling pollution from certain industrial activities. The regime introduced the concept of Best Available Techniques (BAT) to environmental regulations.

4.193 Operators must use the BAT to control pollution from their industrial activities. The aim of BAT is to prevent, and where that is not practicable, to reduce to acceptable levels, pollution to air, land and water from industrial activities. The BAT also aim to balance the cost to the operator against benefits to the environment.

Sustainable and Secure Buildings Act 2004

4.194 The Sustainable and Secure Buildings Act 2004 is a fundamental piece of legislation which amends the Building Act 1984 by:
- furthering the conservation of fuel and power
- preventing waste, undue consumption, misuse or contamination of water
- furthering the protection or enhancement of the environment
- facilitating the protection or enhancement of the environment
- facilitating sustainable development
- furthering the prevention or detection of crime.

4.195 Some provisions apply only to buildings constructed after the regulations came into force, while others apply to refurbishments and alterations to existing buildings. The Sustainable and Secure Buildings Act 2004 limits the use of rare hardwoods and other scarce or non-renewable building materials. It also brings into the scope of the Building Regulations 2000 certain types of buildings that are currently exempted, including schools and operational buildings owned by public utilities.

Clean Neighbourhoods and Environment Act 2005

4.196   The Clean Neighbourhoods and Environment Act 2005 covers a wide range of social and environmental issues including:

- site waste management plans, transport of waste, deposit and disposal of waste
- crime and disorder
- vehicle parking, when causing a nuisance, illegally parked and abandoned vehicles
- litter and refuse
- graffiti and other defacement of property
- advertisements
- control of dogs and stray dogs
- noise from audible intruder alarms
- noise from premises
- the role of Commission for Architecture and the Built Environment (CABE)
- abandoned shopping and luggage trolleys
- statutory nuisance (insects, lighting, etc)
- pollution.

Centre for Corporate Accountability

4.197   The Centre for Corporate Accountability (CCA) provides a "work-related death advice service".

4.198   The CCA is the only national non-governmental organisation in Britain that provides free, independent and confidential advice and assistance to families bereaved from a work-related death. The organisation:

- provides advice on all investigation and prosecution issues arising out of the death
- helps families deal with the police, the HSE, local authorities, the Maritime and Coastguard Agency and the Crown Prosecution Service
- assists families in finding out information, writing letters to different state bodies, and attends meetings along with the families.

4.199   In addition, the organisation helps families understand the process and helps assess whether an adequate investigation has been carried out and the evidence properly scrutinised.

Checklists

4.200   MHCi is an international research and consulting business that focuses on the measurement of CSR. Its approach to CSR is based on the concept of corporate social dynamics that emphasises corporate relationships with all stakeholder groups in the social development area. It has developed a checklist called Corporate Responsibility Index Through Internet Consultation of Stakeholders (CRITICS), which is a self-assessment online tool to measure the level of social responsibility in an organisation. CRITICS is part of a MHCi research project to assist companies to become more socially responsible.

List of Relevant Legislation

4.201
- Construction (Design and Management) Regulations 2007
- Control of Asbestos Regulations 2006
- Environmental Information Regulations 2004
- Environmental Information (Scotland) Regulations 2004
- Building Regulations 2000
- Electricity at Work Regulations 1989
- Energy Bill 2003
- Corporate Manslaughter and Corporate Homicide Act 2007
- Clean Neighbourhoods and Environment Act 2005
- Disability Discrimination Act 2005
- Sustainable and Secure Buildings Act 2004
- Freedom of Information (Scotland) Act 2002
- Freedom of Information Act 2000
- Pollution Prevention and Control Act 1999
- Data Protection Act 1998
- Environmental Protection Act 1990
- Building Act 1984
- Health and Safety at Work, etc Act 1974
- Regulatory Reform (Fire Safety) Order 2005

Further Information

Publications

HSE Publications

The following is available from *www.hsebooks.co.uk*.
- L8 (rev 2000) *Legionnaires' Disease – Control of Legionella Bacteria in Water Systems – Approved Code of Practice and Guidance*

British Standards Publications

The following is available from *www.bsi-global.co.uk*.
- BS 8900: 2006 *Guidance for Managing Sustainable Development*

Organisations
- Association of Chartered Certified Accountants (ACCA)
  Web: *www.accaglobal.com*
  The Association of Chartered Certified Accountants (ACCA) is the largest and

fastest-growing international accountancy body in the world. It works to achieve and promote the highest professional, ethical and governance standards and advance the public interest.

- Better Payment Practice Campaign
  Web: *www.payontime.co.uk*
  The Better Payment Practice Group is a co-operative forum of representatives of the business community and government that seeks to help improve the payment culture among organisations trading in the UK.

- British Institute of Facilities Management (BIFM)
  Web: *www.bifm.org.uk*
  The BIFM is the UK's leading institute representing the interests of those who practise facilities management.

- Business in the Community (BITC)
  Web: *www.bitc.org.uk*
  With 700 member companies, BITC operates a network of 98 local business-led partnerships and works with 45 global partners. It runs the Index of Corporate Responsibility and the CSR Academy.

- Carbon Trust
  Web: *www.thecarbontrust.co.uk*
  The Carbon Trust helps business and public sector organisations to cut carbon emissions and assists with the development of low-carbon technologies.

- Commission for Architecture and the Built Environment (CABE)
  Web: *www.cabe.org.uk*
  The CABE promotes high quality design and architecture to raise standards of the built environment.

- Centre for Corporate Accountability
  Web: *www.corporateaccountability.org*
  The Centre for Corporate Accountability is a charitable organisation that monitors worker and public safety, and undertakes research and provides advice on law enforcement and corporate criminal accountability.

- CSR (Corporate Social Responsibility) Academy
  Web: *www.csracademy.co.uk*
  The CSR Academy was launched in 2004. Now run by Business in the Community, it aims to support companies developing the skills and competencies to integrate CSR into their businesses. It is for companies of all sizes as well as for UK educational institutions.

- CSR Europe
  Web: *www.csreurope.org*
  CSR Europe is a non-profit organisation that aims to help companies achieve profitability, sustainable growth and human progress by placing corporate social responsibility in the mainstream of business practice.

- Department for Business, Enterprise and Regulatory Reform (BERR)
  Web: *www.berr.gov.uk*
  The Department for Business, Enterprise and Regulatory Reform brings together functions from the former Department of Trade and Industry (DTI), including responsibilities for productivity, business relations, energy, competition and consumers. It also drives regulatory reform.

- Eco-Management and Audit Scheme (EMAS)
  Web: *www.emas.org.uk*
  EMAS is a voluntary initiative designed to improve companies' environmental performance. Its aim is to recognise and reward those organisations that go beyond minimum legal compliance.

- Ethical Trading Initiative (ETI)
  Web: *www.ethicaltrade.org*
  The ETI is an alliance of companies, non-governmental organisations and trade

union organisations. It aims to promote and improve the implementation of corporate codes of practice which cover supply chain working conditions.

- European Committee for Standardization (CEN)
  Web: *www.cenorm.be/cenorm/index.htm*
  The CEN contributes to the objectives of the European Union and European Economic Area with voluntary technical standards which promote free trade, the safety of workers and consumers, interoperability of networks, environmental protection, exploitation of research and development programmes, and public procurement.
- Forum for the Future
  Web: *www.forumforthefuture.org.uk*
  Forum for the Future is the UK's leading sustainable development charity.
- Institute of Environmental Management and Assessment (IEMA)
  Web: *www.iema.net*
  IEMA is a not-for-profit organisation established to promote best practice standards in environmental management, auditing and assessment.
- Institute of Social and Ethical AccountAbility
  Web: *www.accountability.org.uk*
  AccountAbility is an international non-profit membership institute committed to enhancing the performance of organisations and to developing the competencies of individuals in social and ethical accountability and sustainable development.
- Investors in People
  Web: *www.investorsinpeople.co.uk*
  Investors in People UK provides national ownership of the Investors in People Standard and is responsible for its promotion and branding, quality assurance and development.
- Social Accountability International
  Web: *www.sa-intl.org*
  The SAI is a US-based non-profit organisation dedicated to the development, implementation and oversight of voluntary, verifiable social accountability standards, notably SA8000.
- SustainAbility
  Web: *www.sustainability.com*
  SustainAbility is an independent strategy consultancy and think-tank specialising in corporate responsibility.
- The Natural Step
  Web: *www.naturalstep.org*
  The Natural Step is a non-profit organisation working to build an eogically and economically sustainable society.

Chapter 5

Model Policies and Records

Model Policies

Contents

Introduction

Policies should be formulated to cover situations where precise rules are necessary. The following policies will not be appropriate to all organisations and they will be used best by adapting them to a company's own particular circumstances. When companies decide to use these model policies merely as a framework to write their own, the following tips might be helpful.

- Keep sentences reasonably short so that they can be easily understood.
- Ensure that the target audience will understand the meaning.
- Ensure that all policies are workable.
- Involve appropriate managerial/supervisory staff in their formulation.
- Check that the policies reflect good practice.
- Do not just make them a guide to "the way we have always done things".

It is important to stress that policies will need to be updated from time to time. A senior member of staff should be given the responsibility of ensuring that proposals are made to update a policy when it becomes out of date. In particular, this person needs to consider:

- whether the policies are still relevant to the operation of the organisation
- whether managers/supervisors are carrying out the procedures contained within the policies and the reasons behind any failure to do so.

Organisations which already have written policies may find that those in this section serve as a useful checklist to ensure that proper consideration is given to important issues in their own circumstances.

1. Accident Investigation

General Statement

This policy outlines the investigation procedures which are to be adopted when any accident, ill health, near miss or dangerous incident occurs on the organisation's premises during the course of any work activity.

It is the policy of this organisation to ensure that where practicable all accidents or incidence of work-related ill health, dangerous occurrences and near misses will be fully investigated by suitably trained staff. Accident or incident investigation is not a means of determining fault or apportioning blame.

The purpose of the investigation is:
(a) to ensure that all necessary information in respect of the accident or incident is collated
(b) to understand the sequence of events that led to the accident or incident
(c) to identify the unsafe acts and conditions that contributed to the cause of the accident or incident
(d) to identify the underlying causes that may have contributed to the accident or incident
(e) to ensure that effective remedial actions are taken to prevent any recurrence
(f) to enable a full and comprehensive report of the accident or incident to be prepared and circulated to all interested parties
(g) to enable all statutory requirements to be adhered to.
(h) This policy will apply to all accidents or incidents involving employees, visitors, members of the public and contractors. The organisation will co-operate with employers of contractors who may be involved in any accident or incident.
(i) The person responsible for the implementation of this policy is
_____ .

Staff Selection

To ensure that the objectives of the investigation are met, suitable and sufficient staff will be selected and trained in investigation procedures and interview techniques.

Staff selected to carry out investigations will be required to attend any necessary training and will be provided with the appropriate information and resources to enable them to carry out their respective roles.

_____ will act as lead investigators for the accidents or incidents as detailed below.

Other staff will be required to co-operate and participate in any investigation if the organisation feels that they have specific knowledge, understanding, experience or skills that may assist in the investigation.

_____ will be required to co-operate and participate in any investigation.

Training

All staff selected to lead investigations will receive suitable and sufficient training in the investigative procedures to be adopted, interview techniques, report writing skills and use of any equipment employed in the investigation process.

Safety Representatives and Employees

The organisation encourages the involvement of employees in the investigation process.

Recognised trade union safety representatives will be given access to any necessary information and workplaces to enable them to fulfil their duties. Safety representatives will also be encouraged to fully participate in any investigation.

Employee representatives will also be encouraged to participate where a safety representative is not present.

All employees will be required to co-operate with the organisation in any investigation.

Enforcing Authority

In the event that the enforcing authority wishes to carry out an investigation, the organisation will strive to meet all of its legal responsibilities when co-operating with the investigating inspector.

Equipment

All necessary equipment required to carry out investigations will be supplied, located in a suitable environment and well maintained. All staff necessary will be trained in the use of such equipment.

Process of Investigation

Staff investigating any accident or incident will be given full access to the scene of the incident/accident and any other part of the workplace deemed necessary to carry out the investigation.

All necessary information will be collected and collated. Physical evidence may be recorded and samples taken as necessary.

Investigating staff will be given access to any necessary documentation and will act in accordance with any requirements of the Data Protection Act 1998.

Interviews of those involved in the accident or incident, witnesses and any other person necessary will be carried out in accordance with the training and guidelines issued.

Remedial Action

The organisation will, so far as is reasonably practicable, implement any recommendations made as part of the investigation. In the event of any remedial action taken, staff will be fully involved and provided with the necessary information, instruction and training.

Records and Reports

All necessary staff will be issued with an accident report as soon as is reasonably practicable. Employees or their representatives will be given access to any report in so far as it is applicable to do so.

Records of any accident will be kept in accordance with the company's policy on record keeping.

Any records kept will be done so in accordance with the Data Protection Act 1998.

---

2. Consultation With Employees

Policy Statement

1. **General Statement**
   The organisation acknowledges the importance of employee involvement in health and safety matters and the importance of the positive role played by safety representatives, safety committees and representatives of employee safety. As such, it is the intention of the organisation to provide the facilities and assistance that such representatives and committees might reasonably require in order to carry out their functions.

2. **Arrangements for Securing the Health and Safety of Workers**
   The organisation undertakes to consult with safety representatives over issues related to health, safety and welfare and to provide the information safety representatives and representatives of employee safety require in order to carry out their functions.

   Safety representatives are required to give the organisation reasonable notice of their intention to carry out inspections, to provide written reports following such inspections and to follow the organisation's procedures when disputes over health and safety issues arise.

   The organisation intends to establish a safety committee that will meet regularly and review safety performance within the organisation. The committee will consist of employer and employee representatives and will be chaired by a senior manager with the authority to act upon the decisions reached by the committee.

3. **Information, Instruction and Training**
   The organisation will offer safety representatives and representatives of employee safety the opportunity to attend relevant training. Additionally the organisation will offer paid leave for any safety representative or representative of employee safety requiring time off to carry out his or her functions or to receive any necessary training.

4. **Safe System Of Work**
   The following procedures should be observed with regard to safety representatives and representatives of employee safety.

   1. In the case of union-appointed safety representatives, unions should inform the organisation in writing of the individual safety representative's appointment.
   2. Safety representatives and representatives of employee safety should understand the way in which the safety consultation and safety committee structure operates within the organisation — they should also be aware of the group or constituency that they represent.
   3. Safety representatives, representatives of employee safety and safety committee members will receive adequate training.
   4. Safety representatives and representatives of employee safety should be aware of the disputes and grievance procedures in operation within the organisation.
   5. Safety committees should meet as scheduled, there should be agendas for meetings and minutes should be carefully recorded — information about these meetings should be available to the entire workforce.
   6. The safety committee chairperson should have the authority to act upon the committee's decisions.
   7. Safety committees should have terms of reference and properly formulated aims and objectives.

8. **Summary Policy Statement**

The three most important steps with regard to employee consultation and safety committees are:

(a) to ensure that committees operate in a positive way, reinforcing the organisation's safety culture and employee participation in solving health and safety problems

(b) to ensure adequate training for safety representatives, representatives of employee safety and safety committee members, thus improving communications, prioritisation of risk control and the approach to solving health and safety problems

(c) to incorporate the safety consultation arrangements and safety committee structure into the organisational structure and health and safety policy.

---
3. Directors' Responsibilities

General Statement on Intent

This policy statement details the responsibilities of the company board of directors. It is recognised that the board of directors needs to take responsibility for health and safety within the organisation.

The board of directors is committed to health and safety, will provide leadership and will ensure that health and safety is taken into account when business decisions are taken.

Directors will be responsible for safety measures at directorate level for matters for which they have control. Directors will assume the employer's responsibility for compliance with the organisation's health and safety policy, relevant legislation and Approved Codes of Practice and Guidance. The board will:

(a) accept its collective role in providing health and safety leadership within the organisation formally and in public
(b) ensure that individual members of the board accept their role in providing health and safety leadership
(c) ensure that health and safety intentions are reflected in board decisions
(d) ensure the active participation of employees in improving health and safety
(e) ensure that it is informed of and alerted to health and safety risk management issues
(f) promote an interest in and enthusiasm for health and safety matters throughout the organisation
(g) set a high personal example of health and safety standards.

Health and Safety Policy

The company chairman and the board of directors will:

(a) administer and interpret the effective implementation of the organisation's health and safety policy
(b) ensure that health and safety policy statements reflect current board priorities
(c) cause the organisation's health and safety policy to be translated into effective action at all levels
(d) make available adequate resources and financial provision for putting the health and safety policy into effect
(e) ensure that the health and safety policy is signed by the chairman and board of directors.

Health and Safety Arrangements

The company chairman and board of directors, to ensure the effective application of health and safety within the organisation, will:

(a) ensure that they have an understanding of the application of the Health and Safety at Work, etc Act 1974 and other legislation relevant to the organisation's business
(b) review the organisation's health and safety performance regularly
(c) ensure that management systems provide effective monitoring and reporting procedures

(d) be kept informed about significant health and safety failures and of the outcome of the investigations into their causes

(e) ensure that implications in respect of health and safety are addressed in all business decisions

(f) ensure that risk management systems for health and safety are in place and effective

(g) discipline any member of staff failing to comply with the requirements of the organisation's health and safety policy

(h) liaise with the person(s) appointed for health and safety over the full range of his or her individual responsibilities

(i) arrange for a senior director to chair the committee on safety

(j) ensure that staff are fully involved in health and safety

(k) ensure that managers and staff are given adequate training in health and safety matters to competently discharge their responsibilities.

4. General Health and Safety Policy

General Statement

It is the policy of _____ (the organisation) to ensure, so far as is reasonably practicable, the health, safety and welfare of its employees and the health and safety of other persons who may be affected by its activities. The organisation will take steps to ensure that its statutory duties are met at all times.

The Organisation's Responsibilities

The organisation will ensure that:
- (a) all processes and systems of work are designed to take account of health and safety and are properly supervised at all times
- (b) a member of senior management maintains specific responsibility for health and safety
- (c) competent people are appointed to assist us in meeting our statutory duties including, where appropriate, specialists from outside of the organisation
- (d) all employees are consulted on matters relating to health, safety and welfare
- (e) adequate facilities and arrangements will be maintained to enable employees to raise issues of health and safety
- (f) each employee will be given such information, instruction and training as is necessary to enable the safe performance of work activities
- (g) all arrangements are brought to employees' attention and are monitored and reviewed to ensure that they are effective.

Employees' Responsibilities

Employees must ensure that they:
- (a) co-operate with management to enable all statutory duties to be complied with
- (b) take reasonable care of their own health and safety and the health and safety of others who may be affected by their acts or omissions
- (c) familiarise themselves with the health and safety arrangements that apply to them and their work functions.
- (d) Full details of the organisation and arrangements for health and safety will be set out in the remainder of this document. (Employers should insert arrangements specific to their organisation).

Signed	on behalf of	(organisation)
_____	_____	
Title: Managing Director	Date	
	_____	

5. Permits to Work

Policy Statement

As part of our duties under the Health and Safety at Work, etc Act 1974 to provide safe systems of work, the organisation has introduced permits to work for the following work activities.

(a) Hot work.

(b) Entry into confined spaces.

(c) Work on high voltage electrical equipment.

(d) Excavation work.

(e) Maintenance of power presses.

(f) Work with asbestos.

(g) It is the intention of the organisation to introduce new permits or modify existing permits as necessary and to review their use.

(h) The permit-to-work system applies to all the identified work carried out on site, and employees, contractors and visitors are all expected to comply with the requirements of any permits that are in force. The person responsible for implementing this policy is _____.

(i) Employees working off-site, ie on another organisation's premises, are expected to abide by all permits to work operated on that site. If no such permits are in use, employees must operate permit procedures as they exist under their employer. If additional permits are deemed necessary for certain off-site work, this should be raised with the appropriate person and the need for the permit determined.

(j) Should employees experience any problems with the operation of permit-to-work systems, they should immediately inform a responsible person (usually a manager or supervisor) so the organisation can investigate and rectify the situation.

6. Principles of Occupational Health

Policy Statement

(Company Name's) policy is to take all reasonable steps to prevent work-related ill health, and to support the general health and well-being of its employees. To implement this policy, _____ (the organisation) will:

  (a) make sure that the causes of ill health that may arise from its activities are, wherever possible, identified, understood, and either prevented or controlled

  (b) manage health problems through early recognition and monitoring

  (c) manage early return to work after sickness certification and, wherever possible, support rehabilitation after prolonged illness

  (d) provide reasonable adjustments for people with disabilities to support them in employment

  (e) provide employees with information and services to help them take personal responsibility for maintaining and improving their own health.

Organisation

The organisation of occupational health provision is the responsibility of _____ .

Responsibilities

In relation to occupational health, this person is responsible for:

  (a) promoting the involvement of employees in health matters through clearly defined roles and responsibilities and access to relevant information and services

  (b) implementing a management system which will undertake risk assessments, manage occupational health risks in proportion to their extent, and measure implementation actions through local audit, including assisting managers to source appropriate training where need is identified

  (c) administrative accountability for the operation of the external occupational health service

  (d) the receipt and dissemination of activity reports

  (e) arranging and reporting on quarterly service review meetings with _____

  (f) maintaining links with all departments, including appropriate committees and groups, to ensure the satisfactory operation of the policy.

  (g) Staff also have a responsibility, as part of the organisation's health and safety policy, to comply with all the health and safety arrangements of the organisation designed to protect their health while at work.

Measurement and Review

The organisation will establish and maintain programmes for the review of occupational health management systems implemented in each department. These will provide information on indicators, such as health and attendance in the workplace, which help to measure health and well-being performance for:

  (a) managers

  (b) employees

  (c) stakeholders.

(d) An addendum to the policy may set out the functions of the external occupational health service, developed in consultation with the provider. A model is outlined.

Functions of the External Occupational Health Service

1. **Fitness for Work and Rehabilitation**
   In many cases, a simple health questionnaire will provide adequate information on the fitness of an individual to carry out the work required of them. For others, an interview or an examination and biological tests may be necessary.
2. For the majority of employees, demonstrating fitness for work will be a routine formality, but a more detailed assessment may be necessary for staff involved with (list of hazards). In some cases the organisation may seek the advice of an independent occupational health doctor on the advice of the occupational health provider. This function applies:
   (a) before employment
   (b) before transfer to a different job within the organisation
   (c) on return to work following illness or injury
   (d) in situations where work performance is being adversely affected by a health problem.
3. The occupational health provider may need to discuss the working situation with the local manager or GP prior to any decision being reached about an applicant's or existing employee's fitness for work or placement. Pertinent medical advice can then be given.
4. When an employee has health problems requiring consideration for rehabilitation after illness, discussions will take place between the employee, the human resource manager and the local managers.

Health Maintenance

There are situations where it will be necessary to review at regular intervals the health of certain staff and the environment they work in. This will be done informally or by confidential interview with the occupational health provider.

Periodic Assessments

Periodic assessments will be completed if staff are exposed to known hazards. Examples of areas where staff are exposed to known hazards include (list of local hazards). Staff with known health problems and chronic conditions will be monitored.

Other Assessments

For staff going abroad on the organisation's business, information will be available on the necessary inoculations/medication that are advised and arrangements made, if requested, for them to be given.

Medico-social Problems

This function covers those areas where investigation, information and advice may be given to assist management and the staff concerned. Examples include the following.
   (a) Absence — staff with recurrent health problems.
   (b) Retirement — health and lifestyle advice to those about to retire and input to pre-retirement courses.

(c) Persons with special needs — advice and guidance not only to management about the recruitment of staff with special needs but also to the staff themselves when they are at work.

(d) Advice on stress management with referral to specialists where appropriate.

Education and Training

It is important that education and training are seen as being part of the remit of an occupational health service. This training can be formal or informal. Through training, occupational health and safety standards can be continually improved and long-term benefits gained. Examples of training include (list appropriate local examples)

Record Keeping

Various records will need to be kept to:

(a) ensure correct medical action is taken on the basis of sound information

(b) meet legal requirements

(c) give an indicator of some of the benefits gained.

In some situations, records must be kept for 30 years or more. Records normally comprise:

(a) confidential medical records — records will be kept of all injuries, sickness, absence, treatments, referrals and advice and are only available to medical personnel and the individual

(b) non-confidential records — these do not refer specifically to any given individual's medical information and may be used without confidentiality restrictions.

Confidentiality

The organisation will have information about the health of staff. Information and records will not be divulged to any non-medical staff, including occupational health management, without the written consent of the individual. Employees have a statutory right of access to their own records.

This does not preclude non-confidential records being reported to ensure the organisation has a basis on which to take remedial measures, safeguards and decisions affecting its employees' interests.

Occupational health staff are guided by their own professional codes of conduct in matters of confidentiality.

7. Risk Assessment: Principles and Techniques

General Statement

Risk assessments form the central strand of a self-regulated safety management system. Successful completion of them provides sound economic benefits to the organisation as well as satisfying legal requirements.

This policy is intended to reduce risks to the health and safety of employees and others who may be affected by the way in which we conduct our business.

Those involved in the risk assessment process will receive appropriate training.

The persons responsible for conducting risk assessments and for reviewing existing risk assessments are: _____ _____.

Arrangements for Securing the Health and Safety of Workers

1. **Elimination of Hazards**
   The organisation will ensure all hazards will be eliminated, so far as is reasonably practicable. If this is not possible, the remaining risks will either be avoided or reduced to an acceptable level. The measures introduced to achieve this will follow the principles of prevention and aim to combat risks at source.
2. **Assessment of Risk**
   If hazards cannot be eliminated or risks avoided, an assessment of risks will be carried out by competent persons. The following factors will be considered during the assessment.
   (a) **Likelihood**
      Whether the likelihood of the harm arising from the hazard is remote, possible, an even chance, probable or almost certain will be considered.
   (b) **Severity**
      Consideration will be made of whether the severity of harm from the hazard is likely to result in:
   - insignificant injury
   - first-aid treatment only
   - absence from work for more than three days
   - a major injury
   - death
   - permanent disability.
   Reference will be made to accident book records, Reporting of Injuries, Diseases and Dangerous Occurrences Regulations 1995 forms, sickness and ill-health records, first-aid records and incident (near miss) records when reaching this decision.
3. **Those at Risk**
   Individuals or groups at risk due to the hazard will be considered. This will include employees, the self-employed and any other persons. If vulnerable persons, such as young people, pregnant women, nursing mothers, those with disabilities, lone workers and those working out-of-hours or at remote locations, etc are likely to be exposed, additional consideration will be given.

Managers' and Supervisors' Duties

Managers or supervisors must ensure:
(a) assessments are carried out where relevant and records are kept
(b) control measures introduced as a result of assessments are implemented and followed
(c) employees are informed of the relevant results and provided with necessary training
(d) any injuries or incidents lead to a review of relevant assessments
(e) employees adhere to safe systems of work
(f) safety arrangements are regularly monitored and reviewed
(g) employees identified by the assessment as being at risk are subjected to appropriate health surveillance
(h) special arrangements are made, where necessary, for vulnerable persons.

Employees' Duties

Employees must ensure:
(a) they report to management (in confidence) any personal conditions which may put them at greater risk when carrying out work activities
(b) they comply with all instruction and training
(c) their own health and safety is not put at risk when carrying out work activities
(d) they use equipment and machinery in accordance with instruction and training
(e) any problems relating to their work activities are reported to a responsible person, along with any shortcomings they believe exist in the arrangements made to protect them.

Information and Training

Suitable information, instruction and training will be provided to all persons involved in the risk assessment process.

Any specific information, instruction and training needs identified will be provided. A responsible person will also regularly review training needs and refresher training will be provided at reasonable intervals.

8. Safe Systems of Work

The organisation recognises that many of its activities present significant risk to the health and safety of its employees and others, such as contractors, visitors and members of the public.

In order to control these risks, the organisation has developed safe systems of work. We are committed, as an organisation, to ensuring that these safe systems of work are effective in controlling our risks. Our policy, therefore, is to:

(a) identify those activities that require a safe system of work in carrying out our normal risk assessment procedure

(b) identify safe methods of work for these activities; where necessary, these will be written formal safe systems of work

(c) implement these systems using the expertise of our employees involved in the work activities

(d) monitor the workings of the safe systems through workplace inspections and reviewing accident/incident statistics derived from our accident reporting procedure.

The person responsible for managing our safe systems of work is _____.

We can only ensure the success of these safe systems with the full co-operation of all our employees.

Records

Contents

Introduction

Records serve to substantiate and document the existence of a health and safety management system and are therefore evidence of legal compliance. All records should be kept in a structure and format that meets both the minimum legal requirements and the needs of the organisation. Increasingly, records may be kept in electronic format. This has obvious updating and distribution advantages.

Minimum requirements for records include the current:

- general statement
- health and safety policy manual comprising organisation and arrangements
- subsidiary documents, such as detailed risk assessments, work instructions and emergency procedures to which the policy manual refers.

Records should be kept of the following.

- Appointment of safety representatives.
- Training record of safety representatives.
- Area with which safety representative is concerned.
- Group of employees represented by safety representative.
- Union to which safety representative belongs.
- Reports made by safety representatives following inspections, etc.
- Action taken as a result of above reports.
- Information provided to safety representatives.
- Membership of safety committee.
- Training given to safety committee members.
- Recommendations made by the safety committee.
- Action following the above recommendations.
- Past safety committee agendas and minutes.
- Accident statistics and ill-health trends for use by safety committee.

ACCIDENT INVESTIGATION — EQUIPMENT ITINERARY

Equipment item	Location	Responsible person	Last inspection date	Comments

ACCIDENT INVESTIGATORS

Staff member	Position	Examinations undertaken	Interviews conducted	Samples taken	Documents examined	Signed and dated

ACCIDENT REPORT

Injured Person

Name

Home address

Job title

Accident

Date

Time

Location

Work process involved

What happened*

Details of injury

Person Reporting Accident

Name

Home address

Job title

Signature

Date of report

* Use a separate sheet of paper if necessary.

One record per page (to conform with Data Protection Act 1998)

CHECKLIST FOR ALL PERSONNEL HANDLING EXTERNAL MAIL

All mail should be checked for the following characteristics:	YES	NO
Is the parcel or letter inordinately heavy for its size or unevenly weighted?	☐	☐
Are there any wires or electronic components protruding from the envelope?	☐	☐
Are there any greasy or sweaty marks present on the wrapping?	☐	☐
Does the package smell like almonds or marzipan?	☐	☐
Is the name and address in obviously disguised handwriting or in cut-out or stencilled letters?	☐	☐
Does the postmark indicate that the package has been sent from an area associated with past incendiary or bomb attacks?	☐	☐
Is the postmark foreign or from an area from which mail is not normally received?	☐	☐
Does the package appear to contain a book which is unexpected?	☐	☐
Is there an excess postage charge?	☐	☐
Is the letter or parcel addressed to an incorrect job title, not a name, and marked personal, private or confidential?	☐	☐
Is the flap stuck down with additional adhesive or tape?	☐	☐
If the package is received in a padded envelope, is the sealing flap reinforced with a staple or staples?	☐	☐
Are there any holes through which a wire could be inserted?	☐	☐
Does the envelope appear to contain a powdery substance?	☐	☐

If the answer to any of the above is yes, contact the person to whom the parcel is addressed to see if it is expected.

If it is not:

- Call the police and the fire-service.
- Do not bend or squeeze the package.
- Place the package on a flat surface away from any windows.
- Do not cover the package with sand or other materials.
- Do not place the package in water.
- Contact the co-ordinator who will activate the bomb incident plan.

FIRE EMERGENCY PLAN

Name of organisation	
Address of premises	
Building number/name (if applicable)	
Date plan produced and/or amended	
Name of person producing plan (print name)	
Job title	
Signature	

Action to be taken by a person discovering a fire

How the fire brigade (and any other emergency services) are to be called and who is responsible

Fire warning system (description of bells/sirens/voice, etc and types of signals and location of system panels)

Evacuation procedures (description of procedures to be followed)

Key escape routes (how access can be gained, where they lead, how they are protected from fire)

Assembly points

Duties and identities of employees with specific responsibilities

Arrangements for safe evacuation of persons identified as being especially at risk from fire

Firefighting equipment provided (locations and details)

Specific arrangements for high fire risk areas

Procedures for liaison with fire brigade on arrival (who, where, what, etc)

Training needed by employees and arrangements for giving such training

GENERAL RISK ASSESSMENT FORM

Date

Assessed by

Location

Assessment number

Task/premises

Review date

Number	Activity/plant/materials, etc	Hazard	Persons in danger	Severity 1–10	Likelihood 1–10	Rate	Measures/Comments	Result*

*Key to result

M = Minor risk   A = Adequately controlled   N = Not adequately controlled   U = Unable to decide

INCIDENT INVESTIGATION REPORT

Organisation/subsidiary involved	
Location of incident	

Date of incident		Time of incident	am/pm

Type of incident

Potential severity	Major ☐ Serious ☐ Minor ☐
Probability of recurrence	High ☐ Medium ☐ Low ☐

Description of how incident occurred (use extra sheet if necessary)

Use this space to sketch site if necessary

Immediate causes: what unsafe acts or conditions caused the event?

Secondary causes: what human, organisational or job-related factors caused the event?

Remedial actions: recommendations to prevent recurrence

Signature of investigator		Date	

Follow up action/review of recommendations and progress

Name of reviewer	
Position/title of reviewer	
Signature of reviewer		Date	

INVESTIGATION CHECKLIST ACCIDENT SCENE

Question	Yes/No	Comments
Have all physical details been recorded (photos, sketches, etc)?	Yes ☐ No ☐	
Has equipment and plant been examined?	Yes ☐ No ☐	
Have samples been collected of substances and materials?	Yes ☐ No ☐	
Interviews		
Have witnesses been interviewed or given statements?	Yes ☐ No ☐	
Has the injured person been interviewed?	Yes ☐ No ☐	
Has the person(s) causing the accident or incident been interviewed?	Yes ☐ No ☐	
Documents		
Have all necessary documents been collected and examined?	Yes ☐ No ☐	
Analysis		
Have all immediate causes been identified?	Yes ☐ No ☐	
Have all underlying and root causes been identified?	Yes ☐ No ☐	
Did the workplace or premises involved contribute to the event?	Yes ☐ No ☐	
Did the plant, equipment or substances being used contribute to the event?	Yes ☐ No ☐	
Did the process or procedures adopted contribute to the event?	Yes ☐ No ☐	
Did the people involved contribute to the event?	Yes ☐ No ☐	
Were those who caused the event or injury adequately trained, informed, competent and experienced?	Yes ☐ No ☐	
Was there suitable supervision and control?	Yes ☐ No ☐	
Was there co-operation among the staff?	Yes ☐ No ☐	
Was there suitable communication among the staff?	Yes ☐ No ☐	
Were those involved in the event competent?	Yes ☐ No ☐	
Was all plant, equipment and the workplace adequately designed?	Yes ☐ No ☐	
Were there adequate implementation procedures to ensure safety?	Yes ☐ No ☐	
Were risk assessments carried out and acted upon?	Yes ☐ No ☐	
Are there any management issues that contributed to the event?	Yes ☐ No ☐	

Remedial Actions		
Are additional controls required?	Yes ☐ No ☐	
Do systems of work need amending?	Yes ☐ No ☐	
Do policies and procedures require reviewing?	Yes ☐ No ☐	

LONE WORKER WORK PERMIT

Permit number	
Applicable to	All workers who work on their own in isolated areas, eg lift motor rooms, plant rooms, electrical switch rooms

1. Issue

Commencement date		Expiry date	
Time in		Time out	
Location of work			
Description of work			

I have examined the location, checked the precautions against the attached checklist and give permission for the work to start.

Name of competent person			
Status			
Signature			
Date		Time	

2. Receipt

I accept responsibility for carrying out the work detailed on this work permit and confirm that no other work will be carried out by me on any other plant or equipment.

Name			
Status			
Signature			
Date		Time	

3. Suspension/Completion of Work

The work for which this work permit was issued is now suspended ☐ completed ☐.
The work is complete ☐ incomplete ☐ ready to recommission ☐.
All work equipment and tools have ☐ have not ☐ been removed.

Name			
Status			
Signature			
Date		Time	

4. Cancellation of Work Permit

This work permit is cancelled.

Name			
Status			
Signature			
Date		Time	

Precautions Checklist

This checklist must be completed and signed by a competent person, following his or her personal detailed inspection of the work area.

	Yes	No
1. I confirm that I have physically checked the work area in order to ensure that the following necessary safeguards have been provided for, *prior to issuing this work permit.*		
(a) Does the work area present any special risks?	☐	☐
(b) Is there safe access and exit?	☐	☐
(c) Can one person safely handle temporary access equipment, plant, substances and goods involved in the work?	☐	☐
2. Is there any medical condition which makes the worker unsuitable for working alone?	☐	☐
3. Does the worker understand any risks involved and the necessary precautions to be taken?	☐	☐
4. Is the worker aware of the building's emergency procedures?	☐	☐
5. Does the worker know where the nearest fire alarm break glass call point is situated and have they been told what to do in the event of a fire?	☐	☐
6. Does the worker have access to first-aid facilities?	☐	☐
7. Will a member of staff periodically visit and visually monitor the worker?	☐	☐
8. Will regular contact, eg every 30 minutes, be made by the worker to the reception desk?	☐	☐
9. Are facilities available in the work area, in order to summon assistance in the event of an emergency, eg telephone, portable radio, alarm system?	☐	☐
10. Is the work permit clearly displayed at the job location?	☐	☐
11. [Add any additional precautions deemed necessary.]	☐	☐
12. [Add any additional precautions deemed necessary.]	☐	☐

Additional precautions (continued)

Name of competent person	
Status	
Signature	
Date	Time

PERMIT TO WORK

Reference number	
PW reference number	
Task or work operation	

This permit to work is issued for the following work. No work other than that detailed must be carried out.

Is work to be carried out when plant, equipment or systems are in operation? Yes ☐ No ☐

Location of work	
Description of work	
Hazards:	
existing	
introduced by work	
Method of isolation/making safe	
Protective equipment	

Authorisation

Name of person issuing permit	
Designation	
Signature	
Time	Date

Receipt

I hereby declare that no work other than that stated above will be carried out, and all precautionary measures will be adhered to

Name (person i/c work)	
Designation	
Signature	
Organisation	

Clearance

I hereby declare that the work stated above has ☐ has not been ☐ completed. Details if not completed.

Name	
Designation	
Signature	
Organisation	

Cancellation

All copies of this permit to work are hereby cancelled.

Name	
Designation	
Signature	
Time		Date	

SAFE SYSTEM OF WORK

Description of activity	
Location of work	
Equipment and plant to be used	
Materials to be used	
Personnel involved	
Safety precautions to be taken	
Sequence of operations	
Prepared by	
Signature	
Date	

SAFE WORK METHOD STATEMENT FORMAT

Where the Client or Principal Contractor specifies a format and its contents clearly, you should comply with it. Otherwise you should create your own, observing certain, basic principles to ensure it is sufficiently comprehensive.

A typical statement should have:

1. Title page	Nature of the work.
2. Contents page	Listing all the sections in the document including appendices.
3. Reference/source documentation	Risk assessments, data sheets, HSE Guidance Notes, Approved Codes of Practice, Safe Working Guidance.
4. Safety	Reference your safety policy/management control system ✓ Organisation ✓ Arrangements ✓ Safe Working Procedures ✓ Training/Competence
5. Equipment	Identify equipment relevant to the work to be carried out ✓ Tools ✓ Machinery/Plant ✓ Safety Equipment ✓ Personal Protective Equipment
6. Method of Work	This is the key part of the document where you must clearly establish the step-by-step detailed procedure for carrying out the work, eg: ✓ Pre-installation work programme ✓ Post-installation work programme ✓ Access requirements ✓ Special handling requirements ✓ Other contractors, service suppliers ✓ Special instructions/training for all workers Clear cross-referencing to the appropriate risk assessments will be necessary and will assist in completing the statement.
7. Appendices	Reference documents identified throughout the previous sections, eg risk assessments, data sheets, drawings, training records, etc.

TELEPHONE BOMB THREATS CHECKLIST

Write down the exact words of the message as told by the caller.

The following questions should then be asked and the responses should be recorded.

What is the location of the bomb?

What time is it set to go off?

What does it look like?

What type of bomb is it?

What sort of explosives does it use?

Why have you planted it?

Who are you?

Where do you live?

As soon as the call is over, check the automatic display (if fitted) for details of the caller's number or trace the call if possible through the operator or through automatic number identification. Complete the following.

Details of the Caller

Male ☐   Female ☐   Child ☐   Adult ☐   Juvenile ☐

Did you recognise the voice?

Did the caller appear familiar with the site?

Manner of Speech

Normal ☐   Hysterical ☐   Garbled ☐   Rambling ☐   Other ☐ *(please specify below)*

Stutter ☐   Lisp ☐   Other speech impediment ☐ *(please specify below)*

Accent (please specify if recognised)

Did the message appear to have been read or was it spontaneous?

Was the caller speaking fast or slow?

Caller's attitude

Records

Background Noise	
Noise on the line	
Call box pay tone or coins	

Operator ☐   Interruptions ☐   Whispering ☐   Children ☐
Giggling ☐   Traffic ☐   Conversation ☐   Typing ☐
Machinery ☐   Aircraft ☐   Music ☐   Church bells ☐
Trains ☐   Other   ☐ (please specify below)

Any other information	
Name of person receiving the call	
Number of telephone on which the call was received	
Date/time of call	

WORKPLACE INSPECTION CHECKSHEET

Condition or activity	Satisfactory		Remedial action required	Priority			Responsible person
	Yes	No		H	M	L	
Manual Handling	☐	☐		☐	☐	☐	
Control of Substances Hazardous to Health Regulations 2002 (COSHH)	☐	☐		☐	☐	☐	
Dangerous Substances and Explosive Atmospheres Regulations 2002	☐	☐		☐	☐	☐	
Machinery	☐	☐		☐	☐	☐	
Operation of safe systems of work	☐	☐		☐	☐	☐	
Contractors' activities	☐	☐		☐	☐	☐	
Access equipment	☐	☐		☐	☐	☐	
Fire	☐	☐		☐	☐	☐	
Portable electrical appliances	☐	☐		☐	☐	☐	
Disposal of waste	☐	☐		☐	☐	☐	
Etc	☐	☐		☐	☐	☐	

Index

Introduction.

Please note the following points.
1. Index entries are to paragraph numbers.
2. The index covers Chapters 1 to 4, but not Chapter 5, for which see the Contents lists in that Chapter.
3. Alphabetical arrangement is word-by-word, where a group of letters followed by a space is filed before the same group of letters followed by a letter, eg "control measures" will appear before "controlling mind". In determining alphabetical arrangement, initial articles and prepositions are ignored.

manslaughter – max sentence = life.

Corporate '' –   ''   ''